PageMaker 4.2
for the Mac

Everything You
Need to Know

PageMaker 4.2 for the Mac

Everything You Need to Know

William B. Sanders

Prima Publishing
P.O. Box 1260SAN
Rocklin, CA 95677
(916) 786-0426

■■

Managing Editor: Roger Stewart
Project Manager: Laurie Stewart
Production: The Cowans
Copy editing: Jeanine Ardourel
Typesetting: Sandlight Publications
Cover design: Kirschner-Caroff Design

Library of Congress Cataloging-in-Publication Data
Sanders, William B., 1944-
    PageMaker 4.2 for the Mac : everything you need to
know / William B. Sanders.
        p. cm.
    Includes index.
    ISBN 1-55958-239-1
    1. Desktop publishing—Computer programs. 2. Macintosh (Computer)—Programming. 3. PageMaker (Computer program) I. Title.
    Z286.D47S24 1992
    686.2'2544536–dc20   92-13782
                                                                            CIP

92 93 94 95 RRD 10 9 8 7 6 5 4 3 2

Printed in the United States of America

HOW TO ORDER:

Quantity discounts are available from the publisher, Prima Publishing, P.O. Box 1260SAN, Rocklin, CA 95677; telephone (916) 786-0449. On your letterhead include information concerning the intended use of the books and the number of books you wish to purchase.

CONTENTS AT A GLANCE

1   WHAT IS PAGEMAKER? 1

2   SYSTEM 7 AND PAGEMAKER 4.2 5

3   QUICK START 21

4   THE WORK AREA 32

5   PREPARING AND PLACING TEXT 68

6   WORKING WITH PLACED TEXT 86

7   USING THE STORY AND TABLE EDITORS 124

8   STYLE SHEETS, INDEXES, AND TABLES OF CONTENT 150

9   GRAPHICS 187

10 STYLE 219

11 LINKING FILES, PRINTING, AND SCRIPTING 240

INDEX 263

CONTENTS

1 WHAT IS PAGEMAKER? 1

WORD PROCESSING AND PAGE MAKEUP 2

THE COMPUTERIZED VERSION OF TYPESETTING 3

NEW FEATURES OF PAGEMAKER 4.0 AND 4.2 3

2 SYSTEM 7 AND PAGEMAKER 4.2 5

MEMORY 5

Adding RAM through Virtual Memory 6

USING AN ALIAS 9

FONTS 10

LaserWriter Font Utility 12

EDITION FILES 15

STATIONERY PADS 16

NETWORKING 17

3 QUICK START 21

PLACING TEXT AND GRAPHICS 21

A STEP-BY-STEP TRIP THROUGH A SIMPLE PAGE 22

Step 1: Bringing Up the Page 22
Step 2: Placing Initial Text 23
Step 3: Completing Text Placement 25
Step 4: Initial Graphic Placement 25
Step 5: Cropping Graphics 26

Step 6: Moving Graphic Blocks 29
Step 7: Using Text Wrap 29
MOVING ON 30

4   THE WORK AREA **32**

MAKING A PAGE 32
Setting Page Sizes 33
Facing Pages 35
Margin Settings 36
Page Number Setup 38
Page Setup Review 39

MASTER PAGES 39
Viewing Master Pages 40
Moving Around a Page 47

USING THE RULERS 48
Setting the Zero Point 49
Guides 51
Columns 56
Placing Page Numbers 59

TOOLBOX 65
Tool Functions 66

5   PREPARING AND PLACING TEXT **68**

WORD PROCESSING TO PAGE MAKEUP 69
Compatible Word Processors 69
Text Files from Any Word Processor 70

TEXT TROUBLES 71
Hard Carriage Returns 71
Spaces Replacing Tabs 73
Story Preparation 74
Tags 74

GRAPHICS IN TEXT 75
Inline Graphics 75

PLACING STORIES 77
Placing Options 78
Format Options 80

Text Flow 81
Working the Flow 82
Drag-Placing 83

6   WORKING WITH PLACED TEXT 86

READING WINDOWSHADE HANDLES 86

TEXT BLOCKS 87
Resizing Text Block Shapes 87
Moving Text Blocks 92
Threaded Text 95

SELECTING TEXT IN LAYERS 99

THE TEXT TOOL 102
Selecting Text 103
Adding Text 104
Editing Text 106

ADJUSTING TEXT 109
Changing Text Windows to Accommodate Cuts and Pastes 110
Controlling the "Ripple" Effect of Text Changes 113
Font Work 114
Exporting Files 122

7   USING THE STORY AND TABLE EDITORS 124

USING THE STORY EDITOR 124
Story View Menus 125
Editing Text 129

SEARCHING, CHANGING, AND SPELL CHECKING 131
Finding Text 131
Find and Replace 133
Spell Checking 135

USING THE TABLE EDITOR UTILITY 137
Making Tables 137
Editing Data 142
Table Editing 143
Preparing Tables for PageMaker 149

8   STYLE SHEETS, INDEXES, AND TABLES OF CONTENT 150

STYLE SHEETS 150

Default Sheets 151

CREATING STYLE SHEETS 153

    Editing Styles 154
    Rules 157
    Creating New Styles 163
    Paragraph Control 165
    Kerning, Spacing, and Hyphenation 168
    Tight and Loose Lines 168
    Track Kerning 174
    Manual Kerning 176

TABLE OF CONTENTS AND INDEX CREATION 178

    Table of Contents 178
    Index 181

9   GRAPHICS **187**

TYPES OF GRAPHIC FILES THAT CAN BE PLACED 187

PREPARING GRAPHICS 189

SCALING GRAPHICS 191

    Cropping Graphics 193

TEXT WRAP AND GRAPHICS 198

    Entering Text in a Graphic Field 201
    Image Control 202

INDEPENDENT AND INLINE GRAPHICS IN TEXT 204

    Placing Inline Graphics 204
    Changing from Inline to
    Independent Graphics 205

PAGEMAKER GRAPHIC TOOLS 205

    Monthly Sales in $100 Increments 205
    Lines 206
    Fill 211

COLORS 213

    Color palette 213
    Defining Colors 214

10 STYLE **219**

WHAT LOOKS GOOD? 220

TEMPLATES 222
    Balance 225
    Unity 228
LAYOUTS 230
    Margins 230
FONTS 233
    Using the Right Font for the Publication 234
    Leading 238
LINE LENGTH 238

11   LINKING FILES, PRINTING, AND SCRIPTING 240
LINKING FILES 240
    Working Links 241
    Book Linkages 245
PRINTING 246
    Setting Printer Parameters 246
SCRIPTS 253
    Scripting Rules 254
    Running Scripts 255

INDEX **263**

PageMaker 4.2 for the Mac

Everything You Need to Know

WHAT IS PAGEMAKER?

Welcome to the world of page design and creation. Page-Maker is a tool that lets you take words and pictures and create a statement on a page. The statement is made not by the words or pictures alone, but rather by the relationship between the text and graphics. By having the right tools and understanding the right techniques, you can create pages that will make the statement you want. Your design will tell the world you are a serious professional, a knowledgeable business person, a sensitive artist, a daring adventurer, or a whimsical muse—all before anyone reads a single word.

Consider for a second the printed pages you see in daily life. You have seen pages that looked good or bad in everything from brochures to books. Begin with this page you are reading. Does it look right? Does it feel right? How was it put together? Now look at a page in another book. Does it look the same or different? Which components are similar, and which are different? Considering other printed materials such as calendars, newspapers, flyers, business cards, time sheets, memos, advertisements, magazines, menus, and even income tax forms, remember that they were designed with some purpose in mind. Some are better than others as far as communicating the "feel" desired. An income tax form is pretty dry, but it was designed so that it could be filled in easily. It looks "official" and not like a lot of fun. Compare the income tax form with a travel magazine cover. The magazine cover evokes images of fun and adventure. None of these designs "just happens," but all are created through the art of page makeup. PageMaker is a tool for such creation.

WORD PROCESSING AND PAGE MAKEUP

Word processing is primarily a means of easily typing and editing text. Ask the typists you know how they got along before word processing, and they'll shake their heads and wonder themselves. Imagine having to retype an entire letter because a single word was omitted. However, while word processing programs were great for dealing with text, they were not very good at combining text with graphics.

Page makeup programs like PageMaker came along to ease the job of combining text and graphics into professional-looking publications. For years, newsletters and similar publications were a combination of word-processed text and pasted-in graphics. The publisher would leave spaces in the word-processed manuscript to literally paste in the graphic components of the publication. Many of the resulting publications looked amateurish; while they served their purpose of putting text and graphics together, they left much to be desired.

What people needed was a way to easily arrange text and graphics on their computer. PageMaker provided that "cut-and-paste" environment whereby word-processed text could be cut and pasted electronically with graphics. The idea was to take the hand work done with scissors, paste, tape, T-squares, and the rest of the paraphernalia of a typesetting shop and put it onto a computer screen.

So the difference between word processing and page makeup lies in the emphasis and ease of what each does. Word processors are great for writing and editing text, but they have limited flexibility for graphic integration and visual layout. Page makeup programs are best suited for laying out a page and organizing a publication, but they are limited in their ability to create and edit text. This is not to say that one cannot integrate graphics with text in a word processor or edit text in a page makeup program, but the point is to acknowledge what each does best.

THE COMPUTERIZED VERSION OF TYPESETTING

As pointed out earlier, the idea behind PageMaker is to provide an electronic equivalent to a typesetting shop. You can put up the page on the screen; size it to the desired dimensions; cut, paste, and crop graphics; and generally do the work that used to be done by hand with hot lead or a glue pot. Not only that, but you can also do it faster, cheaper, and simpler. In addition, several new features—such as automatic indexing and uncropping graphics—that were not available in the old-fashioned typesetting shops are available on the computerized version.

At the core of PageMaker is the *Place* command. With this command, you place word-processed data and computerized graphics onto a page. The *Place* command allows you to position text and graphics on pages wherever you want. With other commands and tools, you can then create any type of page you want. You can change the text, both in form and content, create some graphics with the graphic tools, and fine-tune a page to your most exacting standards. Whether you have wide experience in typesetting and graphic design or this is your first time with page makeup and computers, you will find yourself in possession of powerful tools. This book is intended to have you using those tools to create publications the first time you sit down to use PageMaker.

NEW FEATURES OF PAGEMAKER 4.0 AND 4.2

Those readers who have used earlier versions of PageMaker on their computers will find some major and minor improvements and additions. The following list shows the major additions to PageMaker Versions 4.0 and 4.2.

New Features for PageMaker Version 4.0

- Story Editor
- Spell checker in Story Editor
- Track kerning

- Limited text rotation
- File linkage
- Automatic indexing
- Automatic table of contents generation
- 5 percent to 250 percent text expansion or condensation
- Widow and orphan line control
- Table editor

New Features for Version 4.2

- System 7.0 savvy
- True Type
- Scripts
- New Control Palette
- PrePrint 1.51 Color Separation Utility
- Page sorting
- Make Booklet
- Precise baseline leading
- Automatic drop caps
- Preview tab and indent Settings
- Automatic column balancing

Some minor but important improvements also include automatic alignment of tab bar, toolbox shortcuts, some font editing, improved speed, new indexing features, and other similar enhancements.

CHAPTER 2

SYSTEM 7 AND
PAGEMAKER 4.2

PageMaker 4.2 is the first version of PageMaker designed specifically with the Macintosh System 7 in mind. It takes advantage of a number of System 7 features, and integrates them into PageMaker's system. If you are new to the Macintosh and PageMaker, this chapter is designed to help you get the most out of System 7 for PageMaker 4.2 applications. However, you should be familiar with how to use the Finder and other rudimentary elements of the Macintosh system. Your Macintosh user's guide will help you out there.

The first thing to know about System 7 and PageMaker is that you do not have to use System 7 with PageMaker 4.2. Several versions of System 6 will work perfectly well with PageMaker 4.2, and if you have a small amount of random access memory (RAM), it may be wiser to use the older system. You will not be able to take advantage of certain System 7 features in PageMaker 4.2, such as Editions, but most of what you can do with PageMaker can be handled efficiently with versions of System 6.

MEMORY

The very first item you should consider with System 7 is the amount of memory it uses, the memory used by PageMaker 4.2, other files you may have in memory at the same time, and the amount of RAM memory you have in your Mac. To see how much memory is used by System 7 and your other programs, click the icon in the upper right-hand corner of your screen—the **Application** menu—until it shows the Finder icon—a little Macintosh. Then click the **Apple** menu in the upper left-hand corner of your screen and select *About This Macintosh* option. You will see the dialog box shown in Figure 2.1.

In looking at Figure 2.1, we can see that the System Software 7.0.1 takes up about 1.2MB of RAM, PageMaker 4.2 takes up 1.5MB, and Microsoft Word uses about 1MB. Since there are 5MB of RAM (5,120K), that leaves about 1.3MB for other applications and for adding material to existing documents. If things get too crowded, it's possible to shut down one or more applications to free up memory. However, you cannot turn off the system, and so the System Software value is going to be fairly constant.

Adding RAM through Virtual Memory

Suppose you have only 3MB of memory and you want to use System 7 and PageMaker 4.2. With the memory taken up by just the system software and PageMaker, you'll have less than 1MB for adding text and graphics and/or having another application loaded at the same time.

With System 7, you can add *virtual memory*. Virtual memory is hard-disk space that thinks it is RAM memory. That is, you can add

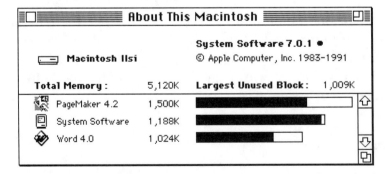

FIGURE 2.1 Determining how much memory is used by your applications and System 7.

RAM memory that is actually part of your hard disk. Here's how to do it:

- From your **Apple** menu, select the *Control Panels* option.
- Open the *Memory* control panel by double-clicking it.
- Click the On button for virtual memory (see Figure 2.2).
- Select the hard drive to be used for virtual memory.
- Adjust the amount of virtual memory by clicking the up/down arrows.
- Restart your Mac from the **Special** menu.

Once you restart your Macintosh, you have a file on your hard disk that acts as an extension of RAM. Loading up beyond your actual RAM capacity is possible. On the sample system, we added 2MB of virtual memory, and loaded it up. Figure 2.3 shows how much it can now hold.

Compare Figure 2.3 with Figure 2.1. Not only can the system with virtual memory added store more, but the System Software itself is using 1MB more of memory. Just as you can add text and graphics to PageMaker or your word-processing application and have it use more memory, with added tasks, your System Software also takes up

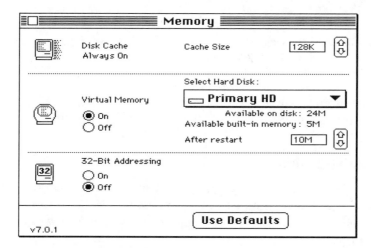

FIGURE 2.2 Adding virtual memory

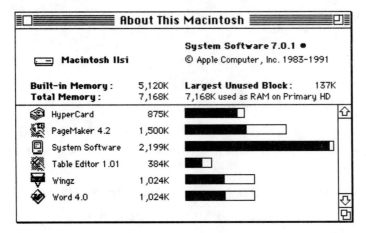

FIGURE 2.3 A 5 megabyte RAM system with 7MB of applications loaded.

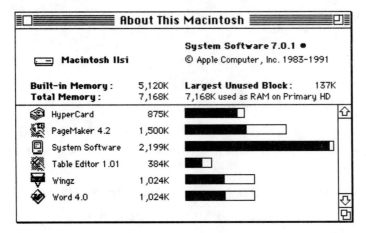

FIGURE 2.4 With fewer applications loaded, the System Software REQUIRES less memory.

more memory space. With only the Finder in use, the System Software takes up much less space as shown in Figure 2.4.

Color and Memory

If you are using a color/grayscale monitor, you can speed things up on the screen by switching to a black-and-white display. Simply choose the Monitors panel from the **Apple** menu's *Control Panels* option, and select the black-and-white display. All color/grayscale figures will be preserved. When you need to use them, just switch back to a color/grayscale display

same method. Try switching to black and white, and you will see a
marked difference in speed immediately.

USING AN ALIAS

A small System 7 feature than can be usefully incorporated with
PageMaker projects is the alias. An alias is an icon you can place
anywhere you want, and it points to the file anywhere else on your
system. For example, suppose you might have a file on your secondary hard drive that is in a folder that is inside another folder. To open
that file, you must open the secondary hard drive, find the first
folder, open it and find the second folder, and then find the file in
the second folder. Now for an ongoing project that you want correctly filed so that you can find it in the future, you want it to stay in
the current location. However, it would be nice if you could just open
it from the desktop without having to dig through a bunch of folders.
That's what an alias does, and it only takes up 1K of space.

To create an alias, from the Finder select the file or folder for
which you want to make an alias. Choose Make Alias from the
Finder's **File** menu. You will then get an icon that indicates it is an
alias for the selected file or folder as shown in following illustration:

You can take that alias file and put it anywhere you want—in a
different hard drive, on the desktop—and when you click it, it will
find the file and open it for you. You can even rename the file, put it
somewhere handy, and open it as soon as you turn on your computer. The next illustration shows the desktop with the *Part 1 alias* file
renamed *Current Project*. Even with the new name, it still finds the
"Part 1" file.

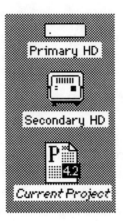

No matter what the name, you can always spot an alias by the use of italicized text in its name. No other file or folder uses text in labels.

FONTS

When you use most screen fonts, they become distorted as you increase or reduce the page magnification or use them in a size not in the system file. However with TrueType fonts, the screen fonts maintain a consistent appearance with sizes and magnifications.

You can tell the TrueType fonts from the bit-mapped (fixed-size) fonts by looking at their icons. The following illustration shows two bit-mapped fonts and a Times TrueType font:

Tiffany 18   Times   Avant Garde 12

TrueType font icons are identified by three staggered A's while bit-mapped fonts have a single letter. Also, the bit-mapped font icons have a number next to them, indicating the fixed size of the font. The screen image of the font is only good for the size specified. The Tiffany 18 point and TrueType Times look fine on the screen in 18 points. However, the Avant Garde 12 point font set to 18 points looks ragged, as can be seen in the following illustration:

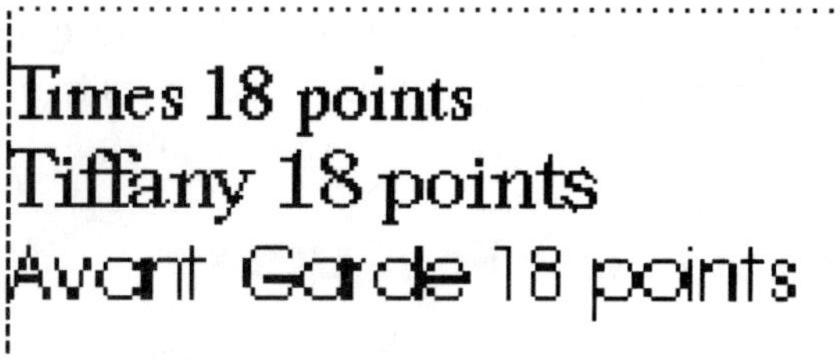

Times 18 points
Tiffany 18 points
Avant Garde 18 points

When we magnify the view to 200 percent, only the Times font still looks relatively clear and clean. The other fonts look rough, as we can see in the following illustration:

Times 18 points
Tiffany 18 points
Avant Garde 18 po

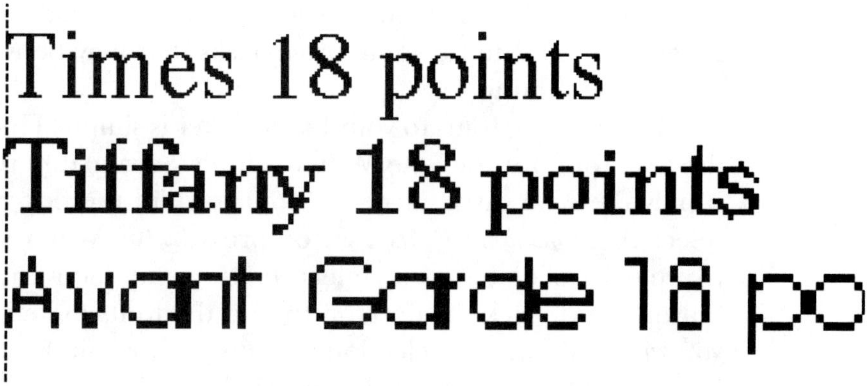

When we reduce the fonts to 12 points, the Times font is still clear, along with the 12-point fixed-size Avant Garde font, but the Tiffany 18-point font is rough and unclear, as the following illustration shows:

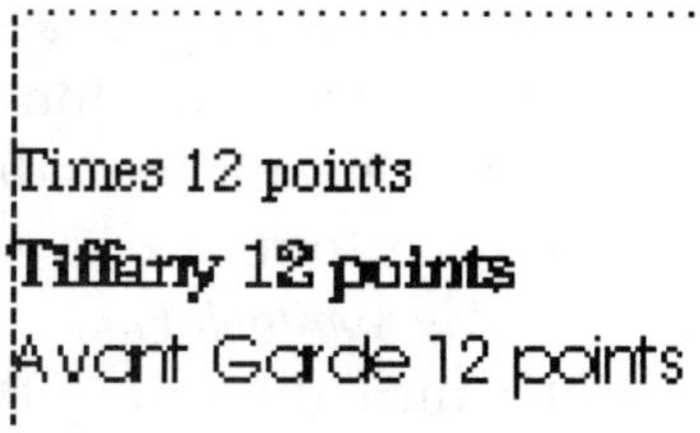

Times 12 points
Tiffany 12 points
Avant Garde 12 points

Fortunately, no matter how ragged bit-mapped fonts appear on the screen, their PostScript representations on laser-printer output are excellent. However, if you want the best screen representation of what your fonts will look like in the context of the other elements on your page, try and get TrueType fonts from your font vendor.

LaserWriter Font Utility

LaserWriter Font Utility

An important utility you will find in the System 7 software package is the LaserWriter Font Utility. It is used to download fonts to your LaserWriter and to do some other tasks that may be important to desktop publishing.

Downloading fonts to your LaserWriter is simple. First, you need the laser fonts for the LaserWriter printer. Several different vendors supply these on disks. Place the fonts disk in the floppy drive and select the *Download Fonts . . .* or press ⌘-Ⓓ. When you see the Download to dialog box, select *Printer,* and then click the Add button. Next, click the desktop to find the fonts diskette, and then you will be shown the selection of fonts as shown in Figure 2.5.

Select the fonts you want and click the Add button. Each font must be added separately. Once you have all the fonts you want, click the Done button, and the fonts you added will be shown in a Fonts to download window as shown in Figure 2.6. Click the Download button, and the fonts will be downloaded to your LaserWriter.

Be sure to add the screen fonts to your system file. They are linked to the printer fonts in your laser printer. If screen fonts are not installed, you cannot access the fonts in your printer, since only the screen fonts appear on your fonts directory in PageMaker.

To find out what fonts are in your LaserWriter, from the **File** menu, select *Display Available Fonts . . .* or press ⌘-Ⓛ. Be sure to have your LaserWriter turned on since the fonts the program examines are in your printer. You will then be shown an Available Fonts window, such as the one shown in Figure 2.7.

If you have ever wondered how to get your LaserWriter to quit printing a test sheet every time you turn it on, the LaserWriter Font

Download to
Printer Fonts
Glyph
GlyphBol
GlyphBolObl
GlyphObl
Printer Fonts
Eject
Desktop
Add
Done
Cancel
Download

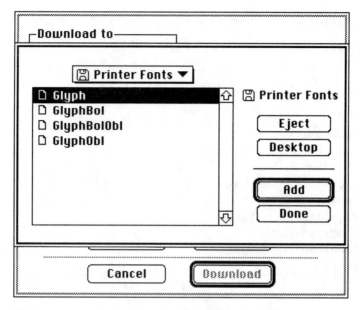

FIGURE 2.5 Selecting fonts from fonts disk

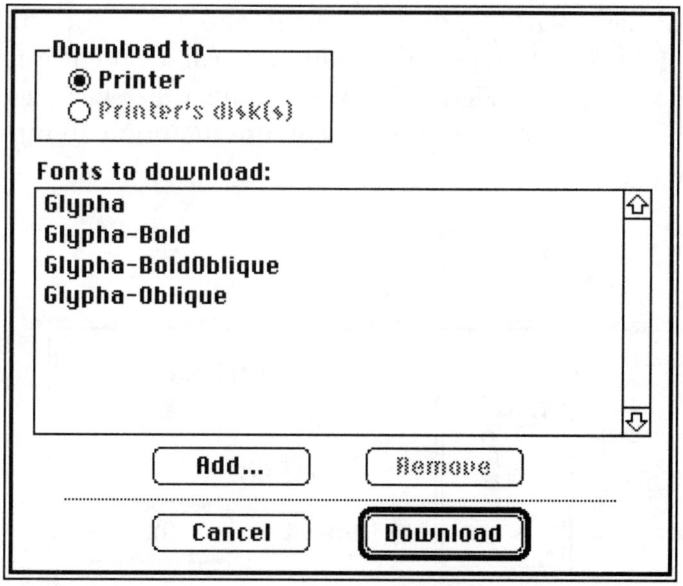

Download to
Printer
Printer's disk(s)
Fonts to download:
Glypha
Glypha-Bold
Glypha-BoldOblique
Glypha-Oblique
Add...
Remove
Cancel
Download

FIGURE 2.6 Fonts downloaded to laser printer

☐ ▤ ▤▤▤▤ **Available Fonts** ▤▤▤ ▤

LaserWriter: LaserWriter Plus

    ◯ Printer's Disk(s)   ⦿ **Printer**
    ◯ Printer's Font Expansion Card(s)

Fonts in printer:

AvantGarde-Book
AvantGarde-BookOblique
AvantGarde-Demi
AvantGarde-DemiOblique
Bookman-Demi
Bookman-DemiItalic
Bookman-Light
Bookman-LightItalic
Courier

[Delete]

FIGURE 2.7 Available fonts information comes from LaserWriter.

Utility has a *Start Page* option to turn it off. Open the **Utilities** menu, select the *Start Page Options . . .*, and you will see the Printer start page window shown in Figure 2.8. You can turn the start page off, and if you later want to print a test sheet, use the utility to turn it back on again.

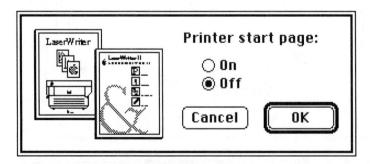

FIGURE 2.8 Turning the start page on or off

EDITION FILES

PageMaker 4.2 running under System 7 can "subscribe to" edition files. Edition files are created with application software that uses special *Create Publisher* options in their **Edit** menu. In PageMaker 4.2, the *Editions* option in the **Edit** menu can subscribe to edition files created by other application software that uses the Publish/Subscribe System 7 features. PageMaker 4.2 *cannot* create edition files—it can only subscribe to them.

Here's how it works. Suppose your spreadsheet program uses Publish and Subscribe. You select the material you wish to publish and create an edition file. You then subscribe to that edition file in PageMaker 4.2. When you change the original file, any changes will then be transferred to the PageMaker files that contain the edition.

To subscribe to an edition file, open the **Edit** menu, and select *Editions* as shown in Figure 2.9.

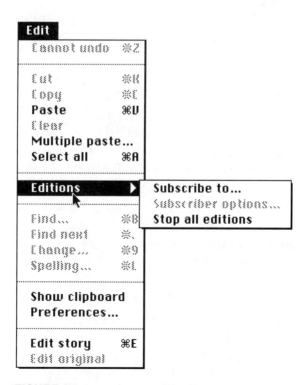

FIGURE 2.9 Importing an edition file

When you subscribe to an edition file, you can then import it into your document. The advantage of using the *Subscribe to . . .* option instead of the *Place . . .* option is that whenever the edition file is changed, it will be updated automatically in PageMaker. Another advantage is that if you want to make a change in the imported edition file, you can select the subscriber, hold down the Option key, and double-click it with the pointer to bring up the application that created the subscriber. For example, suppose you have a graphic in PageMaker that you want to change. Instead of tracking down the application and launching it and then changing the graphic, you can launch the application directly from PageMaker. That makes it handy for changes.

Since many applications may not have the Publish/Subscribe features to create edition files, you can use PageMaker's Link features. Placed linked files are automatically updated if the file is changed. See Chapter 11 "Files, Printing, and Scripting," for a discussion of using links.

Edition files only work with PageMaker 4.2 running under System 7. If you use a version of System 6, it will not work.

STATIONERY PADS

Another System 7 feature that you may find handy with PageMaker is the stationery pad. Essentially, a stationery pad is like a template. You can save PageMaker documents as publications or templates. The only difference between a publication and template is that the template opens a copy of itself. This is handy for letterheads, memo forms, and other fill-in forms you use.

In cases where you forget to save a PageMaker document as a template, all you have to do to change it to a template form, called a stationery pad in System 7, is to select the icon of the document, press ⌘-Ⓘ, and click the Stationery Pad box. Figure 2.10 shows a Page-Maker publication that was changed to a template by selecting the Stationery Pad box.

The advantage of using stationery pads over templates is that they can be easily switched back and forth if need be. On the desktop you

```
┌──────────────────────────────────────────────┐
│ ▤□▤▤▤▤▤▤▤▤▤  Geo Info  ▤▤▤▤▤▤▤▤▤▤▤▤ │
├──────────────────────────────────────────────┤
│  ┌───┐                                         │
│  │P▧ │  Geo                                    │
│  │4.2│                                         │
│  └───┘                                         │
│                                                │
│    Kind : PageMaker 4.2 stationery pad         │
│    Size : 16K on disk (15,872 bytes used)      │
│                                                │
│   Where : Secondary HD : PgMker Bks : PM 4.2   │
│           Mac :                                │
│                                                │
│  Created : Tue, Mar 31, 1992, 8:28 AM          │
│ Modified : Tue, Mar 31, 1992, 8:46 AM          │
│  Version : n/a                                 │
│                                                │
│ Comments :                                     │
│  ┌──────────────────────────────────────────┐ │
│  │                                          │ │
│  │                                          │ │
│  │                                          │ │
│  └──────────────────────────────────────────┘ │
│                                                │
│  □ Locked              ⊠ Stationery pad        │
└──────────────────────────────────────────────┘
```

FIGURE 2.10 Note the Stationery Pad box in lower right corner.

can tell a stationery-pad document by its turned up lower right corner on the icon. In the following illustration, the icon on the left is the original PageMaker icon, and the one on the right is the stationery-pad version:

NETWORKING

When running PageMaker 4.2 on a network, you can work with others on different computers in creating a publication. One person might do the page layout, another the artwork, and another write the text. Each can then use the others' contributions in completing an overall project without leaving a work station.

If you are on a network with other computers, set up file and program sharing with the Sharing Setup control panel accessed from the **Apple** menu's Control Panels. Figure 2.11 shows the Sharing Setup dialog box with its three options.

The options provide the following capabilities:

- **Network Identity**   This is where you identify yourself, your password, and your computer's identity.

- **File sharing**   Click the Start button to initiate file sharing. This allows you and others to use the same file.

- **Program linking**   Some application programs can share information with one another.

When file sharing is up and running, you can then establish sharing parameters by selecting the *Sharing . . .* option from the Finder's **File** menu. If you have more than one hard disk, establish the sharing from one or several disks. In the Sharing dialog box, as shown in Figure 2.12, you will be given the option of allowing

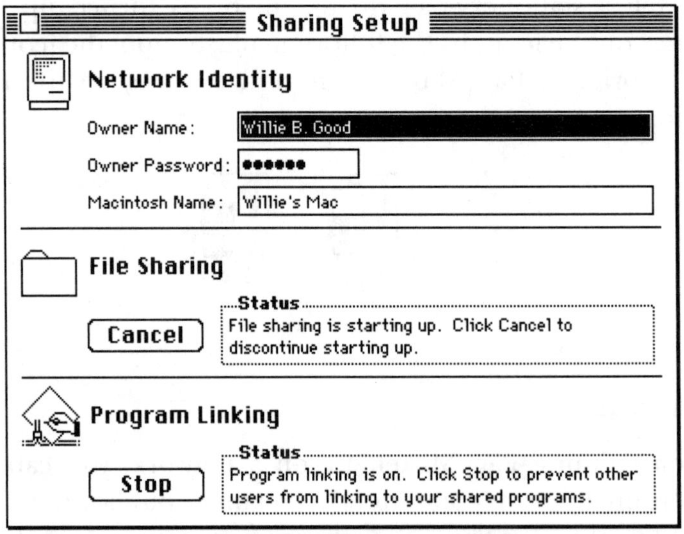

FIGURE 2.11 Initial networking dialog box

```
┌─────────────────────────────────────────────┐
│ ▣▣   ≡≡≡≡≡≡≡≡≡  Primary HD  ≡≡≡≡≡≡≡≡≡ │
├─────────────────────────────────────────────┤
│    Where:        Primary HD, SCSI 0           │
│   ┌───────┐                                   │
│   │ .     │                                   │
│   └───────┘                                   │
│                                               │
│  ☒ Share this item and its contents           │
│  ──────────────────────────────────────────   │
│                         See    See    Make    │
│                       Folders Files  Changes  │
│                                               │
│  Owner: ┌─────────────────┐  ☒     ☒     ☒    │
│         │ Willie B. Good ▼ │                   │
│         └─────────────────┘                   │
│ User/Group: ┌──────────────┐ ☒     ☒     ☐    │
│             │  Artists    ▼ │                  │
│             └──────────────┘                  │
│              Everyone        ☒     ☒     ☐    │
│  ──────────────────────────────────────────   │
│  ☐ Make all currently enclosed folders like this one │
│                                               │
└─────────────────────────────────────────────┘
```

FIGURE 2.12 Choosing the amount of access others may have

differential access to your folders and files, and enabling others to make changes. In the example in Figure 2.12, the owner has allowed others to see his files and folders but not to make changes in them.

The owner of the file let a group called "Artists" have access to his files. Imagine a work situation where there are some groups you want to have access and other you do not. How do you create icons for new groups and individuals? From the control panel, select the Users & Groups icon and open it. From the **File** menu, select *New User.* Type the name of the user or groups you wish to register, and you're all done. Their names will appear in the Sharing dialog box, and their icon will appear in the Users & Groups control panel as shown in the following illustration:

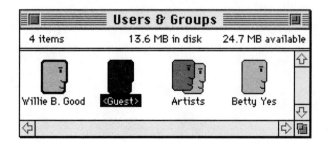

Planning a network correctly can increase a work group's productivity. The more access that interdependent computers have to the parts that go to make up a publication, the easier it is to get a PageMaker project done efficiently. As more and more users begin working on local area networks (LANs) or even a remote access, understanding how to combine your work with that of others to put together a PageMaker publication becomes more important. System 7 helps users do that more efficiently.

CHAPTER 3

QUICK START

T o get started on the right foot, we will examine the core of PageMaker. Once you understand the basics, you can see everything else in the program as an enhancement to the basic core. If you're a new PageMaker user, this method will ensure that you don't waste time with the peripherals before you understand the fundamentals.

PLACING TEXT AND GRAPHICS

As noted in Chapter 1, "What Is PageMaker?," the key to understanding PageMaker is the use of the *Place* command. This command allows you to place text from a word processor and graphics from a graphics program onto a page you have designed. PageMaker recognizes most word-processor files created on the Macintosh. Graphics can be generated by scanners, can be "hand-drawn" graphics you have created yourself on the computer, or can be "clip-art" graphics created by professional computer artists. Further on in the book we will show how to create and edit text and draw graphics with Page-Maker. However, while PageMaker can generate text and graphics, those capabilities are secondary to the purpose of placing text and graphics. When using PageMaker, think of yourself as a typesetter who is arranging stories and pictures created by writers and artists.

Your job is to put them together in an interesting and visually pleasing manner—not to do the writing and artwork yourself. Someone else has done that. The artistry with PageMaker is in bringing the components together so that they look good.

A STEP-BY-STEP TRIP THROUGH A SIMPLE PAGE

In order to see how PageMaker works on the basic level, we will create a simple page. First we will use word-processed text from your template file. Next, we need a graphic, so we will use a graphic file from Lesson 4 in your Tutorial files. Then we will put them together into a page demonstrating some key features of PageMaker 4.2.

The "story" we will use is simply some text you can use to place on the sample page. It is from the "Lorem Ipsum" file that you will find in the "Templates" folder. Remember, the purpose is not to create text and graphics, but rather to place and adjust. The following is a sample of the text you will see in the "Lorem Ipsum" file.

Word-processed Sample
Lorem ipsum dolor sit amet, consectetuer adipiscing elit, sed diam nonummy nibh euismod tincidunt ut laoreet dolore magna aliquam erat volutpat. Ut wisi enim ad minim veniam, quis nostrud exerci tation ullamcorper suscipit lobortis nisl ut aliquip ex ea commodo consequat.

Using a sample written in Latin helps you focus on the text as a block and not as a specific content.

The graphic the Anchor.TIF file, located in the Lesson 4 folder in with the Tutorial files. It depicts a fish wrapped around an anchor. We will first place the text, and then work with a few PageMaker tools to fit the graphic in the middle of the text.

Step 1: Bringing Up the Page

We will start with a two-column page using the default format. Further on in the book, we will examine exactly how to format pages; but for now, we just want to get off to a simple start. To make a page, select *New* from the **File** menu and accept the default page setup (press (RETURN)). Then from the **Options** menu select *Column guides . . ..* From within the

Column guides . . . submenu, simply type **2** where you specify the number of columns. You should now see a two-column page on your screen.

Figure 3.1 shows how the page should look on the screen after you have put in the two columns.

The dotted lines along the sides and bottom show the limits of the page where text and graphics will be placed. The dotted lines down the middle of the page are the column divider. The solid lines around the page represent the limits of the paper size being used. Since we're using a standard 8.5- by 11-inch sheet, the solid lines are 8.5 inches wide and 11 inches high. (When you have the page on the screen at full size, you can measure the 8.5- by 11-inch page. If you have PageMaker rules on the screen, selected from the **Options** menu, you can measure the correct page size from any page magnification.)

Step 2: Placing Initial Text

Once you have the page on your screen, the next step is to place the text in the Lorem Ipsum file. Click the **File** menu and drag the pointer down to the *Place . . .* selection and release the mouse button. (An easier way to select *Place . . .* is to press the ⌘-Ⓓ key combination.

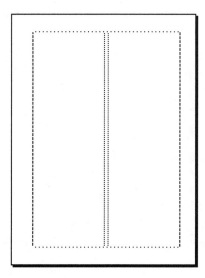

FIGURE 3.1 The initial page with two columns

As you become more familiar with PageMaker, you will find more such substitutions.)

Once you have chosen the *Place . . .* option, you will be presented with a Place File dialog box. In a window on the dialog box will be a collection of files that are in the same folder as your current folder. Find the Template folder, open it, and click the Lorem Ipsum file. Its name will appear in the Name window next to the Files window. Now click OK or press the (RETURN) key. When the file has been loaded into memory and is ready to place on your page, a small text icon will appear on the screen. Hold down the (SHIFT) key, and the icon will change to a curving dotted-arrow. With the mouse, place the icon in the upper left-hand corner as shown in Figure 3.2.

When you click the mouse button, the text will automatically fill to the bottom of the page. Figure 3.3 shows how the page now looks.

Notice that the windowshade handle at the top of the text block is blank and the one at the bottom has a dark triangle in it. The dark triangle indicates that there is more text in the word-processed story to be placed.

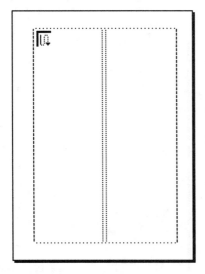

FIGURE 3.2 Placing the icon at the beginning position.

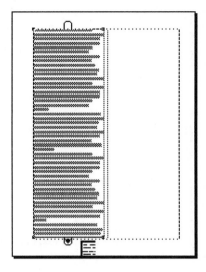

FIGURE 3.3 The first column is placed.

Step 3: Completing Text Placement

The next step is to get the rest of the text from the story and place it in the second column. Place the Text icon at the top of the second column and click the mouse key just as you did when you placed the first part of the story. Figure 3.4 shows how the page will look when you have finished placing the story.

Notice that the windowshade tab at the bottom is now clear. This indicates that there is no more story to place from the word-processed file. This does not mean that you cannot place more text, but rather it indicates that the particular file selected for placement has been exhausted of text.

Step 4: Initial Graphic Placement

Now we are all set to place a graphic. In many ways, placing a graphic is like placing text; however, as we will see, there are many differences. Different icons appear, depending on what type of graphic you place, and graphics do not automatically flow into the columns

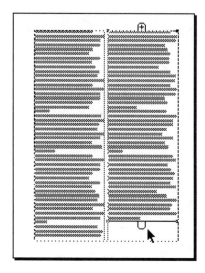

FIGURE 3.4 All the text in the story is placed.

on the page. However, once a graphic is on the PageMaker page, it is handled like all other graphics.

To get started press ⌘-D to get the Place dialog box, and select a graphic file. For this example, we will use the Anchor.TIF file in the Lesson 4 folder found within the Tutorial folder. First, find and open the Tutorial folder. Then open the Lesson 4 folder where you will find the Anchor.TIF file. Get it in the same way you got the Lorem Ipsum file. Position the Graphic icon on the page beneath the last text block on the page. You should see the Graphic icon for TIF files as shown in Figure 3.5.

Next, click the mouse button, and the graphic will appear at the bottom of the page near where you placed the Graphic icon. Figure 3.6 shows the page after the graphic is first placed.

As you can see, the graphic is too big for the space. It will be necessary to do something to the graphic to get it to fit correctly.

Step 5: Cropping Graphics

The term *cropping* refers to cutting graphics. The first thing to do when your graphic is too big to fill the space you have is to determine if there are places where it can be cropped. On the bottom of the graphic there is some debris that can be cut.

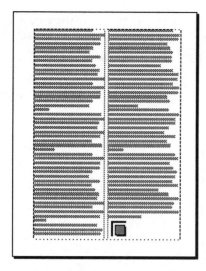

FIGURE 3.5 Placing the Graphic icon.

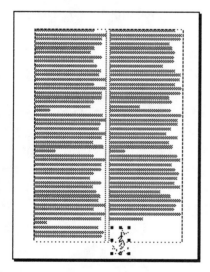

FIGURE 3.6 Graphic figure in initial placement

To crop graphics, select the crop tool from the lower right-hand corner of the toolbox as shown below:

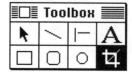

Click the graphic with the Crop tool until you can see all of the "handles" on the graphic image. (The handles are those little dark tabs on the corners and sides of the graphic block.) Magnify the screen to 200 percent by pressing ⌘-2 to make viewing easier. Then, place the Crop tool on the bottom handle as shown in Figure 3.7.

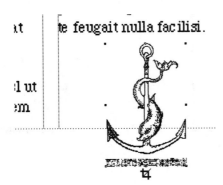

FIGURE 3.7 Positioning the Crop tool

Press the mouse key, and drag the mouse upward to crop the unwanted portion of the graphic. When you begin the actual crop, the Crop tool disappears and is replaced by a Double Arrow icon as shown in Figure 3.8.

Now the picture has been cropped to get rid of the extraneous materials. However, to make the picture appear a more integral part of the page, we want to place it directly above the last paragraph. Therefore, we must see how to move a graphic and prepare it to fit in a text block.

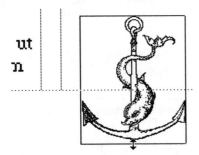

FIGURE 3.8 Cropping the unwanted portion of the graphic.

Step 6: Moving Graphic Blocks

To move a graphic, all we need to do is to place the Pointer tool (the arrow) anywhere on the graphic except on the handles, hold down the mouse button, and drag the graphic block to any position on the page. A four-point arrow appears when the block is set to be moved. Figure 3.9 shows the graphic being prepared for movement.

Try moving the graphic so that the last paragraph is at the bottom of the graphic. When you do that, you will see that the graphic simply sits on top of the text. In order to move the graphic in between the text, we need to use the *Text Wrap . . .* option.

Step 7: Using Text Wrap

To prepare the graphic block for placement in between lines of text, select the *Text Wrap . . .* option from the **Element** menu. When the Text Wrap dialog box appears, select the center top *Wrap* option. As Figure 3.9 illustrates, the icon shows text surrounding a graphic. The icon will darken when it is selected. Then, select the center *Text Flow* option. The icon shows text above and below the graphic, but not surrounding it.

Next, on the bottom portion of the dialog box, you will see a Standoff option in inches. "Stand-off" refers to the amount of space you want between the graphic and the text. On the left and right sides we want to have zero standoff since there is no text except in the adjacent column. To make sure that the graphic does not repel the text in the left column, we will set the left and right standoff to zero.

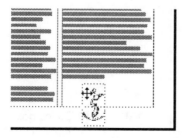

FIGURE 3.9 Preparing to move the graphic.

We will leave the default top and bottom standoff at 0.167 inches to leave some breathing space between the graphic and the text above and below it. When the text wrap is correctly set, the Text Wrap dialog box should appear as shown in Figure 3.10.

Once you have the text wrap set, you can move the graphic block between the two paragraphs. The effect of text wrap with a standoff option is the same as Moses parting the Red Sea. The text jumps above and below the graphic block. Figure 3.11 shows the effect of this new placement.

Notice how the text extends below the bottom margin of the right column. Using the pointer tool, drag the bottom window shade up so that the bottoms of both columns are flush. The overlapping text can be placed on another page. Figure 3.12 shows how this final arrangement should look on your screen.

MOVING ON

Once you understand the basics of placement, positioning, and cropping, you are well on your way to creating professional-looking pages. We have just touched on PageMaker's power, though, and as you read this book, you will find more and more things you can do with PageMaker 4.2. Take things a step at a time; and if you encounter an option or function for which you see no use, don't worry about

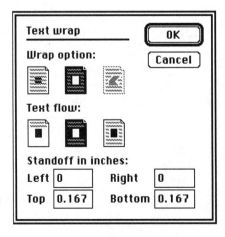

FIGURE 3.10 Dialog box set to have top and bottom standoffs.

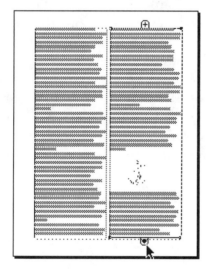

FIGURE 3.11 Graphic between text lines

FIGURE 3.12 Overhanging text removed

it. Later on you may need it, but don't get hung up on anything that impedes your use of PageMaker. Like many other software programs that provide a great deal of power, PageMaker may well have more power than you need for a project. Use what you need, and when you encounter a new typesetting challenge, come back to this book and go over those parts with which you are unfamiliar. In the meantime, experiment with the various options and try to enjoy the learning process.

THE WORK AREA

When people read books, newsletters, magazines, and other publications, they pay little attention to the page format. That is, they are not concerned about the typeface, the margin sizes, the placement of page numbers, and all the rest that goes into creating a page. However, when designing a page with PageMaker, all of these elements are important. The first step in creating a publication is how the page itself should look. A good-looking page will be ignored by typical readers. They only notice when something does not look right. This chapter is the first step in designing your publication so that the readers don't notice how good it is.

MAKING A PAGE

The first step in creating a publication is to set up a page. Normally we tend to think of pages in terms of standard sizes such as 8.5 inches by 11 inches. However, there are several other standard-size pages in publishing. Business cards, labels, invitations, and memos are examples of "pages" that are smaller than the 8.5-by-11 page but standard. Likewise, calendar pages, and "coffee table" books have pages of a larger standard size. Of course, there are all kinds of nonstandard sizes as well. Whatever the size, we need to consider how big the page is going to be before we layout our publication.

Once we have established a page size, we have to consider the orientation of the page. Do we want it in a tall or wide orientation? With an 8.5-by-11 sheet, we normally visualize it in a tall orientation. However, in several applications, we will have to think of it in terms of 11 by 8.5, or a wide orientation. The orientation we choose will depend on the kind of publication planned.

Finally, we have to establish margins for our page. Some pages may have no margins at all, while other pages will have very wide margins. In some cases there will be different margins on different pages, such as on facing pages where the right and left margins in books and magazines will require room for binding gutters.

If some attention and care is given to the page setup, the remaining work in creating a publication will be much easier. For a major printing project, this stage can be crucial, both as part of an overall page design effort and in saving time and money. If changes have to be made after a long or complex document has been created and you find that the page size is wrong or the margins are off, you may have to start all over again. So although establishing your page setup is easy and usually routine, it still deserves careful consideration.

Setting Page Sizes

When you start a publication by selecting *New* from the **File** menu, PageMaker automatically goes to the Page Setup dialog box. The default page size is 8.5 by 11 inches. You may also choose legal size (8.5 by 14 inches) or tabloid size (11 by 17 inches — a double-sized 8.5 by 11 inches). Any other page size requires that you type in the values for the page. If you type in values for the Page Dimensions option that differ from one of the standard sizes, you will immediately see the Custom label appear in the Page window. For example, 6 inches by 9 inches is a fairly standard trim size for a book. If you write in 6 and 9 as the page-dimension sizes, you can see that PageMaker automatically accepts those values and indicates that a custom page size is being used. Figure 4.1 shows what the dialog box will look like when a 6- by 9-inch page size is selected.

```
┌─────────────────────────────────────────────────────────┐
│  Page setup                                ┌───────────┐  │
│                                            │    OK     │  │
│  Page: │Custom│                            └───────────┘  │
│  Page dimensions: │6      │ by │9      │ inches ┌────────┐│
│                                                │ Cancel ││
│  Orientation: ⦿ Tall   ○ Wide                  └────────┘│
│                                            ┌─────────────┐│
│  Start page #: │1    │   # of pages: │23 │ │ Numbers... ││
│                                            └─────────────┘│
│  Options: ⊠ Double-sided  ⊠ Facing pages                 │
│           ☐ Restart page numbering                       │
│                                                           │
│  Margin in inches:  Inside │1      │  Outside │0.75    │  │
│                        Top │0.75   │  Bottom  │0.75    │  │
└─────────────────────────────────────────────────────────┘
```

FIGURE 4.1 Establishing page dimensions

Since the first value is the horizontal dimension and the second value the vertical dimension, the orientation will be tall. From the fit in window view, your page will appear as shown in Figure 4.2.

To change to the wide orientation, you can either swap the values in the first and second Page Dimension boxes or simply click the wide orientation in the Page Setup dialog box. (If you type in the

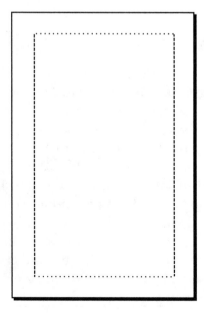

FIGURE 4.2 Tall page orientation

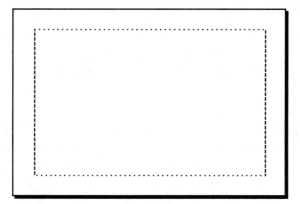

FIGURE 4.3 Wide orientation

values so that the horizontal is greater than the vertical dimension, the orientation will automatically flip from tall to wide, but it will do this only after you have clicked OK.) Figure 4.3 shows what the same page looks like with a wide orientation.

Facing Pages

The next step is to decide whether you want a single- or double-sided page and whether or not you have facing pages. For example, a one-page document may require printing on both sides, but it will not require facing pages. On the other hand, newsletters, magazines, and books are both double sided and have facing pages. Figure 4.4 shows the selection of both a double-sided and facing-page document.

The importance of choosing double-sided and/or facing pages lies in both how they will be viewed on the screen and how the margins will be set up. For example, if we have a 6- by 9-inch document with 1-inch margins on the inside and 0.65-inch margins

Start page #: 1   **# of pages:**

Options: ☒ **Double-sided** ☒ **Facing pages**
           ☐ **Restart page numbering**

FIGURE 4.4 Setting for double-side facing pages

elsewhere, we want to be sure our pages recognize the "inside," or gutter, of the page if we have facing pages. Not only will PageMaker show the facing pages on the screen, but it will also place the inside and outside margins correctly. Figures 4.5 and 4.6 show the different ways PageMaker displays double-sided facing pages and single-sided nonfacing pages.

It may seem like a small detail to decide whether you want single- or double-sided pages at the outset, but it is important. Imagine printing out a large complex publication on a rented laser printer only to find that all of the inside margins are on the left side of a facing-paged document!

Margin Settings

Continuing with the 6- by 9-inch page, we will now set aside a portion of that page that we intend to use for text and graphics. The nonprinting area around a page is the margin. Most publications

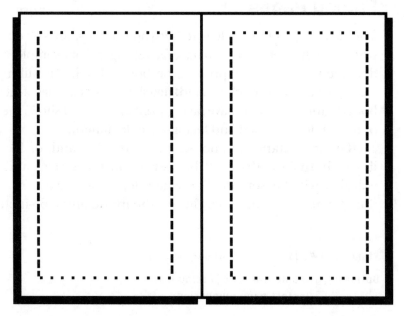

FIGURE 4.5 Double-side facing pages

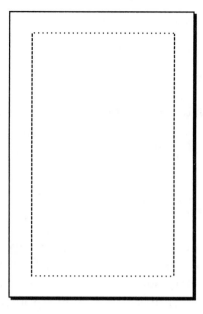

FIGURE 4.6 Single-sided nonfacing page

have some margins. Take a look at some books and magazines for samples, but you can find margins even on invoice forms and business cards.

In deciding how large or small a margin should be, there are many different things to consider; but the key consideration is "how does it look?" for your publication. Single-column publications generally have wider margins than multiple-column publications. For certain effects, you may want no margins at all for graphics. Whatever the case, give the size of margins careful consideration and look at your pages on the screen to see if they have the right appearance. Before making a final decision you may even want to make up some sample pages with text and graphics to see if the margins look like what you want.

At the bottom of the Page Setup dialog box, the inside, outside, top, and bottom margins are given in some units of measure. So far we have been using inches, but PageMaker can measure in other units as well. Further on in this chapter we will discuss these various units of measure, but for the time being, we will stick with inches for the sake of consistency and clarity.

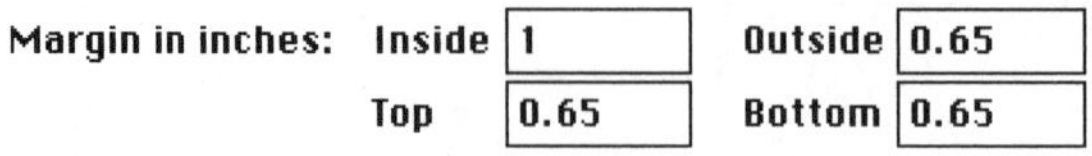

```
Margin in inches:   Inside  1        Outside  0.65
                    Top     0.65     Bottom   0.65
```

FIGURE 4.7 Setting the margins

To set the margins, click the mouse pointer in the margin boxes and type in the values as a percentage of an inch. Figure 4.7 shows how the margin section of the dialog box appears when completed.

Page Number Setup

We need to complete a few more items in the Page Setup dialog box before going ahead. First, it is necessary to decide which page number should go in the Start Page # box. When you are working with several different PageMaker files, this becomes more important. Likewise, when using front and back material, you may find your publication has to have more than a single "page 1," since different numbering systems are used.

Second, you can decide on the number of pages you want at this time by entering them in the # of Pages box. The default is a single page, but if you know approximately how long your publication will be, you can put in any number of pages desired. This step is not that fateful since it is easy to add and delete unused pages in PageMaker once you get started placing pages. However, it might make things a little easier if you add some pages while completing the rest of the page setup.

Finally, another PageMaker option is found in the Page Numbering dialog box. For certain publications, numbering systems other than the default Arabic numbers (e.g., 1, 2, 3, 4, etc.) are required. This is especially true in certain types of technical reports, books, and similar publications that use other alphanumeric symbols. Figure 4.8 shows the numbering options available.

In the Page Numbering dialog box there is also a box for TOC and index prefix. We will see how this works when we discuss creating tables of content and indexes.

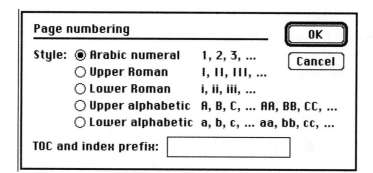

FIGURE 4.8 Numbering options

Page Setup Review

Now that we have gone through the steps in setting up a page in detail, let's take a quick step-by-step review of what PageMaker provides and requires in this first crucial stage in creating a publication.

Page Setup Steps

Step 1　Choose a page size by selecting a standard page or typing in the values for a custom page.

Step 2　Select a tall or wide orientation.

Step 3　Type in page number start.

Step 4　Optionally type in number of pages for publication.

Step 5　Select double-sided or single-sided page.

Step 6　Select facing or nonfacing pages.

Step 7　Type margin sizes.

Step 8　Select type of page number if other than default Arabic.

MASTER PAGES

Once general page size has been determined and the margins set, you can design the Master Pages. Think of Master Pages as being similar to the pages created in the page setup phase. All of the pages in the publication will have the same features found in the Master Pages in the same way that all of the pages will have the same trim size and margins established in the page setup. However, you can do a great deal more with page design on the Master Pages than in page setup.

Viewing Master Pages

In order to work on the Master Pages, select the Master Page icon in the lower left-hand corner of your screen. You can identify the Master Page icons by their "L" and/or "R" labels. Single-sided pages will show only the "R" or right-hand page, while double-sided pages show both left and right pages as shown in Figure 4.9.

The Master Page icons will darken when selected. That allows you to always check to make sure you are working on the correct pages. A common mistake is to set all of the master-page parameters on a regular page and then have to do all the work over again. By looking to see what pages along the bottom border of a publication are darkened, you can always check to see your current page—the page on the screen.

Page Magnification

While discussing Master Pages, we should also take a look at page magnification. There are eight page magnifications for all page viewing. The most commonly-used magnifications are actual-size and fit-in-window. The actual-size view shows the page that will be printed and is used to see how the page or part of the page will look at a normal viewing position. The fit-in-window view provides an

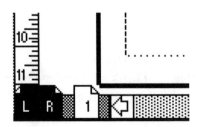

FIGURE 4.9 Darkened Master Page icons

overview of the entire page to give a clear idea of how the publication looks as an overall design.

The fit-in-window view is the default view when you start a new publication. To change a view size, use the Page menu or one of the shortcuts to change the size.

A third magnification is the fit-in-world view, which shows the entire pasteboard. The fit-in-world is achieved by holding down (SHIFT) and selecting the fit-in-window view.

Figures 4.10 through 4.17 show how a page looks on the screen in the eight different different magnifications. The type is a 24-point Souvenir demi-italic font with the message "PageMaker has many magnifications." (The fit-in-world view shows double pages.)

Depending on your monitor screen and window size, your fit-in-window magnifications will appear at different sizes. So if your magnifications look a little different than those shown, don't be concerned.

Since it is common to use many different magnifications while working on a publication, PageMaker provides a number of short-cuts for changing page views. The most important and often-used

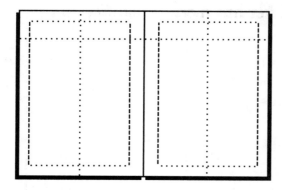

FIGURE 4.10 Fit in world

FIGURE 4.11 25 percent of actual size

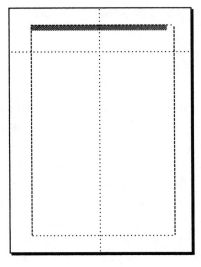

FIGURE 4.12 Fit in window

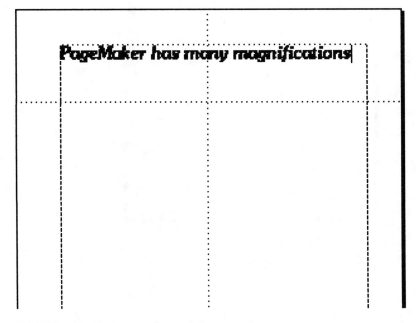

FIGURE 4.13 50 percent of actual size

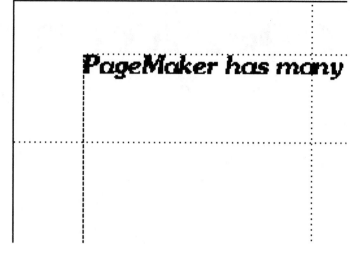

FIGURE 4.14 75 percent of actual size

FIGURE 4.15 Actual size

FIGURE 4.16 200 percent of actual size

FIGURE 4.17 400 percent of actual size

shortcut is with the mouse and pointer. From the fit-in-window view, point to any point on the pages and press the right mouse button. The view will then change to the actual size at the point where you last pointed. You can quickly change from the actual-size view to the fit-in-window view by clicking the right mouse button. Try it a few times to see how easy it is to get the mouse pointer right where you want it on the actual-size view. Table 4.1 shows shortcuts for the different magnifications:

TABLE 4.1 Magnification Shortcuts

View	*Shortcut Keys*
Fit in world	None
Fit in window	⌘-W
25 percent of size	⌘-0
50 percent of size	⌘-5
75 percent of size	⌘-7
Actual size	⌘-1
200 percent of size	⌘-2
400 percent of size	⌘-4

Greeking

In looking at the different magnifications, you will notice that some text at less than 50 percent of actual size is unreadable. (See Figures 4.10 to 4.12.) Instead of using extremely small fonts that would be virtually impossible to read anyway, PageMaker "greeks" the text below a specified size. The greeking process simply involves showing shaded graphic lines instead of text wherever the text size will shrink below a specified point size. In our examples, we used a 12-point font and the greeking was set for below 9 pixels. Since 50 percent of 12-point type is 9 pixels, we can still see text in the 50 percent view. However, below 50 percent of actual size, all that is visible is the area where the text goes.

When using different font sizes in the same publication, you may have some text greeked and some not. For example, Figures 4.18 and 4.19 show how the text looks in several different font sizes in the actual-size and 50 percent of actual-size views.

In Figure 4.18, all of the font sizes are visible, since the smallest font uses more pixels than the maximum greeking size. However, when we examine the page from the 50-percent view, we see that the last three lines are now greeked. All of the bottom three fonts use less than 9 pixels when reduced to half size. The 18-point and 24-point fonts, though, are still at or above the greeking level so they are not greeked.

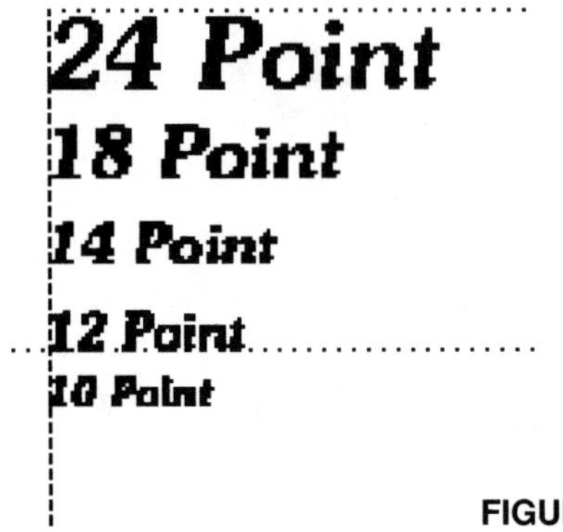

24 Point

18 Point

14 Point

12 Point

10 Point

FIGURE 4.18 Actual size

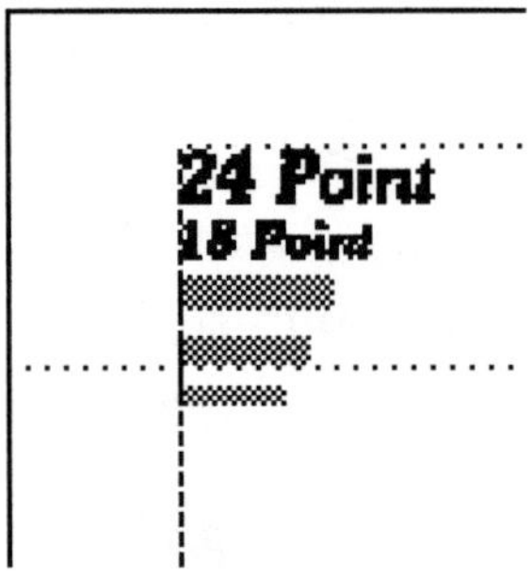

24 Point
18 Point

FIGURE 4.19 50 percent of actual size

The default greeking level is 9 pixels, but if you want to set it at a higher or lower level, it is a simple matter to do so. From the **Edit** menu, select *Preferences . . ..* When the Preferences dialog box appears, you will see,

Greek text below: 9 pixels

or some other value. If you increase the value from 9 to a higher value, you will have more greeked text and less scripted text. Lower the value from 9 pixels, and you will have less greeked text. Depending on the type of screen you have, you will visually see text at a greater or lesser degree. Adjust the greeking level to a comfortable one for you and your system.

Moving Around a Page

In discussing different screen magnifications, we have seen how to look at pages from different perspectives. However, in the magnifications of 50 percent or greater, there is usually a need to move around the page. This is especially true with a double-sided, facing-page publication.

The first tools for moving around that we will discuss are the scroll bars. They consist of a vertical and a horizontal bar along the right and bottom sides of the screen. By placing the pointer on one of the white squares in the bars and holding down the left mouse key, you can move the view of the publication. Figure 4.20 shows the pointer arrow on the bottom square that enables horizontal scrolling.

Besides dragging the boxes on the scroll bars, you may also click in the gray areas between the end arrows and the scroll bar boxes. Further, by clicking the arrows on either end of the scroll bars, you can make small moves horizontally or vertically.

Another way to move around the screen, usually in smaller increments, is by using the grabber hand. When the mouse button is pressed and the (OPTION) key held down, a grabber hand appears when you move the mouse. The effect is like literally grabbing the image on the screen and sliding it in any direction desired. Figure 4.21 shows a grabber hand moving a page on the screen.

A little practice with the grabber hand will show you its best use—usually for fine adjustments and small movements. The grabber hand will not work with the fit-in-world view of the publication.

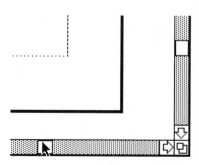

FIGURE 4.20 Pointer on horizontal positioning box

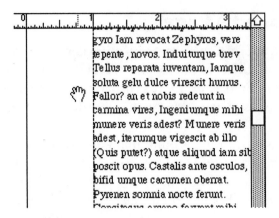

FIGURE 4.21 The grabber hand moves the page.

Best Moves

If you're going to be moving around a page a lot, as you will be in setting up your Master Pages and doing fine-tuning on a publication, there is a better way to move fast than using the scroll bars or grabber hand. When switching from fit-in-window to actual size, you can select the text insertion point or graphic on the screen and then click the right mouse button. It is actually faster to go from actual-size to fit-in-window and back to actual-size than it is to move any distance using the scroll bars. Just select the spot you want and click the right mouse button to toggle back and forth between actual-size and fit-in-window views.

You can also use this method to move quickly to other views as well. To move around a 200-percent view, for example, get the spot you want from the fit-in-window view, jump to actual-size by clicking the right mouse button, and then use the ⌘-②️ shortcut to get back to the 200-percent view. This tip will speed up your moves a lot, and it takes only a little practice.

USING THE RULERS

Once you have your Master Pages on the screen, click on the **Options** menu and select *Rulers.* If they are not already on your screen, you will see rulers appear along the top and left side of your screen. (Be careful; if the rulers are already on your screen and you select *Rulers* from the **Options** menu, the rulers will toggle off and disappear until you select *Rulers* again.)

Setting the Zero Point

Once you have the rulers on the screen, you will see the horizontal and vertical rule marks on the top and left sides of the screen. In the upper left-hand corner of the screen, you will see two intersecting dotted lines (darkened in Figure 4.22). These lines are dragged to set the horizontal and vertical zero points. The default position for the zero points on a PageMaker publication are the limits of the page. The left and top edges of the page are "0" on the rulers. However, you may want to change the zero point to the left and top margins instead of the page edges. To change the zero point, place the pointer at the intersection on the dotted lines, hold down the left mouse button, and drag the zero point lines to the new zero point. In the example in Figure 4.22, the zero points were reset to the left and top margins.

Double-clicking at the intersection of the rulers sets the zero point back to the upper-left corner or the center line of facing pages. This new PageMaker 4.2 shortcut will save you time if you have to change the zero points a good deal for various measurements.

Feel free to change the zero point whenever you want. The rulers are on the page as a reference, and nothing will happen to the page,

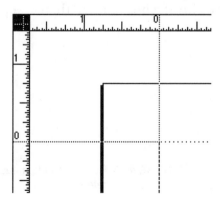

FIGURE 4.22 Zero point is set at margin corners.

text, or graphics if the zero points are changed. For example, in working with multiple columns on a page, there may be occasions when you will want to place something exactly one inch from each column. By resetting the zero point to the left side of the column each time you set your material, you have a simple and accurate reference point.

Ruler Reference

When you move the mouse pointer across the screen, notice how a dotted line moves through the rulers. This moving line shows where the point is on the page relative to the zero point. For example, if you place the pointer on the page 3 inches to the right of the zero point, you will see the dotted line of the horizontal ruler at the 3-inch point. In Figure 4.23, note the dotted line directly above the arrow on the horizontal ruler. That is the ruler reference line; when you are placing text or graphics, it provides you with a measuring reference available to view page position.

Measurement Systems

Before continuing on to discuss placing guidelines on your Master Pages, we will take a quick look at the various measurement systems available on PageMaker. Throughout this book we will be using inches as a unit of measure. However, in the tradition of typesetting, many different units of measure have been used. There will be occasions where you may want to measure in picas, millimeters, or ciceros. Likewise, even if using inches as a unit of measurement, you may prefer to use inches with decimal rather than fractional sub-units.

FIGURE 4.23 Rulers provide measured references.

To change the measurement system, select *Preferences . . .* from the **Edit** menu. In the Preferences dialog box, simply click the measurement system you want. Everything will automatically be changed to the new system. For example, if you changed from inches to picas, an 8.5- by 11-inch page will then be described as 51 by 66 picas. Likewise, your rulers will change to reflect the divisions in picas. Remember, though, it is not a good practice to change from one measurement system to another in the same publication. If you are set on using a certain type of measurement system, stick with it throughout.

Guides

Among the most important tools you will be using with PageMaker are the guides or guide lines. These guides help you place text in graphics in an organized and presentable matter. They appear on the screen, but they do not appear on your page when you print it.

To use the guides, you "peel" them off the horizontal and vertical rules. Place the pointer on the ruler and holding down the left mouse key, drag the line away from the ruler. Figure 4.24 shows a guide being pulled down from the horizontal ruler.

Keep moving the guide until you have it positioned exactly where you want it on your page. When you move a horizontal guide, a double-headed vertical arrow appears. Figure 4.25 shows a line positioned in the top quarter of a page with the double-headed arrow indicating that the line can be moved on the vertical axis.

Figure 4.26 shows the placement of a vertical guide. Note that the arrow in Figure 4.26 is double-headed as well, but it positions guides vertically on the pasteboard or page.

It is possible to drag a guide on top of another guide. Figure 4.27 shows the vertical guide being placed over the horizontal guide.

Since placing guides is an important part of preparing a page for placing text and graphics, a quick exercise in using them will help you understand how they can be positioned vis-à-vis the rulers. Figure 4.28 shows a simple grid made with horizontal and vertical guides. Each of the guides is placed on an inch marker horizontally and vertically to make an even grid pattern. See if you can create this grid, aligning the guides on the inch markers as shown in Figure 4.28.

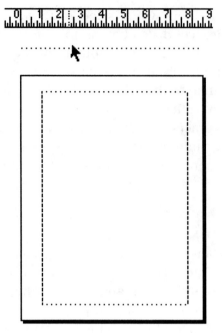

FIGURE 4.24 Pulling guides from the rulers

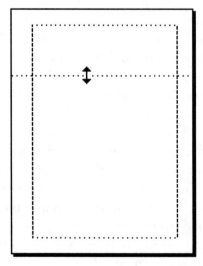

FIGURE 4.25 Horizontal guide positioned on page

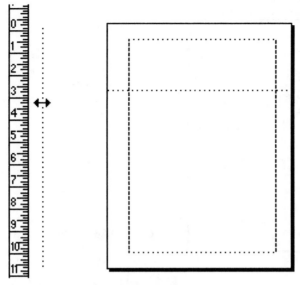

FIGURE 4.26 Vertical guide positioned on page

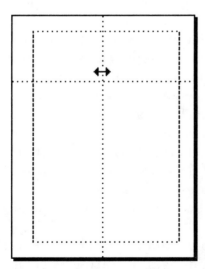

FIGURE 4.27 Horizontal and vertical guides in place

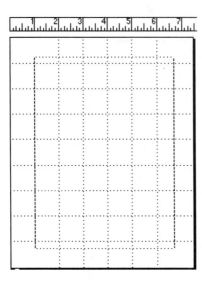

FIGURE 4.28 Practice grid made of guides.

Now that you can see how the guides can be manipulated, let's take a look at a simple practical example of how to use the guides. The goal will be to place running heads on facing, double-sided Master Pages. The running head on the left-hand page will be the publication's title, and the right-hand page will be the name of the section.

Taking a horizontal guide, place it along the top of the publication where the running head is to be placed, as shown in Figure 4.29.

When adding small amounts of text to a Master Page, it is not necessary to use a word processor or text editor to place the text. All you have to do is select the Text tool from the Toolbox and start typing. In this case we will use the Text tool to create running heads for a publication. The title of the publication is *All About Flying*, and the section is *Takeoffs and Landings*. Placing the Text tool on the guide line, we click the mouse and start typing. Figure 4.30 shows how the left-page running head appears. Note that the lettering sits right on the guide line.

Next, we want to put in the running head for the section. Since this will be on the right-hand pages, we will use a right-justified text. To get right justification, simply select *Align right* from the *Type* menu. Select the Text tool and type in **Takeoffs and Landings**. If the

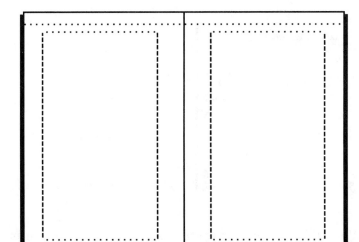

FIGURE 4.29 Horizontal guide across facing pages

FIGURE 4.30 Left page running head.

letters do not sit right on top of the guide, you can adjust them with the Pointer tool. Click on the lettering and hold down the button until a four-way arrow appears and move the text until it sits on the guide as shown in Figure 4.31.

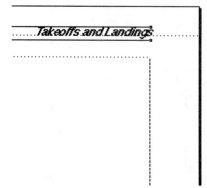

FIGURE 4.31 Right-page running head

When the right-page running head is placed, you cannot see the position of the left-page running head from the actual-size magnification unless you have a very wide screen. However, since the guide extends across both pages, it is a simple matter to have the vertical alignment of the running head be perfectly aligned, for the text for both pages rests on the same line.

Columns

Publications can be divided into one or more columns. The default publication is single-column, but you can have as many columns in a publication as you want. Remember, a publication can be anything from a business card to a newsletter to an invoice sheet. So while we might think in terms of publications having one, two, or three columns, in a lot of applications there may be five, six, or ten columns.

Columns in PageMaker divide the publication into separate channels into which you place text. A single column lets all of the text flow into the space between the margins, while a multiple-column publication guides the text flow into the columns sequentially.

To create multiple columns, select *Column guides . . .* from the **Options** menu. The Column Guides dialog box simply requests the number of columns you want in the publication and the space between the columns. The dialog box also asks whether you want columns for facing pages or only the left or right page. Figures 4.32

FIGURE 4.32 Single-column page

and 4.34 show right and left facing pages with the same text in both. In the single-column publication, the text flows into the single column as shown in Figure 4.32.

In Figure 4.33, the text first flows into the left column and then into the right column. Note that even though the same amount of text is used, the pages look very different.

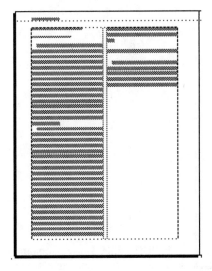

FIGURE 4.33 Double-column page

Custom Columns

When the number of columns is set in a publication, the column boundaries are automatically placed at an equal distance from one another and from the margins. However, it is simple to move a column boundary to the left or right using the pointer. For example, in some applications, it is necessary to have the column boundary moved to the left or right to get even columns. The newsletter cover shown in Figure 4.34 has an unusual arrangement since it uses the left column for part of the newsletter header. In fact, the "Orange County" label is right on the left margin. As a result of this arrangement, the usable portions of the two columns are unequal. A quick fix would be to move the column boundary to the right to make up two equal columns between the heavy dark line on the left and the right margin.

To make the change, first set the zero point over the heavy black line since it will be the boundary for the left margin. Note the distance between the dark line and the right margin—exactly 6 inches. Place the arrow on the column boundary and drag it to the 3-inch position. Now you have two equal columns as shown in Figure 4.35.

It would be an even better idea to set the left margin slightly to the right of the vertical dark line. Then when you designated the

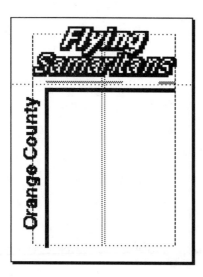

FIGURE 4.34 Uneven columns due to graphic element

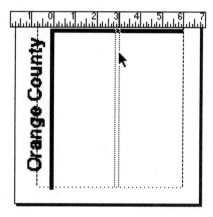

FIGURE 4.35 Columns equalized

publication as two-column, it would automatically set the column boundary in the center of the two margins. However, this example is intended to show how to move column boundaries than to maximize using PageMaker, so we chose to move the boundary instead of the margin.

Columns and Guides

There is a fundamental difference between column markers and the guides. Column markers will force the flow of text within the column boundaries. Guides, on the other hand, have no effect on where the text flows. Both horizontal and vertical guides simply show markers where you plan to place material in your publication. Neither column markers nor guides will print on paper.

A final note about column boundaries and guides involves the placement of graphics in a publication. Elsewhere in this book we will discuss placing graphics, but here it is important to point out that neither column boundaries nor guides have any effect on the flow of a graphic placed on a page.

Placing Page Numbers

Page numbering in PageMaker is handled by placing the page number markers on the Master Pages and setting the number type and starting number in the page setup sequence. Earlier in this chapter, in the Section "Page Number Setup," we discussed setting the beginning page number and how to access different types of numbering options. Now, we will examine setting up the page numbers on the page itself.

Select a position on the Master Pages where you want all page numbers to be placed. Then, once the page number is placed on the Master Pages, all of the regular pages will be numbered sequentially in the position selected. Use the following sequence to set the page numbers:

Step 1 Set the zero position of the ruler to the left bottom margin. (See Figure 4.36.)

Step 2 Place the horizontal guide 3/8 inch below the bottom margin.

Step 3 Place the vertical guide 1/4 inch to the right of the left margin.

Step 4 Choose the Text tool from the Toolbox.

Step 5 Click the position on the left Master Page where the page number is to be placed.

Step 6 Press ⌘-OPTION-P. The letters "LM" (left master) will appear on the page as shown in Figure 4.36.

Step 7 Move to the right side of the page using the slide bar at the bottom of the screen.

Step 8 Reset the zero position of the ruler to the right bottom margin. (See Figure 4.38.)

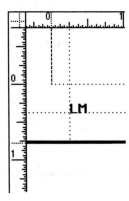

FIGURE 4.36 Using guides to establish page number positions

Step 9 Leave the horizontal guide ⅜ inch below the bottom margin.

Step 10 Place the right guide ¼ inch to the right of the right margin.

Step 11 Select the Text tool and, holding down the left mouse button, drag the mouse from the intersection of the two guides to a position about ½ inch to the left of the right margin.

Step 12 Press ⌘-OPTION-P to get the number marker, "RM," (right master). It should look like the illustration in Figure 4.37.

Step 13 Click the mouse inside the text window with the number marker and select *Align right* from the **Type** menu. That will move the "RM" page marker to the right of the text window.

Step 14 Move the page marker so that it sits in the intersection made by the two guides as shown in Figure 4.38.

The page-number setup is a crucial first step in establishing a Master Page. Once the number positions have been established, take a look at some regular pages and see how everything looks. If the page numbers do not look good in their positions, it is a simple matter to change them on the Master Pages. Of course, once changed on the Master Pages, all of the page numbers in the rest of the publication will be changed as well. (By the way, to quickly reset the zero point, just double-click at the intersection of the rulers.)

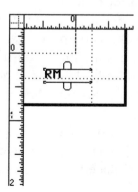

FIGURE 4.37 The right-hand page number is left-aligned.

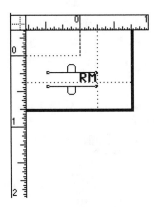

FIGURE 4.38 Use right alignment to correctly position.

Page Number Styles

You can treat page numbers as text and create any page number style you want. To establish a style, use the following steps:

Step 1   Drag the mouse over the page-number marker to darken it.

Step 2   Select *Type Specs . . .* from the **Type** menu.

Step 3   Choose the font and style you want for the page number.

Remember to check the style of page numbers against the rest of the publication's elements to make sure it looks good.

Composite Numbers

Some publications require relative or composite page numbers. Very often, reports, manuals, and technical publications will have the pages numbered by a section or chapter number and a page-number. For example, a reference to page 5-9 or J-15 reflects the section first and the page number next. To make a composite page number, all you need to do is to place the first number and a dash to the left of the page-number marker. For example, Figures 4.39 and 4-40 show how a composite page number appears on a Master Page and on a regular page.

Both elements of the composite number need not be numbers. Figures 4.41 and 4.42 show some other composite page numbers involving other identifiers that can be placed with page numbers.

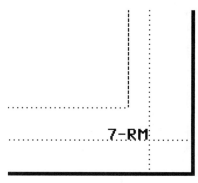

FIGURE 4.39 Master-page composite number

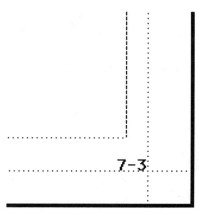

FIGURE 4.40 Regular-page composite number

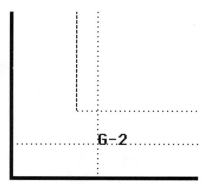

FIGURE 4.41 Lettered-section composite number

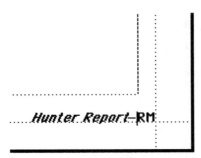

FIGURE 4.42 Descriptive-section
composite number

Non-Arabic Numbers

The "front matter," which includes such materials as prefaces, acknowledgments, and copyright pages in books and other publications, is often numbered with Roman numerals. Other publications, for whatever reason, require a sequential reference without using Arabic numbers. For example, a person may want to create an alphabet book for children and reference the pages with letters. There are limitations, however.

Non-Arabic Number Limitations

- Roman numerals revert to Arabic numbers after 3999.
- Alphabetic characters revert to Arabic numbers after 52.

The page marker placement on the Master Pages looks exactly the same as it does for Arabic numbers. Only on the regular pages can you see the non-Arabic characters. Figure 4.43 shows how lower-case Roman numerals look on a screen page.

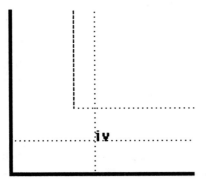

FIGURE 4.43 Roman numeral page
number

TOOLBOX

We have made references to the Toolbox, which is a fairly simple and straightforward part of PageMaker. In this section, we will look at the Toolbox in more detail, discussing its use and some new shortcuts now available in using it. (The two other on-screen boxes, the Color and Style palettes, will be discussed in other chapters.)

If your Toolbox icon is not visible on your screen, click *Toolbox* from the **Window** menu. You should then see the following box:

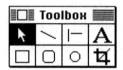

To select Toolbox items, place the pointer on the tool you wish to use and click the left mouse button. Once the tool is selected, the pointer will change to a distinctive image. The following pointing icons are used:

Tool	*Pointer Image*
Arrow	▲
Drawing tools	+
Cropping tool	⊭
Text tool	I

When any of the pointers leave the pasteboard area they change into an outlined arrow. For example, the black pointer arrow will change into a white arrow when placed over the Toolbox. This allows you to use the mouse to move the page, select menu items, and do other things without having to change tools.

Tool Functions

Here we will briefly introduce the eight tools in the Toolbox. In later chapters, tool uses will be elaborated as various other features of PageMaker are discussed.

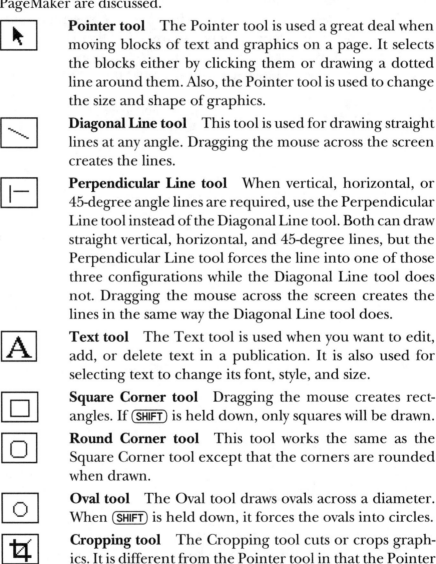

Pointer tool   The Pointer tool is used a great deal when moving blocks of text and graphics on a page. It selects the blocks either by clicking them or drawing a dotted line around them. Also, the Pointer tool is used to change the size and shape of graphics.

Diagonal Line tool   This tool is used for drawing straight lines at any angle. Dragging the mouse across the screen creates the lines.

Perpendicular Line tool   When vertical, horizontal, or 45-degree angle lines are required, use the Perpendicular Line tool instead of the Diagonal Line tool. Both can draw straight vertical, horizontal, and 45-degree lines, but the Perpendicular Line tool forces the line into one of those three configurations while the Diagonal Line tool does not. Dragging the mouse across the screen creates the lines in the same way the Diagonal Line tool does.

Text tool   The Text tool is used when you want to edit, add, or delete text in a publication. It is also used for selecting text to change its font, style, and size.

Square Corner tool   Dragging the mouse creates rectangles. If (SHIFT) is held down, only squares will be drawn.

Round Corner tool   This tool works the same as the Square Corner tool except that the corners are rounded when drawn.

Oval tool   The Oval tool draws ovals across a diameter. When (SHIFT) is held down, it forces the ovals into circles.

Cropping tool   The Cropping tool cuts or crops graphics. It is different from the Pointer tool in that the Pointer tool either moves the graphics or changes their size and shape. The Cropping tool effectively deletes parts of graphics without affecting their shape or placement. The tool is placed on either a side or a corner tab to perform the crop. The tool can also be used for uncropping a graphic.

During any given session with PageMaker you will probably be switching among tools a good deal. A feature of PageMaker for those who like using the keyboard is the availability of shortcuts in switching tools. Most of the shortcuts involve using function keys, and so if your keyboard does not have these keys, just get the tools the regular way by pointing and clicking.

Tool	*Key Shortcut*
Pointer	(SHIFT) (⌘) (or (F1) Spacebar)
Line	(SHIFT) (F2)
Perpendicular Line	(SHIFT) (F3)
TextTool	(SHIFT) (F4)
Square Corner	(SHIFT) (F5)
Round Corner	(SHIFT) (F6)
Oval	(SHIFT) (F7)
Cropping	(SHIFT) (F1)

CHAPTER 5

PREPARING AND PLACING TEXT

As word processors become more and more flexible and powerful, they are often used as page-makeup programs. By the same token the more powerful page-makeup programs are used for word processing. As a result, the difference between word processing and page makeup becomes blurred. The difference between the two activities is best understood in terms of the difference between writing and publishing. Word processors are used for getting the words into the computer. Page-makeup programs are for taking the writing from a word processor and putting it into a publication format. This may or may not involve placing graphics with the text.

Imagine the old-fashioned cut-and-paste procedure where page makeup was done with a pair of scissors and a glue pot. Writers would prepare their stories on a typewriter. Then the various stories would be cut up and arranged in the publication. The arrangement of the stories in the publication is the page makeup function. We are not referring to the arrangement of the paragraphs in a story—that is done by the author. The publisher takes the stories and arranges them in the publication.

When word processors replaced typewriters as the primary tool of writers, the cutting and pasting in publications began to be done not with a pair of scissors and a glue pot but electronically. Now publication composers use page-makeup programs like PageMaker to take files of word-processed text and arrange them in a publication.

WORD PROCESSING TO PAGE MAKEUP

The biggest problem that occurs between word-processing files and page-makeup programs is the attempt to do all the formatting in the word processor. You can transfer certain formatting commands from word-processing files to PageMaker, but much of the formatting done in the word processor may have to be undone when you use PageMaker. For example, an indentation that may look just right on a single-column 8.5- by 11-inch page may look far too deep for a two-column 6- by 9-inch page. So if formatting is to be done on the word processor, either make sure it is consistent with the publication being prepared in PageMaker, or minimize the formatting until you place the story in PageMaker.

Compatible Word Processors

Several word processors can be used with PageMaker, and even noncompatible word processors can be employed if files are handled correctly. First, we will list the compatible Macintosh word processors and then examine how to deal with new versions of word processors and noncompatible word processors. The following word processors are compatible with PageMaker 4.2:

MicroSoft Word Versions 3.02 and 4.0

MacWrite Versions 5.0 and II

MicroSoft Works Version 2.00a

WordPerfect Version 1.02

DCA

RTF

If your word processor is fully compatible with PageMaker you can skip the following section on text files. However, later on if you are using files from someone else's word processor and are getting strange results, you may want to come back and review the following discussion of placing text files.

Text Files from Any Word Processor

If your word processor is not on the preceding list, you can still prepare material for PageMaker by saving it as a text file. Most word processors have a provision for saving written materials as "text" or "ASCII" files. Certain formats may be retained, such as tabs, spaces, and "carriage returns." Depending on how your word processor formats text in a text file, it will be a greater or lesser problem when moved into PageMaker.

A special case where you will find text formats very useful is when you have word-processed files from non-Macintosh computers. For example, if you will be working with files created on WordPerfect 5.1 on an IBM computer, the file can be saved from WordPerfect as a text file. That file can be transferred to your Macintosh via a modem or special IBM-Macintosh conversion program. The text file can then be placed with PageMaker.

In cases where you have a noncompatible word processor and save the file as a text file, avoid even minimal formatting such as indentations for paragraphs. It is a lot easier to format all the text in PageMaker than to first undo certain formatting problems and then reformat the whole thing. The next section, "Text Troubles," helps identify two troublesome text formats and explains how to deal with them.

Since word processors are frequently updated, often with considerable changes, you may find yourself with an updated version of your favorite word processor that can no longer be used with Page-Maker. The best thing to do in this case is to contact Aldus and ask them if an updated import filter for the latest version of your word processor is available. They will either have it available at a nominal fee or tell you where you can get one.

Alternatively, with an upgraded word processor, you have the option of saving the file under the old version that still works with

PageMaker. This second option may not be able to take advantage of some of the word processor's new features, but you can still get everything placed in PageMaker and make adjustments in the page makeup process. If all else fails, you can still save it as a text file.

TEXT TROUBLES

In this section, we will discuss some common problems importing text from word processors. Not only can you import text into Page-Maker 4.2 from Macintosh computer, but it is also possible to import files from IBM/compatible and other computers as well.

Hard Carriage Returns

In most word processors when text has reached the end of a line, the "end of line" is denoted by something other than a "hard carriage return." That is, there is no ASCII code in the text that tells the computer that the position in the text is a carriage return. However, some word processors save the end of a line as a hard carriage return along with the code in the text that makes the text break as a carriage return, no matter what. Figures 5.1 and 5.2 show what happens when text has hard carriage returns in a story.

In Figure 5.1, the original line breaks were set with hard carriage returns. When the text was reformatted in Figure 5.2, note that the narrower margin forces new line breaks, but the original line breaks

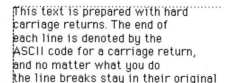

This text is prepared with hard
carriage returns. The end of
each line is denoted by the
ASCII code for a carriage return,
and no matter what you do
the line breaks stay in their original
positions.

FIGURE 5.1 Hard carriage returns in original format

```
This text is prepared
with hard
carriage returns. The
end of
each line is denoted
by the
ASCII code for a car-
riage return,
and no matter what
you do
the line breaks stay
in their original
positions.
```

FIGURE 5.2 Hard carriage returns in
PageMaker text block

are still there, giving the text line breaks in positions before the end of the line. If this happens with the text files you create with a word processor, see if you can change the format in your word processor to save the text with "soft" carriage returns or no carriage returns at all. Compare Figures 5.1 and 5.2 with Figures 5.3 and 5.4, where soft carriage returns are used. In the latter set, the lines are more even, and PageMaker used the hyphenation process to even up the line lengths.

If you cannot have the word-processing software get rid of the hard carriage returns in the text, you can do it "by hand." This involves placing the cursor in front of the first word on the line below the hard carriage return and pressing (BACKSPACE). This is tedious work, and for long publications it is even more so. Therefore, before you do a lot of extra work, consider getting a new word processor to use with PageMaker or even using the Story Editor built into Page-Maker 4.2.

```
This text is prepared with soft
carriage returns. The end of
each line is determined by the
current format and not an ASCII
character for a hard carriage
return.
```

FIGURE 5.3 Soft carriage return in
original document

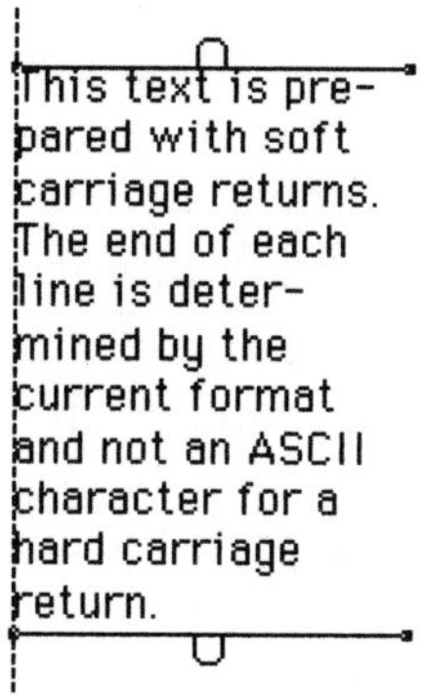

This text is pre-
pared with soft
carriage returns.
The end of each
line is deter-
mined by the
current format
and not an ASCII
character for a
hard carriage
return.

FIGURE 5.4 Soft carriage return in PageMaker text block

Spaces Replacing Tabs

A second major text trouble occurs when word processors save text with spaces replacing tabs. Instead of having a single tab character in the text, the word processor puts in several spaces. Since computer codes for spaces and tabs are different, the spaces-for-tabs situation has to be handled differently from tabs-for-tabs.

A typical problem that occurs when encountering spaces-for-tabs can be seen when you attempt to change the tab setting from within PageMaker. Since PageMaker uses a tab instead of spaces-for-tabs, all spaces are treated as spaces. If there are ten spaces that make up the "tab," there is nothing the Indents/tabs ruler can do to change that ten-space tab.

However, you can fix things without having to use (BACKSPACE) to remove all of the spaces. The trick is to use the *Change* option from the **Edit** menu while in the Story Editor. Selecting the *Change* option, tap in the number of spaces you want to replace in the Find What box of the Change dialog box. In the Change To box, just click the cursor and input nothing. Next to *Options* select *Whole Word*. Finally, click *Change All* and your space-tabs will be gone. Using (TAB), you can put in regular tabs and adjust them with the *Indents/tabs . . .* option of the **Type** menu.

Story Preparation

On the most basic level, preparing text for inclusion into PageMaker is not significantly different from preparing it as you normally would. You can do all of the formatting in PageMaker, or you can do some of it in your word processor and some in PageMaker, depending on how comfortably you can handle the formatting in your word processor. The degree to which PageMaker can read all of the formatted text depends on the import filter and the nature of the word processor. For example, PageMaker can import the page breaks from documents produced by Microsoft Word Version 4.0, but not with MacWrite. Likewise, PageMaker imports graphics imbedded in most word processors by not in Microsoft Works. Experiment some with your word processor to see what you can format in the word processor and what you should leave to PageMaker formatting.

Tags

In our discussion of style sheets in Chapter 8, we will see that various font styles can be created in PageMaker so that an entire paragraph can be selected and the font, style, size, and leading of a paragraph can be changed in a simple operation. Here, though, it is important to know something about tags, since your word processor may not have style definition itself. If it does not, you may want to use tags to define styles from your word processor. (Note: Most word processors do define styles, which you can place in PageMaker, and so the use of tags may not apply to you.)

To tag text, use angle brackets (< >) around the name of the style you wish the paragraph to be. For example, <Headline>, <Caption>, and <Body> show typical styles that can be assigned to a paragraph. PageMaker automatically removes the brackets and style names when the story is placed and provides the selected style to the paragraph. The following two lines show how a word-processed line would look and how it would look in PageMaker once placed:

<Headline> Computers Improve!

Computers Improve!

Of course, you may find it a lot easier to make all of the style changes from PageMaker and will not need to use the tags in preparing text. However, the tag option is available if you need it. In the discussion on defining styles, there will be references to using these tags. Remember they are used only with word processing files that do not define styles themselves.

GRAPHICS IN TEXT

Chapter 9 on "Graphics," has an extended discussion of working with graphics. At this point it is worth introducing the difference between graphics that are added to a publication after the text has been placed and graphics that are embedded in the word processing.

Inline Graphics

Inline graphics was introduced with PageMaker 4.0. Basically, the term *inline graphics* refers to graphics that are attached to text in a publication. With independent graphics, and all earlier versions of PageMaker, the graphics are not part of a text block. If the text is shifted because of addition or deletion of text or text-block adjustments, the text flows above and below the graphic. This is especially troublesome when you have graphics with captions. Consider a page with two graphics and two accompanying captions. Figure 5.5 shows how they are supposed to look.

With independent graphics, if the text is shifted, the captions will be shifted but not the artwork, causing the strange results shown in Figure 5.6.

Wins "Puss of the Year"

Paid millions to model clothes

FIGURE 5.5 Independent graphics in original positions

Paid millions to model clothes

FIGURE 5.6 Shifting text without inline graphics

The easiest way to avoid the problems of shifting captions and other text around graphics is to place the graphic and text together in the word processor. In that way, they automatically are placed as inline graphics. This is an option and it need not be elected. However, when you do have many graphics and captions or other text that must be kept together with the graphics, the simplest route is to first place graphic and text together in the word processor. (In Chapter 9, "Graphics," we will discuss how to get inline graphics after text and graphics have already been placed.)

PLACING STORIES

The heart of PageMaker is the *Place* . . . command in the **File** menu. If you are going to place a story or graphics, all that is required is that the file be compatible with PageMaker. Using the ⌘-Ⓓ shortcut or clicking *Place* . . . in the **File** menu, you select the file you want placed in your publication.

The Place dialog box shows the files available for placement. The window shows the various files and folders that are in the current folder. Point and click at the file or folder your want. If you press the folder name above the window, you will see the folders and disk higher in the hierarchy. For example, in Figure 5.7, the current

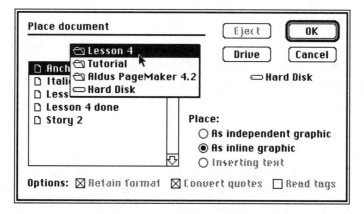

FIGURE 5.7 Finding a file from the Place dialog box

folder is named Lesson 4. It is in a folder called Tutorial, which is in a folder called Aldus PageMaker 4.2 that is on the hard-disk drive. They have the following hierarchy:

```
Hard drive (contains)
        Aldus PageMaker 4.2 (contains)
                Tutorial (contains)
                        Lesson 4 (contains)
                                Anchor.TIF
                                Italic.TIF
                                Lesson 3 done
                                Lesson 4 done
                                Story 1
```

Think of the drive as the base of the hierarchy, and all the folders as building up on it to the current folder. Click the Drive button to find folders and files on a floppy drive or other hard drive. Experiment with finding different files, folders, and disks. It takes a little hunting and pecking before it becomes a simple task.

Placing Options

When placing a file, you have three options. Usually, you will be using the default placement of a story as a new item. We will examine each option in turn.

As a New Item

When you are placing a story as "a new item," whatever you place is independent of anything that has already been placed. The story or graphic is treated as something that is to be added to the pages you are making.

Replacing an Entire Story

Before you can use this option, you must first select a story by clicking an existing story's window block. Figures 5.8 and 5.9 show what happens when this option is selected. Using the Pointer tool, "Story

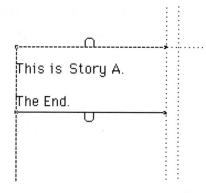

FIGURE 5.8 Original story in place

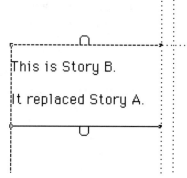

FIGURE 5.9 After selecting *Replace Entire Story* option

A" in Figure 5.8 was selected. The outlines and tabs showing on the screen indicate it is the story to be replaced.

The new story that is to replace the original story is placed in the location of the original story. Figure 5.9 shows the replacement story, "Story B," having replaced and deleted "Story A."

Inserting Text

A final placement option allows you to insert text in a story to replace selected text. This may occur when you want to replace only a paragraph or two instead of an entire story.

To insert text with the *Place* command, first select the text you wish to replace using the Text tool. Drag the pointer over the text to darken it, as shown in Figure 5.10.

Then click *Replacing Selected Text* as the *Place* option. The text you place will replace the selected text, as shown in Figure 5.11.

Note that when the replacement text did not fit within the parameters of the column, it simply made room for itself. Also note that it is no longer darkened.

Format Options

At the bottom of the Place Document dialog box are three format options. The first two, *Retain Format* and *Convert Quotes*, are default options, while the third, *Read Tags*, is not.

- **Retain Format**   When you opt to retain the format, it simply means that the format you used in your word processor is

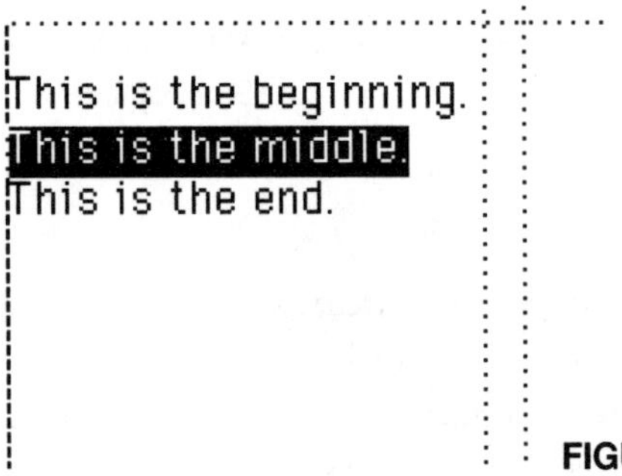

```
This is the beginning.
This is the middle.
This is the end.
```

FIGURE 5.10 Selecting text to be replaced

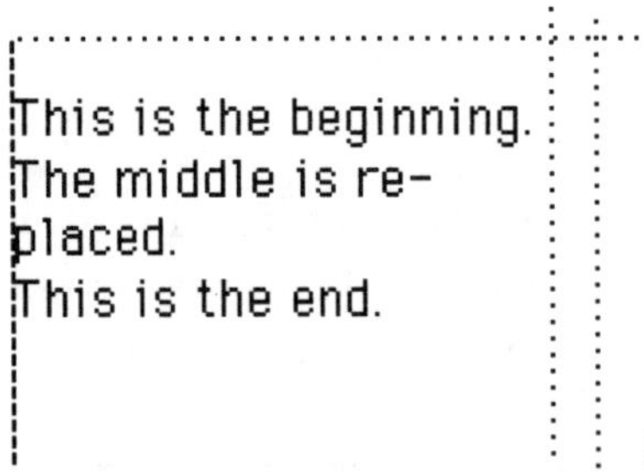

```
This is the beginning.
The middle is re-
placed.
This is the end.
```

FIGURE 5.11 Replacement text in place

retained. Otherwise, the format will be formatted according to PageMaker's default format.

- **Convert Quotes** This feature of PageMaker saves a lot of time. If your word processor does not do so automatically, PageMaker converts straight quotes and apostrophes into curved ones. Double quotes are converted to "open" and "closed" ones.

- **Read Tags** The option to read tags refers to those word processors that can only format text using the tag method discussed elsewhere in this chapter. It is very important to remember to click this option if you have used the angle bracket method to indicate styles in your word processor.

Text Flow

When you place text in a publication using the default place selection (As new item), you have three placement options for the flow of the text. Depending on the type of publication you are creating, each option has its uses.

Manual The default configuration for placing text is the manual one. The Text icon shown to the left appears on the screen. Placing the icon pointer and clicking the left mouse button "releases" the text and it flows into the column until it reaches the bottom margin. The manual option is most useful when you have to place text in various parts of the page or on nonsequential pages.

Autoflow For longer publications, especially books and other publications where you want the flow to go from top to bottom and left to right, the *Autoflow* option is a real timesaver. By placing the Autoflow pointer at the beginning point of your publication, it will place the story in sequential columns and pages, starting in the leftmost column and proceeding until the entire story is placed. It even automatically adds pages. The *Autoflow* option can either be selected from the **Options** menu or be keyed by holding down ⌘ while the manual flow icon appears.

Semiautomatic Flow   The *Semiautomatic Flow* option will automatically prepare for the next placement but waits until the user positions the pointer and clicks the mouse button before continuing the flow. Holding down (SHIFT), with either the automatic or manual flow will generate the semiautomatic flow.

Working the Flow

In this section, we will go through a step-by-step flow to show exactly what you will be doing when placing text. We will use the *Manual Flow* option.

Step 1   Once you have selected the story to place, you will have a "loaded" icon that you will position at the location where you want to begin the text flow. Figure 5.12 shows how your screen will appear.

Step 2   Click the button, and the first segment of the story will flow to the bottom of the first column. The manual Text icon will be replaced by the Arrow icon. At the bottom of

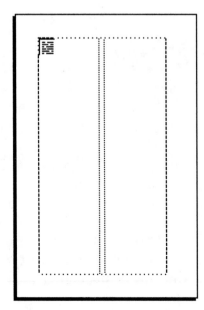

FIGURE 5.12 Story loaded in icon and ready to be placed

the text block will be a windowshade tab with a dark point in it. That indicates there is more text in the story to flow. Figure 5.13 shows how the page appears after the first text has been flowed.

Step 3   Click the bottom windowshade handle and a "loaded" manual Text Flow icon will reappear. Place it in the top of the second column and click the left mouse button to continue the flow. When the story has been fully placed, a blank windowshade tab appears at the bottom of the text block as shown in Figure 5.14.

Using the Automatic Flow option, you would simply execute the first step and all the rest would be done automatically. With the Semiautomatic Flow option, there would be no need to click the bottom windowshade handle, as was done in the second step, since a "loaded" icon would automatically appear.

Drag-Placing

In some applications, you will want to place your text somewhere other than within the standard margins and columns of your publica-

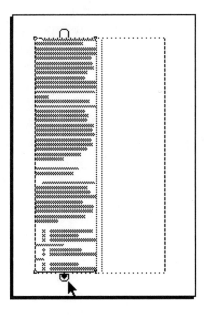

FIGURE 5.13 Dark triangle shows there is more text to be placed

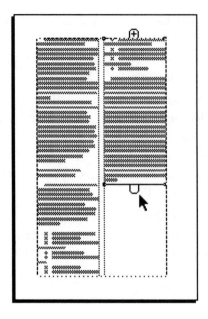

FIGURE 5.14 Clear tab means all text in story is placed.

tion. However, at the same time you want to delimit where the text will go. For example, you may have a small announcement that goes in the corner of a newsletter. Using drag placement, you can place the announcement in a specified area by dragging the loaded icon around the area into which you want to place it.

Once the icon is loaded and the text is ready to place, drag a rectangle around the area where you want your text to flow. Figure 5.15 shows what you will see on your screen when the area is correctly dragged.

If you hold the left mouse button while dragging the defined area, the text will automatically flow into the block as soon as the button is released. Figure 5.16 shows the block in between the

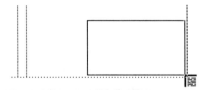

FIGURE 5.15 Area dragged by loaded icon

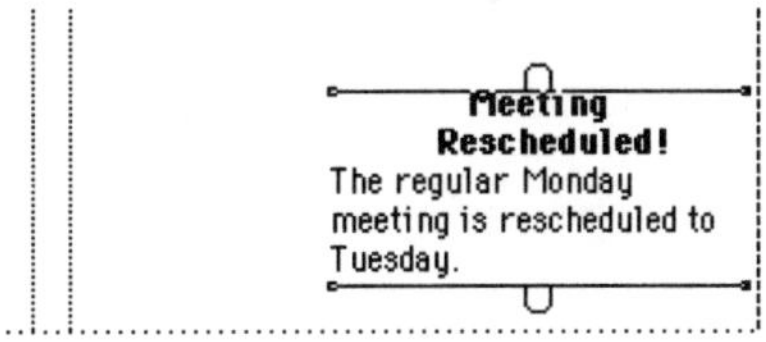

**Meeting
Rescheduled!**
The regular Monday
meeting is rescheduled to
Tuesday.

FIGURE 5.16 Text block is in dragged area only.

margin and the column using only the area defined when the icon was dragged around it.

To further offset the announcement, you can drag a graphic line around it as shown in Figure 5.17. Further on in the book when we discuss graphics, there will be several applications where drag-placing will be important so that graphics can be placed around text blocks without running into other columns.

Before you try your first serious publication with PageMaker, practice some with the placement options. In this way you will become familiar with placing text and not be afraid of ruining a layout. It won't take much time, and it will allow you to experiment with the different options.

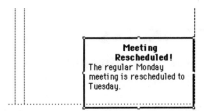

**Meeting
Rescheduled!**
The regular Monday
meeting is rescheduled to
Tuesday.

FIGURE 5.17 A graphic rectangle frames text.

WORKING WITH PLACED TEXT

O nce you have your story placed in a publication, you still may have a lot of adjustments to make. This chapter covers all of the different ways of working with text from the layout view in PageMaker. In Chapter 7, "Using the Story Editor and Table Editors," we will discuss two features that allow further work with text from within PageMaker.

READING WINDOWSHADE HANDLES

In Chapter 5, we briefly discussed what the different windowshade handles mean when placing text. Further clarification follows.

Beginning handle   A clear window-shade handle at the top indicates the beginning of a story.

Further-story handle   A bottom handle with a plus sign indicates further blocks in the story. This occurs at the bottom of a text block when continuing blocks have already been placed.

Prior-story handle   A top handle with a plus sign indicates there are previous blocks in the story. This would occur at the top of a text block that is a continuation of a previous text block.

More-to-place handle The arrow-head handle means there is still more story that can be loaded into the icon and be placed.

 End-of-story handle The bottom clear handle means the block is the last one in the story, no more blocks come after it, and there is no more story to place.

TEXT BLOCKS

Identifying text blocks is done by locating the beginning and ending windowshade handles. Whenever text is clicked with the arrow pointer, the text block will appear. A text block is made up of the top and bottom windowshade handles and four corner handles. Figure 6.1 shows a text block with the lower right-hand corner handle circled.

Resizing Text-Block Shapes

Either windowshade handle or any of the four corner handles can be used to change the size and shape of the text block. The purpose of having text blocks in a flexible format is to give the user maximum control over the placement of text in a publication. For example, suppose you decide that the column is too narrow, and you want to change the column size. After changing the column, you find the text block does not fit. Instead of having to re-place the text, you can use the pointer to drag one of the corner handles and stretch the block to fit the new column as shown in Figures 6.2 and 6.3.

Whenever you change the size of a text block, the text in the story is automatically redistributed. If you enlarge a text block, text from another part of the story will flow into the enlarged area. If you decrease a text block's size, the text will be pushed up ahead into another text block.

Using the top and bottom windowshade handles, you can also change the size of a block within a column. For example, if you find you want to move a text block up to fill in a space you had previously used for a graphic but now want to fill with text, you can drag the top

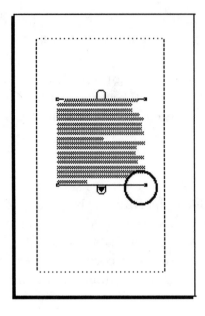

FIGURE 6.1 Each corner of a text block has a handle.

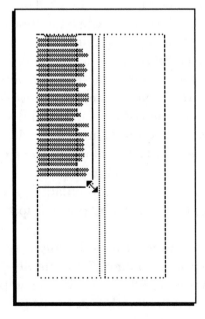

FIGURE 6.2 Dragging a corner handle to resize text block

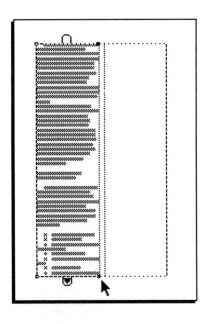

FIGURE 6.3 New text block is filled with text.

windowshade upward to the top of the column. The rest of the block will move up and fill in the column with text. Figure 6.4 illustrates dragging the windowshade handle up to the top of the column.

Text blocks often must be adjusted when you need to insert a graphic in a text column. Beginning with the block shown in Figure 6.5, we will see how to make adjustments to place a graphic in the middle of the column with text above and below the graphic.

First, we'll need to shorten the text block by dragging the bottom windowshade handle upwards to make room in the center of the column for the graphic. Figure 6.6 shows how the truncated block appears after having been shortened. Note also that the bottom windowshade tab has changed from a clear one to one indicating there is more text in the story. We have shortened the text block and thereby removed some text that we'll need to add after the graphic.

Once room has been made for the graphic, place the graphic below the top text block. Figure 6.7 shows how the page appears after the graphic has been placed.

The final step is to click the pointer on the bottom windowshade handle of the top text block to load the pointer. Then place the

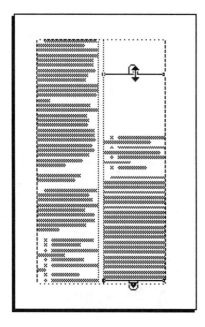

FIGURE 6.4 Dragging text block to top margin

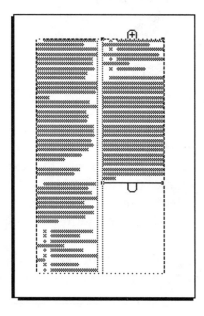

FIGURE 6.5 Text block follows handle to top.

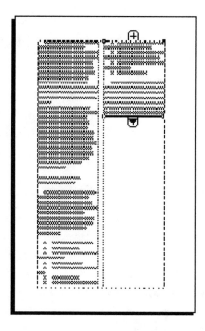

FIGURE 6.6 More-to-place handle appears when block is shortened.

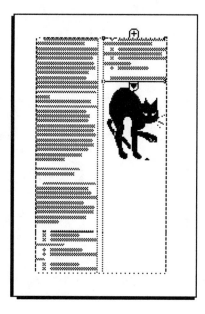

FIGURE 6.7 Graphic is placed below shortened text block.

pointer below the graphic, as shown in Figure 6.8, and click the mouse button to replace the text that was removed when the text block was shortened.

Once the text has been re-placed below the graphic, the rest of the text in the original block has been restored, and the graphic is placed in the middle of the column with text above and below it, as seen in Figure 6.9.

Moving Text Blocks

In addition to changing the size of a text block, it is possible to move an entire text block. To move a block of text, place the pointer anywhere on the text block except one of the corner or windowshade handles. Press the mouse button down until there is a four-sided arrow on the text block. Then move the text block in any direction you want. Figure 6.10 shows a text block being moved from one page to another. Note the four-pointed arrow in the lower right-hand portion of the text block. Remember to wait until the four-pointed arrow appears before attempting to move the text block.

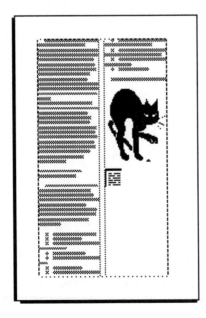

FIGURE 6.8 Icon is loaded with text from the shortened text block.

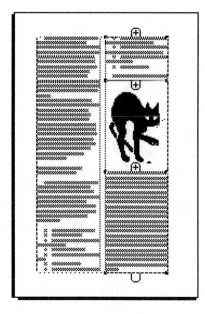

FIGURE 6.9 Remaining text is placed below graphic.

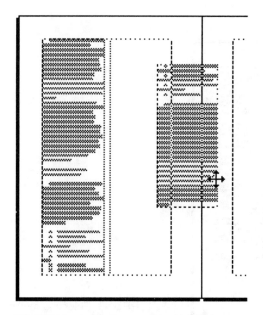

FIGURE 6.10 Moving text block across page

Selecting Multiple Blocks of Text

To move multiple text blocks, you first need to select them. There are two ways to do this:

Method 1   Click one text block to be selected, and then holding down Shift click on the other blocks you wish to select.

Method 2 With the Pointer tool, draw around the text blocks you wish to select. Using this method, it is best to make the selection from a fit-in-window or fit-in-world view so that you are sure to surround all of the text blocks. Figure 6.11 shows three text blocks and a graphic being surrounded by the broken-line rectangle made when the pointer tool is dragged around objects on a page. When the mouse button is released, all three text blocks and the graphic will be selected.

Once the blocks are selected, proceed to move them as you would a single block. Figure 6.12 shows two text blocks being moved from one page to another.

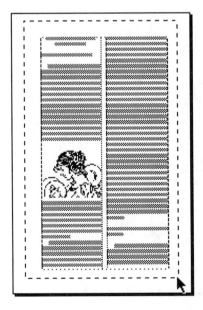

FIGURE 6.11 Selecting multiple blocks of
text with Pointer tool

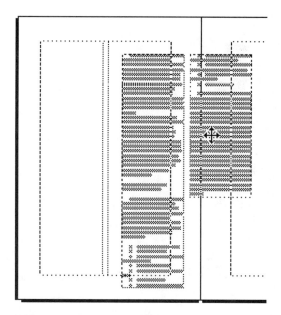

FIGURE 6.12 Moving multiple text blocks simultaneously

Threaded Text

A key concept to understand when working with text blocks and PageMaker in general is that of threaded text. When a story is placed in PageMaker, all of the text is treated as a sequential unit. Page-Maker remembers where all of the words go; and no matter how you change the text blocks, it maintains the word order and shifts text forward and backward as text blocks are changed.

In order to understand text threading in PageMaker, we'll go through a practice session that will give you the "feel" of threaded text. Using a four-column page, we will see how threading works. Beginning with the page shown in Figure 6.13, we see four text blocks constituting an entire story. We can see that it is a complete story because the beginning windowshade handle and the ending windowshade handle are both blank. (The windowshade handles with a plus mark indicate the text block has more text before or after it.)

Imagine that the four columns represent a single story in four pages instead of four columns. They were put on a single page so you

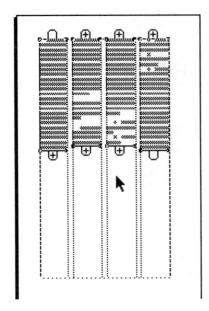

FIGURE 6.13 Single story in four text blocks

could see what happens to the rest of the story when changes are made in the text blocks.

The first thing we will do in this exercise is to elongate the text block in column 3 by pulling downward on the windowshade handle of the third text block. The result is that the text block in the fourth column disappears, and all of the fourth text block's text flows into the elongated text block of the third column. Figure 6.14 shows how the page appears when the third text block is elongated.

At this point, the page has only three text blocks, but it is important to understand that there is the same amount of text. Text blocks are like containers. The text is like liquid within the container. As prior containers in the sequence are expanded, the text from the later containers flows to the prior ones. However, if later containers are expanded, the text does not flow forward. It only flows backwards in the sequence to prior text blocks. Also, keep in mind that while all of the text blocks in this exercise are on one page, the same thing will happen across multiple pages in your publication when all of the text is in the same story.

To see one text block shrink, but not disappear, when a text block is expanded, pull the bottom windowshade handle of the text block in the first column to the bottom as shown in Figure 6.15.

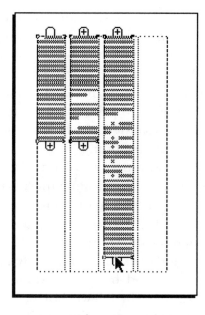

FIGURE 6.14 One block disappears as another block is expanded.

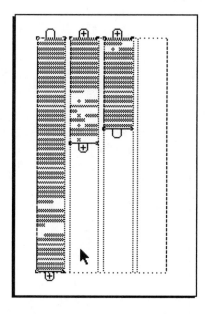

FIGURE 6.15 Text blocks shrink when prior blocks with threaded text are expanded.

As you will see, the third text block shrinks as its text flows into the prior blocks in the sequence. However, it does not disappear since all of the text did not flow out.

Now to see that text does not flow forward and expand later text blocks, move the bottom windowshade handles of the first two columns so that they are as shown in Figure 6.16. Notice that the arrow appears now at the bottom of the third text block. That's because later text blocks will not expand to accept new text even though they can shrink as text flows to prior blocks that have been expanded. Since they cannot be expanded, the block indicates there is more text to be placed in the publication.

To put things back to the way they were initially, it will be necessary to click on the windowshade indicating there is more text, and then place the loaded icon pointer into the fourth column to re-place the text, as shown in Figure 6.17. Once it is re-placed, the page should look like it did originally as shown in Figure 6.13.

The more you experiment and work with threaded text, the more you will intuitively understand it and how to maximize its use in PageMaker. If it is a little confusing at first, it will be clearer each time you use the program. In the meantime, experiment with the exercise illustrated in Figures 6.13 to 6.17.

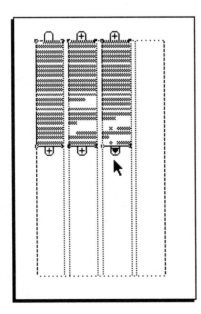

FIGURE 6.16 Threaded text does not flow forward—only backward

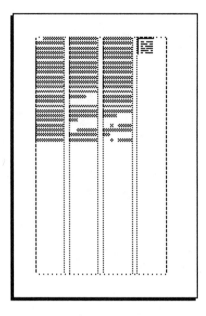

FIGURE 6.17 Original block is restored by re-flowing the text.

SELECTING TEXT IN LAYERS

New PageMaker users often encounter a problem when they attempt to select text or a text block and find they cannot make the desired selection. The problem usually lies in overlapping text blocks. The text the user wants to select is below another text block, but because neither block is selected, the user cannot see the overlap. This occurs most commonly when a headline with some blank spaces on the bottom overlaps the body text. For example, look at Figure 6.18. There is nothing to indicate overlapping text blocks.

However, when we step back and select all of the blocks on the page, we see there are two overlapping text blocks, as shown in Figure 6.19.

Zooming back in, we can see that there is a good deal of overlap of the headline over the body text. In fact, the first three lines of body text are overlapped by the text block of the headline as shown in Figure 6.20.

PageMaker has layers of text blocks dependent on the last block that was placed. If the body text were placed before the headline,

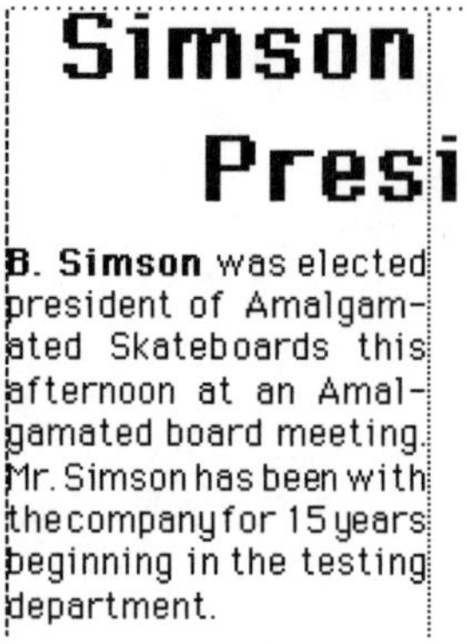

Simson
Presi
B. Simson was elected president of Amalgamated Skateboards this afternoon at an Amalgamated board meeting. Mr. Simson has been with the company for 15 years beginning in the testing department.

FIGURE 6.18 Overlaps are not visible unless blocks are selected.

Simson Elected
President

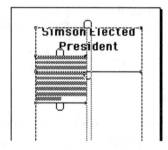

FIGURE 6.19 Once selected, block overlaps become apparent.

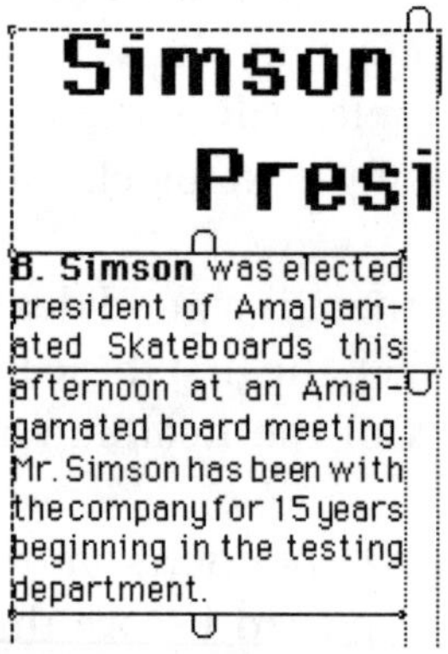

Simson
Presi
B. Simson was elected president of Amalgamated Skateboards this afternoon at an Amalgamated board meeting. Mr. Simson has been with the company for 15 years beginning in the testing department.

FIGURE 6.20 Identifying where overlaps occur

then it would lie beneath the headline text. If you attempt to select either the block or individual lines of text in the first three lines of the body text, either no text at all would be selected or the headline block would be selected. Figure 6.21 illustrates what's going on. As long as the top layer overlaps the bottom, the bottom is inaccessible.

The solution to the problem is to bring the body layer to the top. This is done by clicking on a portion of the text block that is not overlapped by the top block. With the arrow pointer selected, click on the nonoverlapped portion of the bottom layer of text as shown in Figure 6.22.

Once the underlying text block has been selected, select *Bring to Front* from the **Element** menu. A shortcut is to use ⌘-Ⓕ (SHIFT) to place the text block in front. Now, in the layout view, you can select the text in the body text block.

Top layer

Bottom layer

FIGURE 6.21 Text blocks may be layered two or more deep.

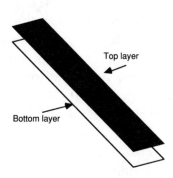

FIGURE 6.22 Selecting text block to be brought to front.

In some cases, one block of text will be entirely covering another text block. When this happens, there is no way that the *Bring to Front* command can work, since it is impossible to click on a portion of the bottom text block that is not covered by the top block. For example, the following illustration shows a situation where the bottom text block, made up of a standing cap (the large bold "Q"), is engulfed by the body text:

Quite a bit was
written about her, but
none of it was as good as
what she wrote herself.

In order to select either the text block of the standing cap or the letter itself, the element is going to have to be moved to the top or front layer. To do this requires not moving the standing cap to the front, but rather moving the body text to the back. This is done by selecting the body-text block using the Pointer tool and choosing *Send to Back* (or use ⌘-Ⓑ) from the **Element** menu. Now the standing cap block is in front and the body text is in the back. If you have several layers, you want to send all the layers to the back until you reach the desired block.

A shortcut you can employ is to place the pointer on the area of the desired block and click the mouse button while holding down ⌘. It automatically selects the background text block. With more than two layers of text, using this method is a little tricky if you want an in-between layer.

THE TEXT TOOL

The Text tool is employed for entering and editing text. For the most part, PageMaker is not designed for entering a lot of text the way a word processor is, but many times you will need to add a little text here and there and change the size, style, or even shape of text. To select the Text tool, either click the "A" in the Toolbox or press

(SHIFT)-(F4). When the Text tool has been selected, you will see an I-beam-shaped icon. The following illustration shows the Text Tool icon selected:

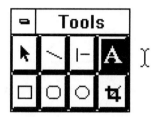

Selecting Text

In order to edit text, it is first necessary to select it. When text is selected, it will be shown in inverse video on the screen. The background will turn black and the text white. When using text of different colors, the inverse of the text will depend on the color. For example, green text turns violet when selected.

To select text, the common method is to use the mouse, holding the button down and dragging the pointer over the desired text. When the text turns inverse, you know it has been selected. Large amounts of text can also be selected by clicking the pointer at the beginning of the desired text, and then holding down Shift and clicking at the end of the desired text. Finally, for smaller amounts of text, placing the cursor to the left of a word and clicking the mouse button twice will select the entire word. Clicking the mouse three times anywhere on a paragraph will select the entire paragraph.

Select All

A special case where you want to select all blocks, both text and graphics on a screen or all text in a single block, is done with *Select All* from the **Edit** menu or using ⌘-Ⓐ on the keyboard. If the Text tool is being used, all of the text in a story is selected. This is useful for making major changes such as text type or size in a single operation in an entire story. If the pointer tool is being used, all of the text blocks and graphic blocks on a screen are selected. If two pages are shown, then everything on both pages is selected. Table 6.1 provides a quick summary.

TABLE 6.1 Text Selection

Amount	*Method*
Moderate	Drag with Text tool.
One word	Double-click to left of word.
One paragraph	Triple-click in paragraph.
Several Lines	Click cursor at beginning of selection, hold down (SHIFT) key and click at end of selection.
Entire screen or text block	Use *Select all* from **Edit** or text block menu or ⌘-(A).

To cancel a selection, just place the pointer off to the side of the page and click or select something else.

Adding Text

If a lot of text must be added to a publication, use the Story Editor. The next chapter explains how to use the Story Editor in detail. For smaller amounts of text, you can add text to a story in two basic ways. First, you can add text to an existing story that has been placed in the publication by selecting the Text tool and inserting the text anywhere you want in an existing text block. Click the mouse button at the point of desired insertion. From that point, simply type in the added text. The new text will be threaded with the rest of the text in the story block, shifting text forward. When adding text this way, be sure to check the end of the story to see if the last text block was expanded beyond the margins. Figures 6.23 to 6.26 show a text

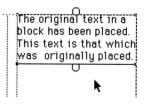

FIGURE 6.23 Beginning with a placed document

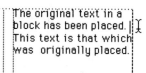

FIGURE 6.24 Making an insertion point by clicking the mouse pointer at the desired point of insertion

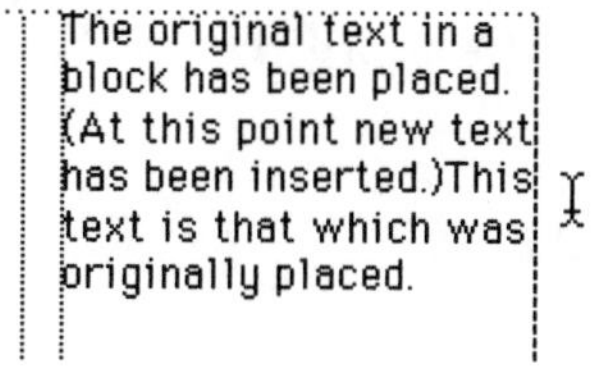

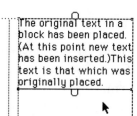

FIGURE 6.25 Adding the new text

FIGURE 6.26 The text block automatically expands to encompass the added text.

insertion sequence where new text is added and the text block expanded.

Drag-Placing

In some applications it may be necessary to define a new text block. This second basic way to add text uses *drag-placing,* or creating a new block by dragging the Text Tool icon around the area in which you wish to create a text block. The following illustration shows a rectangular area that has been dragged with the Text tool. The text icon is only partially visible when this is done:

When the block is complete, the outline disappears and the cursor is set in the upper left-hand corner of the block. Begin writing, and the text will fill in only the blocked area. Drag-placing is useful for creating blocks within margins, making marginal notations or even making notes off the page on the pasteboard. As can be seen in the following illustration, a block created with drag-placing lies between the column boundary and the margin:

In some applications you may need to create a block within another block of text. For example, if you want to highlight a certain statement with a clearly different format, you can draw the block outside the existing block and then move the new block inside the existing block. However, you cannot create a block inside an existing block using the drag-placing technique.

As we will see in Chapter 9, "Graphics," drag-placing is used extensively to place text inside a graphic. With some types of graphics, the text is repelled like similar poles on magnets, and the most efficient way to place text inside the graphic is to use drag-placing.

Editing Text

For any sizable amount of editing, use the Story Editor described in the next chapter. However, when you have just a little editing or editing on a small project, it is possible to edit directly on a Page-Maker layout page. We will start with the options for editing in the **Edit** menu.

Undo

For new users *Undo* is the most important single command you can remember. If you make a mistake, before you do anything else, you can undo the mistake. To execute an *Undo* command, either select *Undo* from the **Edit** menu, or press ⌘-Ⓩ on the keyboard. The undo operation has to be done before you enter any more text or change pointers.

Cut

There are two basic ways to use the *Cut* command. Using the Text tool to cut a segment of text from a publication, first select the text. Then choose *Cut* from the **Edit** menu or ⌘-Ⓧ on the keyboard. The selected segment of text will be put into a buffer and may be pasted elsewhere or left unused. With the next cut or copy operation, the originally cut material will be permanently deleted.

A second way to use the Cut command is with blocks of text. Using the Pointer tool, select a single block or several blocks of text. Then using *Cut* from the **Edit** menu or ⌘-Ⓧ on the keyboard, cut the text block(s). These blocks will be placed in a buffer and can be pasted elsewhere before any further material is cut or copied.

Copy

To execute a *Copy* command, select the material to copy, using either the Text tool or pointer, and choose *Copy* from the **Edit** menu or ⌘-Ⓒ on the keyboard. The *Copy* command works much like the *Cut* command in that the selected material is placed into a buffer. However, the selected material is not removed from the original position as it is with the *Cut* command. The copied materials may be pasted elsewhere until something else is copied or cut and placed into the buffer.

Paste

To insert material into your publication that has been cut or copied, use the paste operation. Select *Paste* from the **Edit** menu or press ⌘-Ⓥ on the keyboard to replace the material on the screen. When using the Text tool, click the cursor in the position you want the material to be pasted and then execute the paste procedure. Using the pointer to paste blocks seems a bit more random, but the paste is always right in the middle of the screen of whatever view is current. In a two-page fit-in-window view, the pasted block appears right between the two pages. From a 400 percent view, the pasted block is in the middle of the screen as well; but since from a 400 percent view much less screen is shown, it is a way to place a pasted block more precisely.

Another way of pasting text is a Paste/Replace operation. A selected bit of text is replaced by the contents of the copy buffer. This operation is useful when you want to replace a single word or sentence with one that has been cut or copied from somewhere else. To execute a Paste/Replace, first cut or copy the replacing text into the buffer. Next, select the text to be replaced and deleted. Finally, execute a normal paste operation from the menu or keyboard. The following four illustrations show how text can be replaced:

Begin with the original text:

It was a big surprise
when her husband came
home unannounced.

Cut or copy replacement text:

Select text to be replaced:

It was a big surprise
when her husband came
home unannounced.

Paste in replacement text:

```
It was a gigantic sur-
prise when her husband
came home
unannounced.
```

Once this operation is completed, the only way to get back the original text is to execute immediately the undo procedure. Otherwise, it is a handy way of saving a cut or clear when you want to replace one portion of text with another.

Clear

The *Clear* command is used only when you are absolutely, positively certain that you want to erase something. The *Clear* command does not place the deleted material into a buffer as does the *Cut* command. To erase using *Clear*, first select the material to be cleared, then choose *Clear* from the **Edit** menu or press (BACKSPACE) on the keyboard.

If you accidentally clear something, immediately execute the undo sequence. About the only advantage of using *Clear* instead of *Cut* is that the *Clear* operation does not erase whatever is in the buffer. Therefore, you can cut or copy from your publication and preserve its contents in the copy buffer while using the *Clear* command to erase other material. However, unless there is a good reason to keep material in the buffer, using the *Clear* command is a little like walking a tightrope without a net, and you would be generally better off using the *Cut* operation.

ADJUSTING TEXT

The more elaborate your publication, such as advertisement layouts, flyers, announcements, brochures, chapter headings, and certain types of newsletters, the more you will need to make adjustments. Earlier in this chapter we discussed making changes to windows and text blocks, and in this section we will discuss further adjustments.

Changing Text Windows to Accommodate Cuts and Pastes

When cuts and pastes are made, text blocks can be thrown out of alignment with other text and graphics. In the Chapter 9, "Graphics," we will discuss coordinating text and graphics, and here we will discuss adjusting for cuts, pastes, and adding text.

Making Room for Added Text

When text is pasted or added to a placed document, the text block frequently cannot accommodate the added text. The text then runs over the bottom margin of a column and must be adjusted. Repairing this requires that the text block be shortened by moving the bottom windowshade handle upwards to the bottom margin and then placing the overflow text at the top of the next column. The following four illustrations show the steps for making this adjustment.

Initially, end of text fits nicely, ending at the bottom margin:

```
    The pear growers'
meeting was well at-        I
tended by both young
and old pear growers.
```

New text is added or pasted and the text runs over the bottom margin:

```
    The pear growers'
meeting was well at-
tended by both young
and old pear growers.
Especially satisfying
was the number of
women pear growers.
```

Using the Pointer tool, the bottom of the text block is moved up to the bottom margin:

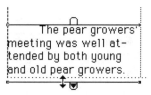

The bottom windowshade handle is clicked to load the cursor, which can then place the overflow text in the next column or page:

Adjusting for Cut or Cleared Text

Usually, cutting or clearing text does not cause the same problems in a publication as adding text. When text is removed, everything ripples backwards, and so there is no margin overflow as with adding text. However, in some instances when text is removed, you can get results that ruin the effect of a publication. For example, a common problem when text is removed is the oddly placed header. A header that was at the top of a column might be dropped to the bottom of the previous column, with no text following the header.

The adjustment for moving text after a hole has created an oddity in the publication is similar to adjustments with added text. By pushing and pulling on the text block windowshade handles, you can ripple the text back and forth until you have the desired results. Let's take a look at the problem of a misplaced header and see how easy it is to fix with PageMaker. This next series of illustrations and text show how to "shove" a header back in place.

At the outset, everything is fine. The following illustrations show the bottom left column and the top of the right column:

From 711 AD to 1492, the Moors occupied most of Spain. Composed of Berbers and Arabs, the Islamic Moors set up city states called *taifa states* The northern boundary of the taifa states ran from Lisbon to south of Barcelona with a bulge upward in Tudela and Huesca.

El Cid in Spain

During the mid-period of Moorish occupation, Rodrigo Diaz, better known as *El Cid* was a major military leader who fought for the Moors and Christians.

When text is deleted in the left column, the header falls to the bottom of the page, as the following illustration shows:

From 711 AD to 1492, the Moors occupied most of Spain. Composed of Berbers and Arabs, the Islamic Moors set up city states called *taifa states* The northern boundary of the taifa states ran from Lisbon to south of Barcelona
El Cid in Spain

Pushing windowshade handle up puts the header back where it belongs in the right column, and the bottom of the left column has a little white space above the bottom margin, as shown in the following illustration:

From 711 AD to 1492, the Moors occupied most of Spain. Composed of Berbers and Arabs, the Islamic Moors set up city states called *taifa states* The northern boundary of the taifa states ran from Lisbon to south of Barcelona.

After the adjustment, the top of the right column again appears as shown on the right in the first of the four illustrations. There is a blank space at the bottom of the column after the text block has been moved up; but as we will see in Chapter 10, "Style," white space in a publication is not necessarily a bad feature.

Controlling the "Ripple" Effect of Text Changes

One of the most frustrating things that can happen in a publication is to get everything just right and then have to make a small change that "ripples" everything out of line. The ripple effect is caused by the threading of the text in a story. However, there is a trick to save a lot of time readjusting the text if you have to add or delete a little text.

Consider the following problem. Your publication is complete, but you must add a crucial line that was omitted—such as the address of the company. If you add the line, the headers will be shoved forward a line; and instead of beginning at the tops of columns, they will be one line down.

The solution is to unthread the text. To do this requires cutting the block of text to which you wish to add the new material. After cutting the block, simply paste it back in; you will see that instead of having the plus handle at the bottom of the block, it has the end-of-story handle. That means the text is no longer threaded to the blocks further on in the story, and so whatever is added to the block will not ripple forward to affect the placement of text. Figures 6.27 and 6.28 show how this works.

The second block in Figure 6.27 requires added text. However, if the text is added, it will ripple everything forward, including the

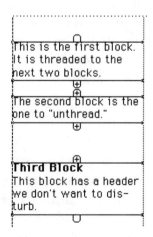

This is the first block. It is threaded to the next two blocks.

The second block is the one to "unthread."

Third Block
This block has a header we don't want to dis-turb.

FIGURE 6.27 Three threaded—but separated—blocks of text

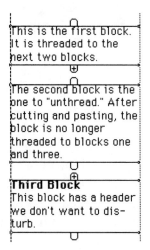

This is the first block. It is threaded to the next two blocks.

The second block is the one to "unthread." After cutting and pasting, the block is no longer threaded to blocks one and three.

Third Block
This block has a header we don't want to disturb.

FIGURE 6.28 The middle block is no longer threaded to the first and third

header in the third block. By cutting and pasting the second block, we create an "unthreaded" or independent block that neither affects nor is affected by the other two blocks. As can be seen in Figure 6.28, the blank top and bottom windowshade handles of the second block show it as an entire story. The plus signs have been removed from the handles of the second block. However, the first and third blocks are still threaded to one another.

"Rethreading" Text

If after unthreading text you find it was a big mistake, you can "rethread" the text. To do so, first use the Text tool to cut all of the text from the unthreaded block. Then paste the text at the bottom of the previous block. You can then place the text in a new block that will be threaded to the blocks before and after.

Font Work

Once you have placed your work and straightened out the blocks, there is still much work you can do with text. Making headlines or special characters and even changing the appearance of fonts is all possible with PageMaker 4.2. In this section we will examine how to set special text into an existing text block and how to change the shape of characters.

Headlines

In newsletter and magazine composition, a common page-makeup task is to place a headline over body text. With multiple-column layouts, it is necessary to resize the headline text block so that it fills the expanse of the top margins. It is a simple matter of using the "drag-placing" technique discussed earlier in this chapter. First, drag a block over the area into which you wish to place your headline, as shown in Figure 6.29. Note that the block goes across a column marker.

Once you have made the text block, simply type in your headline. Next, from the **Type** menu, select *Type Specs . . .* or press ⌘-Ⓣ on the keyboard. Select from the available fonts and the size and style of your font. Use center alignment from the *Alignment* option on the **Type** menu or ⌘-Ⓒ to place the headline right in the middle of the publication as shown in Figure 6.30.

Large Caps

Drop caps, standing caps, and other large caps are often used to begin chapters, articles, or sections of publications. Using the information from this chapter, we will see how to create them. A new feature of PageMaker 4.2 is the *Drop Cap . . .* selection in the **Aldus**

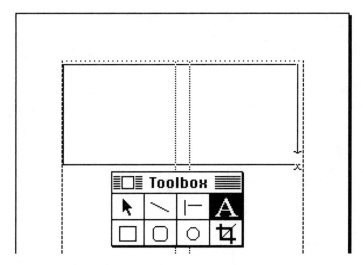

FIGURE 6.29 Dragged area crosses over column divider.

FIGURE 6.30 Placing headlines are placed without changing column setting

Additions submenu in the **Options** menu. This feature automatically puts in drop caps. However, there are other things you can do with large caps, and we will look at them as well.

Starting with a drop cap, the first thing to do is to insert a tab between the letter to be made into a drop cap and the rest of the paragraph. (Inserting the tab is optional, but it might help.) Be sure not to have the first line of the paragraph indented. Figure 6.31 shows how your text should look when you begin.

Once your text is set up as in Figure 6.31, you are just about ready to select *Drop Cap . . .* from **Aldus Additions** in the **Options** menu. To give it a bit more professional style, make the letters of "he big travel" into small caps using the *Small Caps* option in the *Type Specs . . .* submenu. Select the number of lines you want wrapped around the drop cap (we used three in the example), and you will have your drop cap sunk into your text automatically. Figure 6.32 shows how it will look when you are finished. Note that the hyphen that should connect "Be-sides" in lines two and three is missing. This is due to the

T   he big travel bargain
this year is Sri Lanka. Besides having been an inexpensive island paradise for
as long as I can remember,
the civil war there has kept
tourists at bay. As a result of
the conflict, there are plentiful low-cost accommoda-
tions.

FIGURE 6.31 You may optionally insert a tab after the letter to be made a drop cap

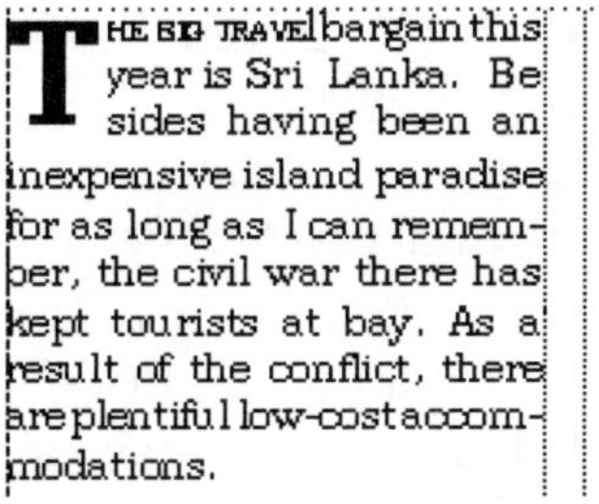

THE BIG TRAVEL bargain this year is Sri Lanka. Besides having been an inexpensive island paradise for as long as I can remember, the civil war there has kept tourists at bay. As a result of the conflict, there are plentiful low-cost accommodations.

FIGURE 6.32 The drop cap is created automatically with the *Drop Cap* addition.

soft carriage returns that the script for *Drop caps* uses. You have to type in the hyphens.

Once you have created a drop cap with the *Drop Cap* addition, be careful about resizing the text block or reflowing the text. In fact, putting the drop cap in should be done after you are sure that the page is set up the way you want it. However, leave a little extra room at the bottom for the space that will be inserted with the tab characters in the lines next to the drop cap.

If you want a cap to stand above and below a line, you have to do a little more work, but it is not difficult. First, using two separate text blocks, create a large cap and the text except for the first letter, as shown in Figure 6.33.

Next, insert tabs in the first three lines of the body text. After the last word in the indented lines, place a soft carriage return. This is

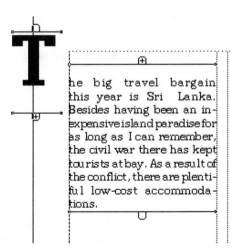

he big travel bargain this year is Sri Lanka. Besides having been an inexpensive island paradise for as long as I can remember, the civil war there has kept tourists at bay. As a result of the conflict, there are plentiful low-cost accommodations.

FIGURE 6.33 Create the cap and body text in two different blocks.

done by holding down (SHIFT) and pressing (RETURN). Figure 6.34 shows how the body text now looks.

Finally, place the large standing cap in the space inside and above the body text. Figure 6.35 shows the final placement of the body text and large cap.

With the text blocks deselected, the large cap fits in with the rest of the text, as shown in Figure 6.36. However, you may find that when

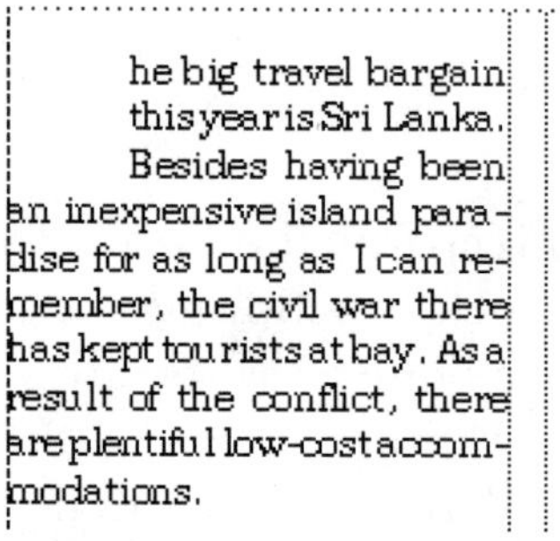

he big travel bargain this year is Sri Lanka. Besides having been an inexpensive island paradise for as long as I can remember, the civil war there has kept tourists at bay. As a result of the conflict, there are plentiful low-cost accommodations.

FIGURE 6.34 Use indents and soft carriage returns in the first three lines.

The big travel bargain this year is Sri Lanka. Besides having been an inexpensive island paradise for as long as I can remember, the civil war there has kept tourists at bay. As a result of the conflict, there are plentiful low-cost accommodations.

FIGURE 6.35 Bring the two text blocks together

The big travel bargain this year is Sri Lanka. Besides having been an inexpensive island paradise for as long as I can remember, the civil war there has kept tourists at bay. As a result of the conflict, there are plentiful low-cost accommodations.

FIGURE 6.36 The large cap appears to fit seamlessly with the body text.

you print the page, there will have to be adjustments. That's because the printed letters may be slightly different than they appear on the screen. This is especially true if you are using System 6.x instead of System 7.

Width Control

Another font adjustment available on PageMaker 4.2 is the width control of fonts. If you select *Set Width* from the **Type** menu, a submenu provides different percentages that you can use to expand or condense your type. Simply select the type to expand or condense, select the percentage from the *Set Width* window, and see the results on the screen. The following two illustrations show how the word *Expand* looks before and after it is widened to 250%:

To get the 250 percent expansions, select *Other . . .* from the **Set Width** submenu and type in **250**. You can enter values from 5 percent to 250 percent in the **Other . . .** submenu.

Going in the other direction, the next two illustrations show what you can do by narrowing the width of a font. The samples shows the word *Narrow* before and after condensing the font by 50 percent:

The distortions shown on your screen will not appear on PostScript printers. Depending on the type of monitor you have, the distortions will look better or worse. Experiment with the width changes to see what looks best with your printer and publication. Do not worry how distortions look on your screen, but use the screen to place the widened or narrowed words in your publication.

Text Rotation

Another tool on PageMaker 4.2 is text rotation. Text is rotated in blocks, not individual characters, so the operation requires the use of the Pointer tool. To see a practical use of text rotation, we will see how to make a chapter heading with it.

First select the text block with the Pointer tool, shown in the following illustration:

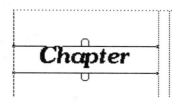

After selecting the text block, select *Text Rotation . . .* from the **Element** menu to get the Text Rotation dialog box. Using the pointer, choose one of the four rotation angles as shown in the following illustration:

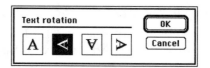

After you select the rotation angle, your text block will appear as shown in Figure 6.37. Note that part of the block is outside the margins.

After rotation from the standard position, the text block cannot be treated as a text block. The block appears to be a graphic block, but it cannot be stretched or cropped like a graphic. From the layout view, any and all changes to the text that is rotated must be made before rotation. If you want to make such changes after rotation, you must rotate the text back to the standard configuration—the leftmost

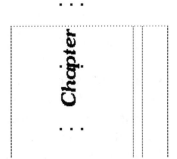

FIGURE 6.37 Text is rotated.

selection shown in the illustration of the Text rotation dialog box. (Rotated text can be edited in the story view. See Chapter 7, "Using the Story and Table Editors.") Then make the changes with the Text tool, and then rotate it back the way you want.

To finish up the example using text rotation, Figures 6.38 and 6.39 show how a large chapter number is added next to the rotated text.

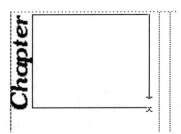

FIGURE 6.38 A drag-placing block is created for the chapter number.

FIGURE 6.39 The chapter number is added and the heading completed.

Exporting Files

On some occasions you will need to export files from PageMaker to your disk. For example, you may wish to send an ASCII file over a modem or do some more work in your word processor on a story that has been expanded already in PageMaker. The file export is the opposite of *Place* in that it takes what is in PageMaker and puts it into either a text file or word-processor file, depending on what import/ export filters are in your system. During the installation process, you will be given the option of an ASCII (text) and installed word-processor file export filters. When exported from PageMaker the file will be either in a text file or the format of the selected word-processor file.

In order to export a file using the Text tool, place the cursor in the story you wish to export or select only a limited amount of text. Then, from the **File** menu select the *Export . . .* option. If you have selected a chunk of text, the *Export* option will default to *Selected Text Only,* but you can click the option to export *Entire Story.* If you have just placed the text cursor in a story, only the *Entire Story* option will be available. The File Format window will show the filters you have installed. Select the file format in which you wish to save the exported story.

Also, you may elect to save the story with Export tags. These tags are the same ones discussed in Chapter 5, "Preparing and Placing Text," that use the angled brackets (<>) to enclose style callouts. The export tags create tags in text files or word-processing files that cannot import styles. Thus, with a headline style, the export tag would place <Headline> before the headline style paragraph. With other styles, appropriate tags would be placed as needed.

Users who are familiar with only a single word processor have a tendency to place only the import/export filters for their word processor in the system for PageMaker. This makes sense because it saves space on the hard disk and unclutters selection windows. However, it is strongly suggested that text (ASCII) filters be included because ASCII is a standard among computers. You may find yourself needing a story from another computer. Your Macintosh may not be able to read a word-processing file from a non-Macintosh, but it can read a Text/ASCII file produced by any computer as long as you have a text (ASCII) filter on your Mac disk.

USING THE STORY AND TABLE EDITORS

T he Story Editor and Table Editor are two powerful tools included with PageMaker 4.2. The Story Editor is a small text editor or word processor used for making intermediate-sized changes in a story. Small changes in stories are made in the Layout View, right in the placed text. Large changes are made in your word processor. However, for those many changes in between, the Story Editor is a terrific tool. It is also valuable for making global changes in style and other text characteristics.

The Table Editor provides a simple way of making tables to import into a publication. Word processors and all versions of Page-Maker can be used for making tables. The Table Editor just makes it a lot easier. For complex tables, it is an even more valuable tool.

USING THE STORY EDITOR

The Story Editor is initiated in several ways. Its most common use will probably be in cases where placed text needs editing. Selecting *Edit story* from the **Edit** menu or pressing ⌘-E on the keyboard will do the trick. Using the Pointer tool, triple-clicking a text block with the story you want also brings up the Story Editor. For a finer positioning of the point of entry into a story, using the Text tool, click an insertion point. When you enter the Story Editor, you will be able to begin editing at that point. The other methods place you at the beginning of the story.

Once in the Story Editor, you are in the "Story View." If you have a placed story in the editor, the file name for that story is the first several words from the file; not the file name on the disk. From the Story View, you cannot use any of the graphic tools, and so the Toolbox is unavailable for use. You can change and adjust text, add and delete index entries, and remove inline graphics. If your story has independent graphics in it, you will not see them. Only inline graphics have a marker to show you where they belong. Other markers show where there are index entries and page numbers. Figure 7.1 shows a typical Story View. The inline graphic and index graphic can be seen in sentences 1 and 2.

If you make a style change, you will not necessarily see the actual style change. If a style is bold or italicized or both, the font in the story view will be bold, italicized, or both. But when in the story view, you see only the font and font size selected in the *Preferences* option in the **Edit** menu. So, if you have a bold italicized font in 18-point Times Roman as a style and your story view is in 12-point Helvetica, all you will see is a 12-point bold italicized Helvetica font in your Story Editor. Unlike the rest of the screens in PageMaker, what you see in the story view is not necessarily what you get when you print out the results. The following illustration shows where the story view font type and size are selected from *Preferences*:

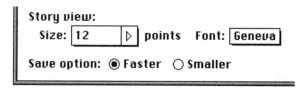

Story View Menus

When you enter the Story Editor, you are in the story view. (The "Layout View" is the view from which you have been placing text and

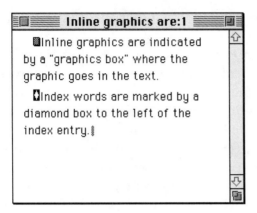

FIGURE 7.1 Typical Story View

graphics up to now.) There are subtle but important changes in the menus:

Layout View	Story View
File	File
Edit	Edit
Options	Options
Page	Story
Type	Type
Element	Windows
Windows	

For the most part, the menus with the same names do the same thing in both the Layout View and story view. However, the **Options** and **Story** menus are very different, and so we will look at them.

Options Menu

The first four choices in the story-view **Options** menu are the same as the last four in the *Layout View* menu. However, the *Display ¶* and *Display style names* choices are unique to the story view. The *Display ¶* option gives a better idea in the unformatted text where paragraphs, tabs, and spaces are located. The ¶ character shows that a paragraph ends with a carriage return. An arrow shows where a tab has been placed and a dot (·) depicts a space. Figure 7.2 shows some examples of tabs, paragraphs, and spaces in this mode.

You can choose whether or not to have the separate column with the style names. The decision not to display style names may come in handy when the story is a single-column style and you want more

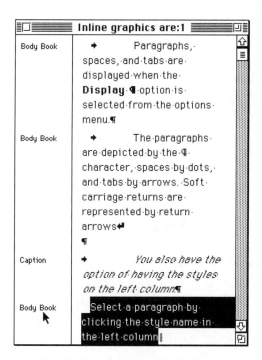

FIGURE 7.2 Style names can be displayed in a separate column.

screen room to edit the story. You can use the style palette as shown in Figure 7.3 to change styles just as you would when in the layout view.

Story Menu

This unique **Story View** menu provides three options:

1. New story
2. Close story
3. Import

The *New Story* option is equivalent to the *New* option in the **File** menu from the layout view. It brings up a blank window into which you may enter text. When the text has been entered, it must be placed into the publication before closing the window. If you decide you do not want the text in the publication, it can be discarded. If you exit by pressing ⌘-Ⓔ on the keyboard, you will automatically be given a filled icon with the text from the Story Editor. Otherwise you will get the dialog box shown in the following figure:

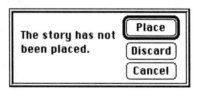

Clicking Place will generate the loaded Place icon, Discard will return to the layout view, and Cancel will return to the Story Editor.

It is important not to confuse the *Close* options in the **File** and **Story** menus. In the **Story** menu, *Close* simply closes the Story Editor, but if you select *Close* from the **File** menu while in the story view, you will close the entire file, not just the Story Editor. You can also return to the layout view by clicking any part of the layout view, pressing ⌘-Ⓔ or clicking the "close box" on the Story Editor window.

The *Import . . .* option in the **Story** menu is equivalent to the *Place* option in the layout-view **File** menu. When you select *Import . . .* you will be given the option of choosing from available files for which

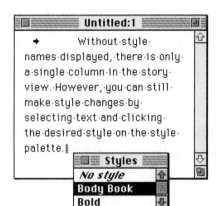

FIGURE 7.3 Use of the style palette, eliminating the style column, permits more work room.

you have installed import filters. Once you have edited the text, you will be given the same options for placing or discarding it as with any other unplaced text.

Editing Text

Editing text in the Story Editor is fairly straightforward. All of the text editing tools used for editing in the layout view are also used to edit in the story view. It is important to remember, though, that while the changes made in the Story Editor will be transferred to the layout in the correct font, style, and size, only limited font style changes are shown in the story view. There are several things you must consider when editing in the Story Editor. In the remainder of this section, we will look at some key elements.

Entering and Deleting Text

When adding or cutting text in a story that has been placed, you must remember that what is done in the Story Editor will affect the placed text blocks. For example, if you add a paragraph of text in the story view, it will be added and threaded into the story being edited.

Therefore, when you return to the layout view, you must examine the text blocks to make sure that everything still fits. Likewise, when you delete text it will be necessary to go back and check to see if the publication still looks right. Especially important will be the effect of changes on independent graphics. While inline graphics will stay with the text when it is flowed forward or backward, independent graphics will not. Therefore, when you return to the layout view, check the independent graphics to make sure they are still correctly placed.

Changing Rotated Text

In Chapter 6, "Working with Placed Text," we discussed how the character of rotated text changed in the layout view when it was not in the normal horizontal position. However, from the story view, rotated text at any angle can be edited. For example, the following illustration shows two blocks of text, one of which has been rotated. In order for the rotated block to go with the unrotated block, it needs to be bold. Since rotated text cannot be changed from the layout view, the Story Editor must be used.

To get the rotated text into the Story Editor, use the Pointer tool. Select the block with the rotated text, "California", and click the mouse button three times. The rotated text will then appear in the story view. Any changes you want can be made including changes in letters, fonts, sizes, and styles. For example, you could change a 12-point "California" in normal Helvetica font into "Kentucky" in a 24-point Times Roman bold italicized font if you wanted. In this case we just want to change the style from normal to bold, as shown in the following illustration:

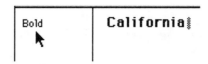

In the illustration, we just happened to have a style "Bold" that was used, but using regular type-style changes from the **Type** menu or ⌘-[BACKSPACE] on the keyboard would have worked as well.

When you return to the layout view, you will be able to see the changes made in the Story Editor, as shown in the next illustration:

SEARCHING, CHANGING, AND SPELL CHECKING

One of the major functions in PageMaker's editor is the Search and Change editing tools. These tools are available only in the story view, but they are quite powerful and useful. They will be especially welcomed by publishers who have to contend with unedited manuscripts and making global changes in a publication. You may have noticed that the editing options for finding, changing, and spell checking have not been available from the layout view—the options in the **Edit** menu were "ghosted." However, they are now available to work on any text that you can get into the Story Editor.

Finding Text

Finding key parts of a story can sometimes be best accomplished by using the *Find . . .* option in the **Edit** menu in the Story Editor. The find operations in PageMaker 4.2 provide options for matching upper and lower case and whole or partial words as well as for searching selected text, the current story, or all stories in a publication. Thus, rather than simply being a tool for locating words in single stories, the *Find* option can be used to search for all of the stories in a publication. Figure 7.4 shows the Find dialog box and part of a window showing that it had found *behold* in the word *beholder*. All text that is found is highlighted. (Selected text is not highlighted during the search procedure so that found-text can be.)

In Figure 7.4, there are options for *Match Case* and *Whole Word*. The *Match Case* option means that it will find the word only if the cases, upper and lower, match. For example, in looking for the word *Father*, the search will find only *Father* and not *father* if the match case option is selected. Likewise, a search for *sugar* would not find *Sugar* or *SUGAR*.

In the example in Figure 7.4, the search word is *behold* and the word *beholder* was found. That is because the search was not for the whole word but only the letters in *behold*. If the *Whole Word* option is selected, the match will occur only if the word in the search window is exactly the same as in the text. If you are looking for a small word, it is a good idea to check the whole word option since your word may be found in a lot of places. For example, the sentence,

"[Is] it w[is]e to w[is]h for h[is] return?"

has *is* in it four times. If you were searching just for the word *is* in a long story, it would take much longer to search for it without the *Whole Word* option.

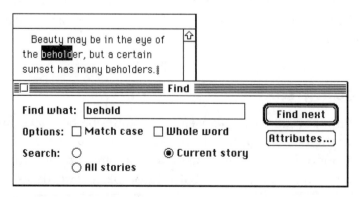

FIGURE 7.4 When a string is located, it highlights in the Story view.

Another feature of the *Find* routine in PageMaker 4.2 is the finding of attributes. By clicking the Attribute button, you can then select from a number of attributes in your publication for search. For example, Figure 7.5 shows several different attributes selected for search targets.

Using the *Attributes* option in the *Find* routines makes it easy to find such things as heads and subheads that you want to check for inclusion or correct style. For example, you may have have some first-level subheads entered as second-level ones. If they have style tags, it is an easy matter to locate them.

Find and Replace

The *Change . . .* option in the **Edit** menu works very much like the operation for the *Find . . .* option. Essentially, it is a find and replace operation that lets the user enter any word or partial word and replace it throughout the publication. Figure 7.6 shows the change dialog box with a change from *mouse* to *rat* being executed.

As a rule, it is generally wiser to use the options for matching cases and changing whole words. The matching cases may not be as crucial in a *Change* operation, but having a whole word is. Unlike the *Find* operation where nothing is changed, the *Change* operation, as its name implies, certainly does change things. So if you change *is* to *was* without specifying that the whole word is to be found first, words like *his, wish* and *mister* turn into *hwas, wwash,* and *mwaster.*

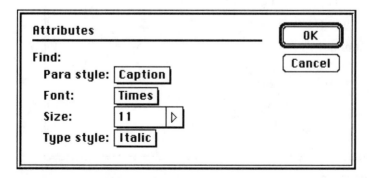

FIGURE 7.5 Attributes are legitimate "find" items as well.

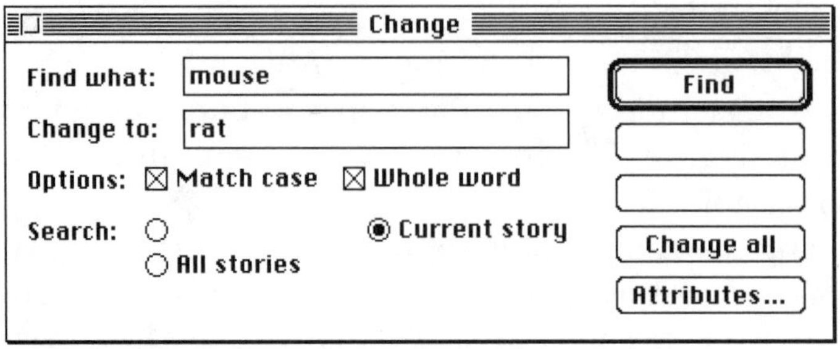

```
┌─────────────────────────────────────────────────┐
│ ▤□▤▤▤▤▤▤▤▤▤▤ Change ▤▤▤▤▤▤▤▤▤▤▤▤              │
├─────────────────────────────────────────────────┤
│ Find what:  │mouse                │  ┌─────────┐ │
│                                      │  Find   │ │
│ Change to:  │rat                  │  └─────────┘ │
│                                      ┌─────────┐ │
│ Options: ⊠Match case  ⊠Whole word    └─────────┘ │
│                                      ┌─────────┐ │
│ Search:  ○          ⦿Current story   └─────────┘ │
│          ○All stories                ┌─────────┐ │
│                                      │Change all│ │
│                                      └─────────┘ │
│                                      ┌─────────┐ │
│                                      │Attributes…│ │
│                                      └─────────┘ │
└─────────────────────────────────────────────────┘
```

FIGURE 7.6 Making global changes in the Story View

Anyone who has put a large publication together only to find that the client did not like the font, style, or some other attribute of the work knows that the option to change attributes the way words are changed is an important enhancement to PageMaker. Like the *Find* operation, the *Change* operation can change paragraph style, font, font size, and type style. For example, Figure 7.7 shows how to change any Subhead 1 paragraph style with the Times font of any size with normal type style to a Subhead 2 with Helvetica font in bold type.

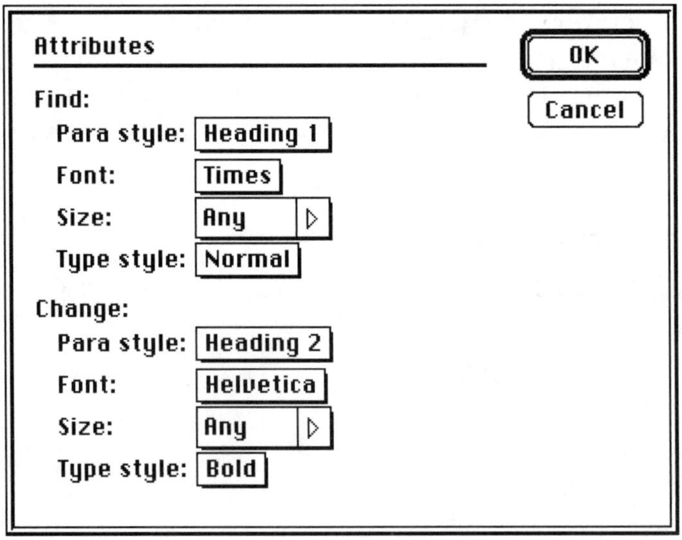

```
┌───────────────────────────────────────────────┐
│                                                │
│  Attributes _____    ┌──────────┐   │
│                                 │    OK    │   │
│  Find:                          └──────────┘   │
│    Para style: │Heading 1│      ┌──────────┐   │
│                                 │  Cancel  │   │
│    Font:       │Times│          └──────────┘   │
│                                                │
│    Size:       │Any   │▷│                      │
│                                                │
│    Type style: │Normal│                        │
│                                                │
│  Change:                                       │
│    Para style: │Heading 2│                     │
│                                                │
│    Font:       │Helvetica│                     │
│                                                │
│    Size:       │Any   │▷│                      │
│                                                │
│    Type style: │Bold│                          │
│                                                │
└───────────────────────────────────────────────┘
```

FIGURE 7.8 A wide range of attributes can be changed.

Remember this technique allows you to make global changes in a publication instead of using the style palette to individually change paragraphs. You will save a considerable amount of time.

One of the interesting things you can do with changing attributes is to change one or more attributes of a style. For example, if a style has bold type as a defined part of its makeup, you can change that to normal if you so desire. That means you can essentially keep the style while changing parts of it for one reason or another in the text.

Spell Checking

A normal prudent step to take before placing text is to use a spell checker to make sure all of the words are correctly spelled. However, if your word processor does not have a spell checker, or if you have made a number of changes in the text after placing it in PageMaker, then you can use the spell checker in the Story Editor.

From the story view, initiate the spelling checker by selecting *Spelling . . .* from the **Edit** menu or pressing ⌘-Ⓛ on the keyboard. You may search spelling errors in any of the following types of text:

1. Selected text

2. Current story

3. All stories in publication

Click the Search button and PageMaker goes through the search area looking for unrecognized words. For example, Figure 7.8 shows an unrecognized and, in this case, misspelled word. If a word is misspelled and not in the dictionary, it can be typed in.

Once the unrecognized word is found, the spelling dictionary provides several words that may possibly be the one misspelled. Click the word you want to select, as shown in Figure 7.8 ("combinations"), and then click the Replace button. The misspelled word is now replaced with the correctly spelled word.

Adding New Words

Sometimes you have a word you need to use a good deal in your writing, and the word is not in the spelling checker dictionary. It is an

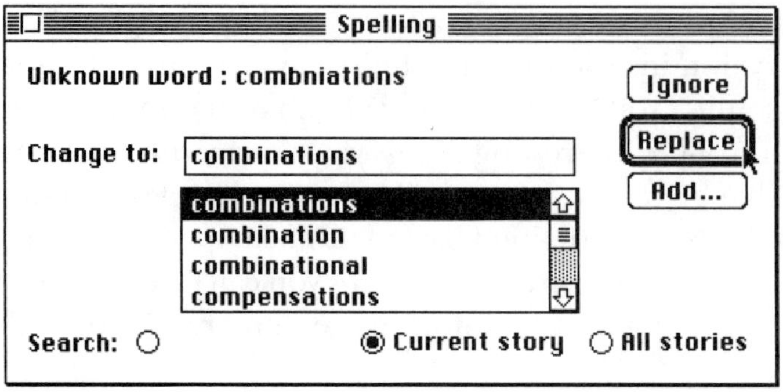

FIGURE 7.8 Typing and spelling errors can be caught and changed.

easy matter to add a word to your dictionary with the *Add* option. For example, suppose the spell checker encountered the following sentence:

> The term *ethnomethodology* was coined to describe a sub-field in sociology.

When the spell checker finds *ethnomethodology*, it will bring it up as an unrecognized word and will not provide alternative words. Click the Add button (Figure 7.8), and the Add Word to User Dictionary dialog box appears as shown in Figure 7.9.

If you have more than a single dictionary, specify the one you want. Also, if the word is not a proper noun that is normally capitalized then be sure to select the *As all lowercase* option. For example, if you had the sentence,

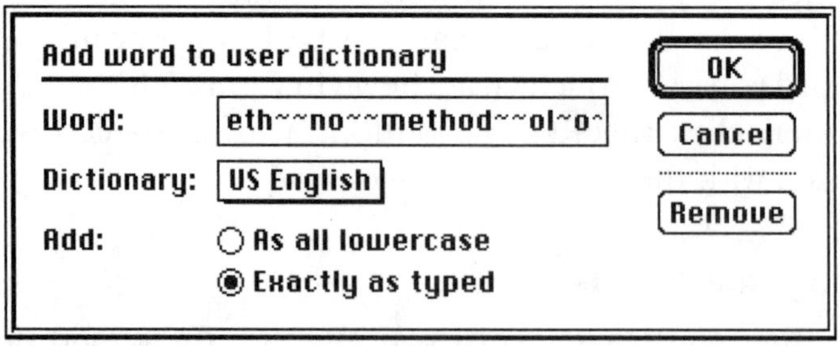

FIGURE 7.9 Adding unknown words to the dictionary

Ethnomethodology is a sub-field of sociology.

then the spelling checker would want to add *ethnomethod-ology* as *Ethnomethodology*. Since the word is not normally capitalized, you would not want it capitalized in your user dictionary.

Caution: Over-reliance on the spelling checker can court disaster if you do not carefully go over your manuscript. The spelling checker does not check to see if the word is correctly spelled for the context of the word's use. For example, the sentence,

The too brothers vent to ton,

was intended to be,

The two brothers went to town.

Not only will the spelling checker not catch the use of *too* for *two*, but it also recognizes *vent* and *ton* as legitimate words not to be corrected. So while your spelling checker can find unrecognized words, it won't help in catching typing errors. Go over your publication carefully to check that the words that are correctly spelled are correctly used.

USING THE TABLE EDITOR UTILITY

The Table Editor is a separate entity from the main program. Unlike the Story Editor, which is operated from within PageMaker, the Table Editor is wholly independent. It is used for easily creating tables to be used independently or in conjunction with PageMaker. If you are familiar with spreadsheets such as Excel or Wingz, then you will be familiar with some of the terminology and uses of the Table Editor. However, the Table Editor is not a spreadsheet, even though several of its operations and terms have qualities similar to those of spreadsheets.

Making Tables

The first step in making a table is to set up the parameters of the table. When you first start a new table, the Table Setup dialog box appears. You enter the size of the table in inches and how many columns and rows you want. If you are not sure, you can always change the table size later—both the number of columns and rows and the size in inches. At this time, the gutters (space between the cells) are also defined in whatever unit of measurement you have selected from the *Preferences* option in the **Edit** menu. The units of measurement are the same as those in PageMaker. We will use inches in our examples. Figure 7.10 shows the default setup.

When the table first appears, it is arranged in a grouping of blank cells using the same reference system as spreadsheets. The cell in the upper left-hand corner, for example, is Cell A1. Alphabetic characters define the columns and numbers define the rows. If there are more than 26 columns, the extra columns are labeled AA, BB, CC, etc. Figure 7.11 shows the default table.

Once the table is on the screen, you can change the width of the cells by placing the pointer on a cell boundary line and dragging the line to the left or right. Figure 7.12 shows Column A being narrowed by dragging the line to the left.

Likewise, the height of a row of cells can be changed by dragging the horizontal line in the left margin up or down, as shown in Figure 7.13.

Once the changes are completed, the table is a smaller size. The advantage of dragging the row and column lines to change cell size over giving an overall table size in inches in the Table setup dialog

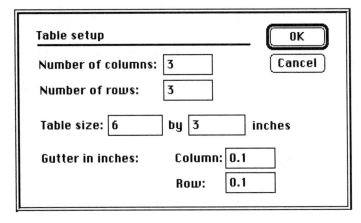

FIGURE 7.10 Dialog box for setting up a table

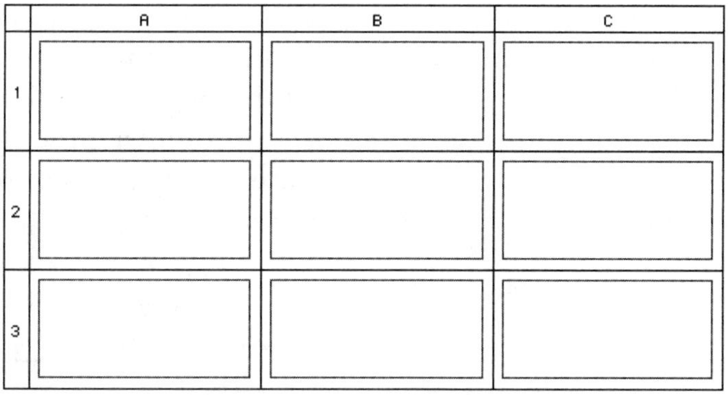

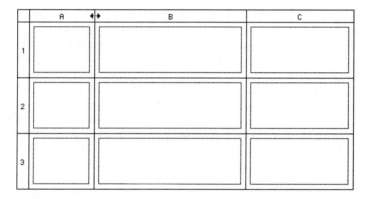

FIGURE 7.11 Table with default parameters

FIGURE 7.12 Narrowing a column

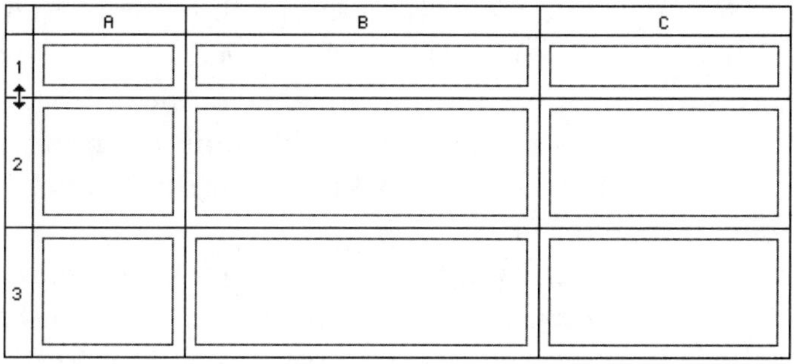

FIGURE 7.13 Narrowing a row

box is that you can better visualize the table's size. However, if you have a large table and limited size in your publication, consider attempting to size it correctly in the Table Setup dialog box and then making further changes, if necessary, by dragging the column and row boundaries. The following illustration shows the reduced table. (Note that the cells in Columns B and C are wider than those in Column A.)

	A	B	C
1			
2			
3			

One further way of changing cell size is to specify the number of inches wide and high in the Column width . . . and Row height . . . in the Cell menu. First select the cell or cells you wish to change and then put in the values. The advantage of this method, especially in conjunction with dragging the boundaries, is that it enables you to provide a uniform size for each cell after getting a rough idea of the size you want by moving boundaries.

The next step is to place data into the table. You can either import data or enter them manually in the Table Editor.

Importing Data

Importing data is something like placing data in PageMaker, but a little different. While the Table Editor will recognize several different formats, it works the best with data saved as text. For example, if you save some data in a Wingz spreadsheet file as text, they can be loaded into sequential cells in the Table Editor. On the other hand, Wingz data saved as a regular Wingz file or some other nontext file generate strange results.

Before importing data, there are two things you may need to do. First, check the *Define Flow* . . . in the **Edit** menu. The Define Flow dialog box, shown in Figure 7.14, provides options for the direction of flow. Select the flow sequence you want for your data.

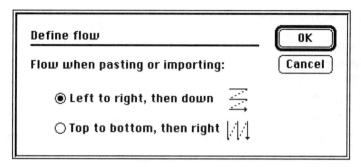

FIGURE 7.14 Defining flow controls imported data placement in table

Once the flow is defined, there is an optional cell selection you can make. You select cells by clicking them. Holding down (SHIFT) and clicking cells allows you to select several cells in a matrix. Clicking a row or column heading will select the entire row or column, and clicking the upper left-hand corner will select the entire table. However, if you select cells, the imported data will flow only into the selected cells.

In the event that there are more cells to be imported than are available in your table, you can either cancel the operation or import only the data that fit your cells. If you want all of the data imported, cancel the import operation and add the new cells through the Table Setup dialog box or the **Cell** menu with the *Insert . . .* option.

Once everything is ready to receive the imported data, use the Import option from the **File** menu to place the data into the table. The following figure shows a table imported from a Wingz spreadsheet that had been saved as a text file:

	A	B	C
1	Bob	Sue	Maurice
2	$67321.00	$78219.00	$92444.00
3	$53856.00	$62575.00	$73955.00

Note how the data are all skewed to the upper left-hand corner of each cell. That is the default placement of data in the Table Editor. Further on in this chapter we will see how to align text in the cells.

Manual Data Entry

Using the Text tool, you can type data in each cell. Using the mouse, select the Text tool and click the cell into which you wish to type. Use (TAB) to move right and (SHIFT)-(TAB) to move left through the columns. Pressing (RETURN) lets you move down to the next row. To move up a row, use the mouse to click the cell to which you want to move. The (SHIFT)-(RETURN) combination will force a carriage return in a cell; otherwise text simply wraps around to the next line as you type in text or numbers.

Editing Data

Editing the data in a table is very much like doing the same thing in PageMaker. Select the data to be edited and use the various editing menus to change the data. For example, to align the data to the center of the cells, select the entire table by clicking in the upper left-hand corner. Then from the **Type** menu select *Align center* or press ⌘-(C) on the keyboard. Next select *Align Middle* from the **Type** menu to complete the centering of text. If you want to change the style of a single row, select the row by clicking the row number as shown in the following illustration:

	A	B	C
1	Bob	Sue	Maurice
2	$67321.00	$78219.00	$92444.00
3	$53856.80	$62575.20	$73955.20

Next, from the **Type** menu, select the desired style. For more detailed changes use the *Type Spec . . .* option (⌘-(T)) to change the font, font size, leading, and type style. For example, Figure 7.15 shows the text in the first row changed to a bold font.

	A	B	C
1	Bob	Sue	Maurice
2	$67321.00	$78219.00	$92444.00
3	$53856.80	$62575.20	$73955.20
4			

FIGURE 7.15 A fourth row is set up.

The other major editing tool, one not found in PageMaker, is the *Number Format . . .* option in the **Cell** menu. Using a currency format, the following table shows values over 1000 with commas:

	A	B	C
1	$123.45	$543.21	$4,345.65
2	$345.66	$123.22	$9,876.54
3	$33.44	$7,654.32	$433.56

You may select other number styles that meet your needs as well. So before typing in special characters for your numbers, check the number formats available to automatically enter your formats.

Table Editing

In addition to editing the contents of the cells, you can edit the table as well. The first thing we will do with the example table is to add another row that will be used to add up the numbers in the second two rows. To do that, we simply go back to the Table setup dialog box and type in **4** for the number of rows. Figure 7.15 shows the added row on the bottom after it has been selected.

Now that we have a row where we can put the sum of Rows 2 and 3, we can use the *Sum* option in the **Cell** menu to have the Table Editor automatically add up the rows. The sum that will go into the fourth row is calculated by the total of the selected cells, automatically ignoring cells with no numeric values. Figure 7.16 shows how to select Column A for preparing a sum.

Next, from the **Cell** menu, select *Sum,* and your screen will show a loaded pointer that can be used to place the cell where you want the sum of the column or row. Figure 7.17 shows the loaded cursor in Cell A4.

When the left mouse button is clicked, the sum is placed in the targeted cell. Using the same operation on Cells B and C, the table

FIGURE 7.16 Selecting column for sum operation

FIGURE 7.17 Cell A4 has loaded-sum cursor

now has the sum of each column in the bottom row, as shown in Figure 7.18.

In order to further clarify the table, we will insert another row that will be used to label the bottom row with the column's sum. However, instead of adding a row using the Table Setup dialog box, we will use the *Insert . . .* function in the **Cell** menu. To insert a row or column, select the row beneath the row you wish to add or the column to the right of the column you wish to add. *Select Insert . . .* from the **Cell** menu and choose the number of rows or columns you wish to insert. Be careful to also select *row* or *column* as well. Figure 7.19 shows the inserted row, Row 4, and the old Row 4 now labeled as Row 5.

	A	B	C
1	**Bob**	**Sue**	**Maurice**
2	$67321.00	$78219.00	$92444.00
3	$53856.80	$62575.20	$73955.20
4	$121,177.80	$140,794.20	$166,399.20

FIGURE 7.18 All columns are totaled in Row 4.

	A	B	C
1	**Bob**	**Sue**	**Maurice**
2	$67321.00	$78219.00	$92444.00
3	$53856.80	$62575.20	$73955.20
4			
5	$121,177.80	$140,794.20	$166,399.20

FIGURE 7.19 A row is inserted.

To label Row 4, type in the word **Total** in Cell A4 only. Since it is superfluous to have three labels saying "Total," we can change it so that there is one long "grouped" cell across the row. To group a row, first select all of the cells you wish to be grouped. Then, click *Group* from the **Cell** menu. Figure 7.20 shows that Row 4 is now one single cell with the "Total" label that had been Cell A4.

Borders and Shades

Two final enhancements that can be made to tables with the Table Editor are borders and shades. Borders surround the cells with different lines to make them stand out. The default borders are 1-point lines, but any of the lines in the **Line** menu can be used as borders. Shades are screens that overlay the cells.

To create a border, first select the cell or cells that you want to be surrounded by lines. Next, from the **Cell** menu, choose *Borders . . .* or press ⌘-Ⓑ on the keyboard. The Borders dialog box, shown in Figure 7.21 appears, providing options for applying the borders in and around the cells as well as the style of line you want. (You may also select the line type from the *Line* option in the **Cell** menu.)

After selecting the perimeter and interior options, click OK or press (RETURN), and your borders will be in place as shown in Figure 7.22 in Row 5.

	A	B	C
1	**Bob**	**Sue**	**Maurice**
2	$67321.00	$78219.00	$92444.00
3	$53856.80	$62575.20	$73955.20
4	Total		
5	$121,177.80	$140,794.20	$166,399.20

FIGURE 7.20 Row 4 is grouped.

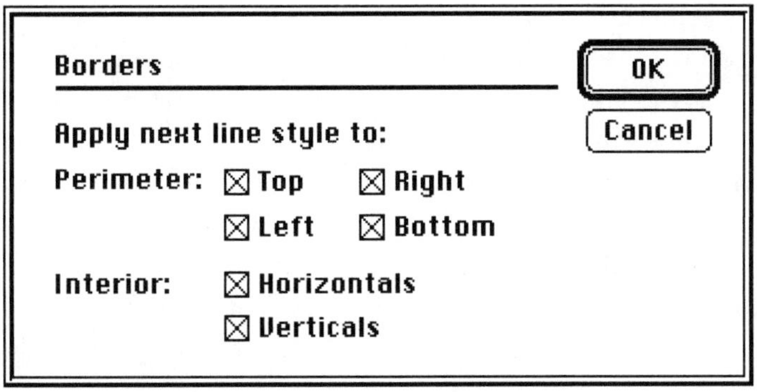

```
┌─────────────────────────────────────────────────────┐
│  Borders                           ┌───────────┐     │
│  _____      │    OK     │     │
│                                    └───────────┘     │
│  Apply next line style to:         ┌───────────┐     │
│  Perimeter: ⊠ Top     ⊠ Right      │  Cancel   │     │
│             ⊠ Left    ⊠ Bottom     └───────────┘     │
│                                                       │
│  Interior:  ⊠ Horizontals                             │
│             ⊠ Verticals                               │
│                                                       │
└─────────────────────────────────────────────────────┘
```

FIGURE 7.21 Border dialog box provides options for line placement.

Applying shades only requires selecting the cells to shade and then selecting the shade itself. If you choose *Alternate Rows* while selecting the shade, every other row of the selected cells will be shaded.

Figure 7.22 shows Row 1 with a 10 percent screen. If a black or heavily screened shade is selected, it may be difficult to read the print. When using the very dark shades, you might try reversing the color of the text. To reverse text color, first select the text and then click *Reverse* from the **Type** menu.

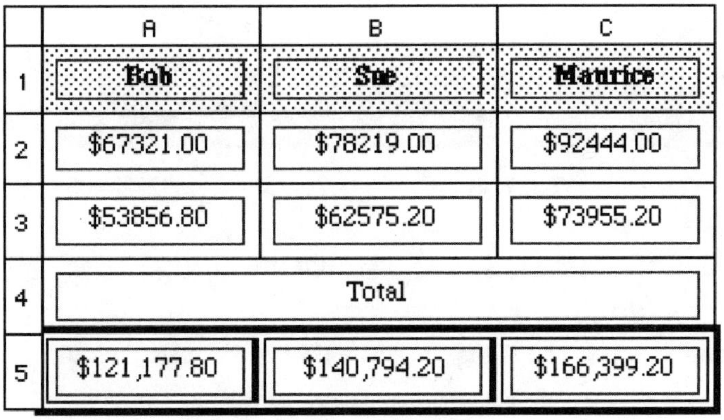

	A	B	C
1	Bob	Sue	Maurice
2	$67321.00	$78219.00	$92444.00
3	$53856.80	$62575.20	$73955.20
4	Total		
5	$121,177.80	$140,794.20	$166,399.20

FIGURE 7.22 The table with screens and borders

By removing the shades, lines, grids, and labels, your table can be opened up into columns of names and numbers. Using your imagination, you can make any design you want. Figure 7.23 shows a simple revision of our sample table accomplished by selecting the entire table and choosing *None* for lines and *None* for shades. Then we clicked off *Grid Lines* and *Grid Labels* in the **Options** menu.

With a little imagination, you can make all types of tables and reports with Table Editor and PageMaker. Figure 7.24 shows the sample table with different fonts and a few other simple rearrangements.

Bob	Sue	Maurice
$67,321.00	$78,219.00	$92,444.00
$53,856.80	$62,575.20	$73,955.20
	Total	
$121,177.80	$140,794.20	$166,399.20

FIGURE 7.23 The lines and labels are removed.

	Bob	Sue	Maurice
	$67,321.00	$78,219.00	$92,444.00
	$53,856.80	$62,575.20	$73,955.20
Total	**$121,177.80**	**$140,794.20**	**$166,399.20**

FIGURE 7.24 Style flexibility is built into Table Editor.

Preparing Tables for PageMaker

The Table Editor is an independent program that can be used for preparing all types of tables. It is not an exclusive program for making tables just for PageMaker. Table Editor can prepare and print its own documents, and Table Editor files are not inherently compatible with PageMaker. If you use the *Save* command in the **File** menu, the files so recorded cannot be placed in PageMaker.

Export Preparation

In order to get a file ready for PageMaker, it is necessary to first export the file as either a text file or an object-oriented graphic. If you export the table as a text file, all you get when you place the table in PageMaker is the text organized in rows and columns. The following text shows what the sample table used in this chapter would look like if imported into PageMaker as a text file:

Bob	Sue	Maurice
$67,321.00	$78,219.00	$92,444.00
$53,856.80	$62,575.20	$73,955.20
Total		
$121,177.80	$140,794.20	$166,399.20

There may be some occasions when you need to place tables as text files, but in order to keep the table looking like the table created in Table Editor, export the table as a PICT file. When placed into PageMaker the graphic table can be manipulated just as any other PICT file. (See Chapter 9, "Graphics," for a full discussion of cropping and sizing graphics.)

STYLE SHEETS, INDEXES, AND TABLES OF CONTENT

T his chapter examines several different aspects of PageMaker 4.2. The discussions of style sheets and paragraph control deal with making your pages look better and doing it easily. Style sheets are often overlooked by users, but once you know their value, they become indispensable tools for PageMaker. The index and table-of-content (TOC) tools help create a TOC and index with very little effort. Used in conjunction with the style sheets, a TOC can be made for an entire book in just a few seconds.

STYLE SHEETS

Style sheets are formats defined with specific characteristics. The characteristics include type, paragraph, tab, and color characteristics. In other words, every characteristic you can define as a text style can be defined with a style sheet. The big advantage of style sheets is that they let you define everything you would want in a paragraph and then incorporate those characteristics in any other paragraph with a single simple operation.

For example, suppose you want to have a style that includes an 11-point Times Roman font, with 13-point leading, 0.25-inch indents, justified text, auto pair kerning above 9 points, and tab stops at every 0.27 inches that have a dotted leader; all text would appear as blue on your screen. (These terms will be discussed later in the chapter.) To set up such a paragraph using the menus discussed in this book up to now would take some doing. If you had to make every other paragraph match that style, you would be getting a workout, since you would have to go through all of the steps to change and unchange the style with each new paragraph.

However, if you had this sample style in a style sheet, all you would have to do would be to select the paragraph and click the desired style. With just a single click you could change any paragraph to those parameters.

Default Sheets

In order to see quickly and easily how style-sheets work, we will use the default styles that are included in the style-sheet palette. They will demonstrate how to use style sheets. For purposes of illustration, we will employ the following one-sentence paragraph:

Use style sheets to enhance getting a job done quickly and professionally.

Type in the preceding example paragraph and bring the style palette onto the screen, if it is not already there by selecting *Style Palette* from the **Window** menu. The following illustration shows the default-style palette box:

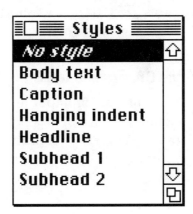

Next, select the Text tool and click anywhere on the paragraph. Now move the pointer to the style palette and select a style by clicking it. Whatever style you clicked transformed the paragraph into that style. For example, if you clicked the "Headline" style, you saw the paragraph change into a 30-point bold Times Roman font style. A "Subhead 1" selection was the same as the headline except it was done in an 18-point font instead of a 30-point font. The "Caption" style turned the paragraph into a 10-point italic Times Roman font style.

The preceding little exercise shows how easy it is to use the style palette and change paragraphs to any style you want. Not only can the style palette be used in the layout view, but it can also be used in the story view. In Chapter 7, "Using the Story and Table Editors," in the section "Using the Story Editor," you may remember that the editor's two-column window had the style name of the paragraph to the left of the text. If the style is selected in the story view and then the style palette clicked, it is possible to change the style in the editor. Of course the story view provides limited screen changes representing the style, but any style changes made in the Story Editor will be seen in the layout view.

In PageMaker 4.2, the style palette was given a new default style, "Hanging indent," to help quickly place bullets or numbered lists at the left-indent marker. Also, there are a number of new shortcuts for users with the Apple Extended Keyboard with the F keys. For the first twelve styles, press ⌘ (F1) through (F12). To apply styles 13-24 press (SHIFT) ⌘ (F1) through (F12). For example, to get the fourteenth style, you would press (SHIFT) ⌘ (F2). (A shortcut for this shortcut would be to point and click with the mouse.)

Global Style Changes in the Story Editor

In the Story Editor a major important feature is the ability to change styles throughout a story or publication. Through the *Change Attribute* operation, an entire publication's styles can be changed in a few mouse moves and keystrokes. For example, if you have three "body text" styles called "Body1," "Body2," and "Body3" that you wish to compare, after looking at the publication in the "Body1" style, you would simply select "Body2" to replace the attribute "Body1" in the Attribute dialog box. Then select *Change All* to have the entire story or or all linked stories changed to the new style. Similarly, "Body2" could then be changed to "Body3."

CREATING STYLE SHEETS

Making your own style sheets is very simple and entails little more than selecting menu choices of various style features. To begin, first select the *Define Styles . . .* option from the Type menu or press ⌘-3 from the keyboard. This will bring up the Define Styles dialog box. The dialog box will show several default styles that have already been defined. However, you can add to the styles or change the existing styles. At the bottom of the dialog box is the definition of the style selected. For example, in Figure 8.1, the *Body Text* style shows the font to be New Century Schoolbook, in 11 points with 13-point leading. The paragraph indents the first character 0.25 inches in justified alignment

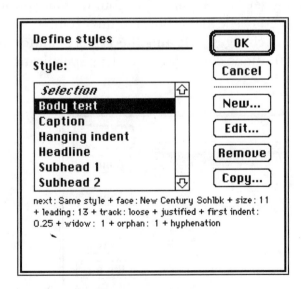

FIGURE 8.1 Define styles dialog box

with loose tracking. That is different from the default PageMaker definition of *Body Text*. In order to understand how we got the *Body Text* that way, we will go through the style-editing process.

Editing Styles

Select the style you want to edit, and click the Edit . . . button. The Edit Style dialog box appears. The name of the style being edited appears in the top box. The second box shows the style, if any, on which the style is based. Finally, the third box shows the style of the paragraph following the current style. Usually the current style is the same style, but sometimes the next paragraph will have a different style. For example, paragraphs following heads are often not in-dented, whereas all other paragraphs are indented. Figure 8.2 shows a typical Edit Style dialog box showing Body Text based on no styles with the next style being the same.

Type

To begin editing, select from one of the four bottom buttons on the right side of the Edit Style dialog box. For this example, we will begin with the Type . . . changes. Selecting the Type . . . button brings up the Type Specifications dialog box. Any type specification changes

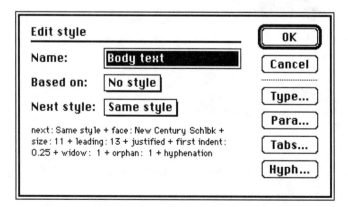

FIGURE 8.2 Edit style dialog box

made in this context will become part of the entire style; not just a selected amount of text. Figure 8.3 shows the Type Specifications dialog box with the characteristics selected for the Body Text.

For unusual styles, you may wish to have the width set to something other than Normal. For example, you may wish to have a "Fat" style with the width of fonts 130 percent of normal or a "Skinny" style with a width of 80 percent. Likewise, for a change of pace in a publication, a style might be all small caps, controlled by the *Case* option.

Finally, further options for type are available in the Type Options dialog box, accessed by clicking the Options . . . button. Figure 8.4 shows the default options for special type size and superscript and

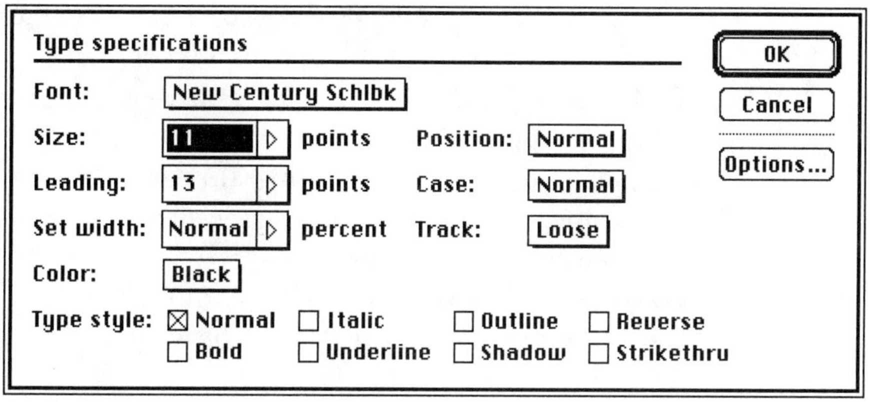

FIGURE 8.3 Type specifications dialog box

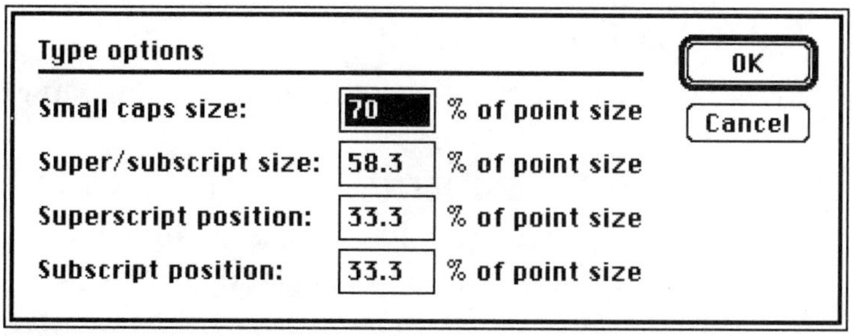

FIGURE 8.4 Type options dialog box

subscript positions. However, to make a really interesting style to get attention, you might want to adjust these type options.

Paragraph

The next part of editing a style is the paragraph format. Click the Para . . . button to open the Paragraph Specification dialog box. The five areas to adjust are the indents, paragraph space, alignment, dictionary, and the seven options.

- **Indents**   The indents refer to the distance from the margins that the text will be spaced and also the amount of indent from the left margin for the first line of a paragraph.

- **Paragraph Space**   The space that precedes or follows a paragraph can be adjusted. If zero space is selected, then the space will be based on the leading between lines.

- **Alignment**   Alignment can be left, center, right, justify, or force justify.

- **Dictionary**   The dictionary will probably be US English, but for other foreign languages, special dictionaries can be installed and used in a style.

- **Options**   All of the options refer to how the paragraph is to be kept together and if it is to be included in the table of contents.

    Keep Lines Together   If you want all of the lines in a paragraph to be on the same page, select this option.

    Column Break Before   When there is a new paragraph, begin a new column.

    Page Break Before   When there is a new paragraph, begin a new page.

    Include in Table of Contents   Usually used with heads and subheads, the head(s) is included in the table of contents if this option is selected.

    Keep with next . . . Lines   If the paragraph is to be broken by a page break, this keeps a specified number of lines with the paragraph on the next page.

Widow Control If the first line of a paragraph appears by itself at the bottom of a page, it is called an widow. The widow can be sent to the top of the next page with widow control

Orphan Control If the last line of a paragraph appears by itself at the top of a column or page, it is called an orphan. To control for that, an extra line or two can be added to accompany the orphan. (For a full discussion of widow and orphan control, see the Section "Widows and Orphans," later in this chapter.)

Figure 8.5 shows a typical Paragraph Specifications dialog box with both widow and orphan control turned on. The indent is set for 0.25 inches, and the text is justified. While no paragraph space is specified in the sample dialog box, for headers and subheads, it is usually a good idea to provide extra space before and after the paragraph.

Rules

It is possible to specify a style to have rules above and/or below a paragraph. This option can be used for certain types of reports or in

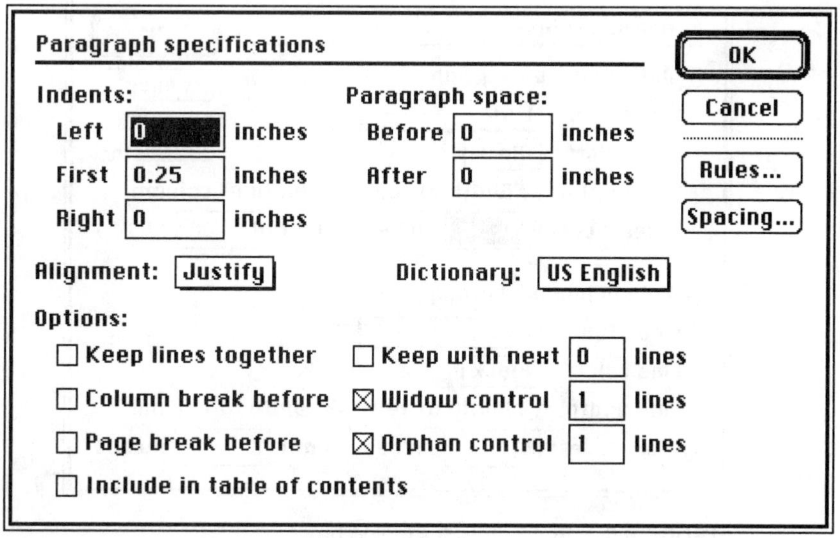

FIGURE 8.5 Paragraph specifications dialog box

any type of publication where lines above and below each paragraph will be useful. Often headers will have a rule above them for separating sections. By incorporating a rule in a header style, the rule will automatically be placed. Click the Rules . . . button to bring up the Paragraph Rules dialog box shown in Figure 8.6.

The selections are the same for a rule above and below the paragraph. You can establish line style with rules from 1 to 6 points in width. If color is important, colors other than black may be selected, and the rule can be as wide as the text or the column and indented on the left or right. Figure 8.7 shows how a paragraph would look on your screen if a rule were placed above each paragraph.

If you do not want to have the rule right beneath the paragraph, you can use the *Paragraph Rule* options. By clicking the Options . . . button in the Paragraph Rules dialog box, you open the *Paragraph Rule* options dialog box. In this box, you can set the rule a specified number of units above or below the baseline.

Grid Alignment

An important option is hidden away in the Paragraph Rules dialog box. This is the *Align to Grid* option. *Align to Grid* has more to do with

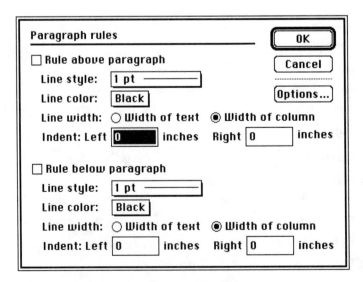

FIGURE 8.6 Paragraph Rules dialog box

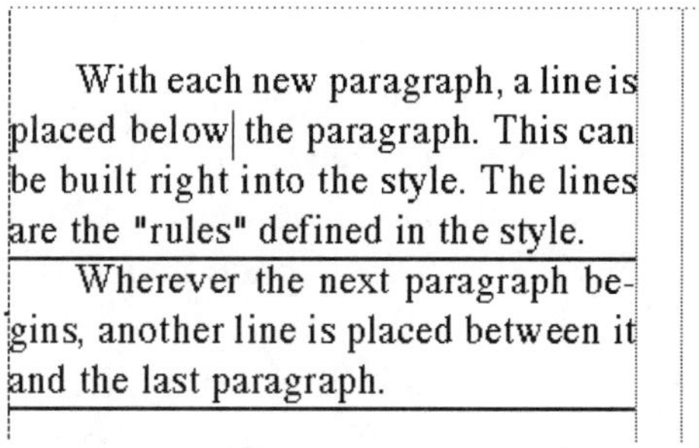

> With each new paragraph, a line is placed below the paragraph. This can be built right into the style. The lines are the "rules" defined in the style.
>
> Wherever the next paragraph begins, another line is placed between it and the last paragraph.

FIGURE 8.7 Rules can be placed below each paragraph.

aligning lines of text in adjacent columns than it does with rules per se. If two columns of text exist side by side, you want to make sure that the lines of text in one column are on the same grid as the text in the adjacent column. In situations where the alignment is thrown off by headers or graphics, the *Align to Grid* option will make sure that the two columns are lined up with one another. The grid size should be the same as your body text leading. Figure 8.8 shows the Paragraph Rule Options dialog box in its default setting.

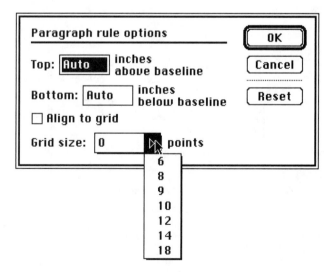

FIGURE 8.8 Paragraph rule options dialog box showing grid sizes

Spacing Attributes

The final paragraph specification is spacing. Clicking the Spacing . . . button brings up the Spacing Attributes dialog box. On it you can specify word and letter space, pair kerning, leading method, and percent of autoleading. Word spacing refers to the "space band" that is created by pressing the space bar. The minimum, desired, and maximum space band can be reset from the default, but the minimum must be less than the desired, and the maximum more than the desired. Letter spacing is the distance from the right edge of a letter to the left edge of the next letter—known as the pen advance.

Pair kerning can be turned off and on by checking the automatic kerning box and the kerning size above a given point. Leading can be selected to be either proportional or top of caps. Proportional is usually preferable. Finally, autoleading sets a leading to be a percentage of the font size. For example, a 12-point font with 120 percent leading would automatically make the leading be 14.4 points. Autoleading should be at least 100 percent to prevent vertical overlap. Figure 8.9 shows the various options in the Spacing Attributes dialog box. If your letters and words look "wrong" use the spacing attributes to make your text look right.

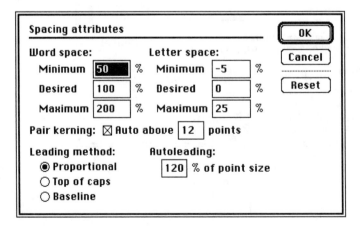

FIGURE 8.9 Spacing attributes dialog box

Tabs

The third style aspect you can edit is the tab styles. Editing tabs allows you to specify what special tab characteristic a style will have without having to worry about uneven tab stops or styles.

The four arrows on the left side of the Indents/Tabs dialog box refer to left, right, center, and decimal tabs from left to right, top to bottom. The Set Leader button provides different leading characters before a tab stop. For example, if the leader is set to "...", then when the tab bar is pressed, a line of periods precedes the character at the tab stop. A typical example would be a tab stop with a "dotted" leader in a roster of players:

```
Jones, Bob.....................32
Smith, Tom...................59
```

The tab would have been pressed after the number name and the stop would be where the player's number begins.

Besides the three leaders provided—periods, dashed line, and solid line—you can create a custom leader. If you want a custom leader, then in the box next to the Set Leader button, type in the leader you want. For example, a leader of pound signs (###) might be useful in certain applications.

To set an indent, drag the top triangle above the ruler as shown in the illustration below. The top triangle sets the indent of the first line of a paragraph, and the bottom triangle sets the indent for the rest of the lines. (The triangles pointing downward on top of the rule are the default tabs—not used for indenting.)

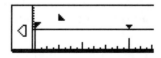

The large triangle at the right side (see Figure 8.10) is used to set the width of the text. The default size of the text is the size of the column into which it is placed; so while working with style sheets, do not move the big triangle on the right.

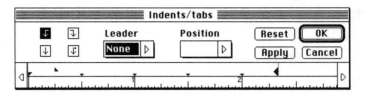

FIGURE 8.10 Indent/tabs dialog box and ruler

Pushing the position arrow opens a little dialog box shown in the following illustration:

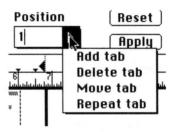

Each of the four actions is fairly self-explanatory except the *Repeat Tab* option. Using an example, we will see how the *Repeat Tab* can be a very handy command. Place a single tab on the ruler by placing the mouse pointer where you want it to go. Then, click the mouse button to make the tab marker appear. Select *Repeat Tab* and tab stops will be placed with the same interval as the selected tab. For instance, if your tab is at 0.25 inches, automatically a tab will be placed at each 0.25-inch interval—0.25, 0.50, 0.75, etc. If things get messy, you can always press the Reset button to go back to the default condition shown in Figure 8.10.

A new feature in PageMaker 4.2 is the Apply button. This allows you to preview the tabs before your final OK. When you click Apply, the page changes to the selected tabs and indents. If you don't like what you see, make further changes and apply them until it is just right. This saves a lot of time compared to going back and forth between the Indent/Tabs dialog box and the text.

Hyphenation

The hyphenation for a style can be set by pressing the Hyph . . . button. The hyphenation process is described further on in this chapter in the discussion of kerning. All of the features of hyphenation that can be applied to selected text can be applied to styles.

Creating New Styles

Making new styles uses all of the features used in editing a style. The only difference is that you select *New* from the Style dialog box instead of *Edit.* From that point you define all of the style features as you did in editing a style. You can either create an entirely new style based on nothing or you can "chain" one style onto another. When you create a brand new style, you have to go through all of the type, paragraph, tabs, and hyphenation dialog boxes or accept their default values. With "chaining" on the other hand, you can use all of the features of the "chained" style and make only a few changes to get an entirely new style.

"Chaining" Style Sheets

We will refer to the process of making a new style based on an existing style as "chaining." The reason for the reference is that the style is made up of another style with only minor changes—a different font size or style (e.g., bold instead of plain.) From a base style, it is possible to chain several other styles. For example, the default styles of "Headline," "Subhead 1," and "Subhead 2" are all chained in that both subhead styles are chained to Headline. In the style definition, Headline is defined as:

```
next: Same style + face: Roman 10cpi + bold
+ size 30 + leading: auto + track: none + flush
left + incl TOC
```

On the other hand, Subhead 1 is simply defined as:

```
Headline + next: Same style + size: 18
```

Everything is the same except that Subhead 1 uses an 18-point font instead of the 30-point font in Headline. If you look at Subhead 2, it is defined as:

Subhead 1 + next: Same style + size: 12

As you can see, Subhead 2 is "chained" to Headline, with Subhead 1 being the link between the two. (Subhead 2 could be defined as "Headline . . . size: 12" just as well.)

Using Style Sheets

Once a style has been defined, using the style sheets is simple. There are several ways to apply style sheets to text. The first thing to do is to bring up the style palette by selecting it from the **Windows** menu or pressing ⌘-Ⓨ from the keyboard. The following list summarizes how styles can be applied to text:

- From the layout view, place the text cursor anywhere in a paragraph and click the desired style for that paragraph in the style palette.

- From the layout view, select a range of text with the Text tool and click the style from the style palette.

- From the Story Editor, click the style type for the paragraph in the left margin; from the style palette, choose a style for the paragraph.

- From the Story Editor, click anywhere in a paragraph and select the style from the style palette.

- From the Story Editor, select a range of text with the Text tool and choose the style from the style palette.

- From the Story Editor, select *Change* . . . from the **Edit** menu or press ⌘-Ⓙ on the keyboard. From the Change dialog box, select *Attributes* . . . and indicate the paragraph style (Para Style:) changes desired using the *Change and Find* or *Change All* options.

As a general rule, fix as many style characteristics as possible in the word processing stage so that when you place the text you immediately get a fairly clear idea of how much space is taken up by a story. However, for making special changes in headlines and headers, or for changing styles when the style used in placement is too big or small for the publication, the style sheet system will save a lot of time.

Transferring Style Sheets

In situations where you need to use the same style sheet in different applications, it is not necessary to redefine the same style sheet with each new publication. PageMaker can copy the style sheet from another publication. Here's how:

1. Select *Define styles* . . . from the **Type** menu or press ⌘-③ on the keyboard.
2. From the Define Styles dialog box, click the Copy . . . button.
3. From the Copy Styles dialog box, select the document from which you wish to copy.
4. When you copy the styles from the source document, it will overwrite the styles in your target document. A warning box will ask if you are certain that is what you want to do.

That's all there is to it. You will find it saves a great deal of time working in this manner. Otherwise, you would have to "reinvent the wheel" with every new document where a standard style sheet is required.

Paragraph Control

From the layout view, all of the paragraph options discussed when we examined editing styles earlier in this chapter may be controlled. From the **Type** menu, select *Paragraphs* . . . or press ⌘-Ⓜ to bring up the Paragraph Specifications dialog box. Figure 8.6 shows the same Paragraph Specifications dialog box used in setting paragraph options. All of the paragraph operations are identical to those discussed in editing styles. Since it is far easier to have paragraph controls in styles than it is to set parameters and options for each individual paragraph, we have already discussed most aspects of paragraph control. Simply refer to the preceding section for instructions on setting paragraph specifications.

Widows and Orphans

One of the important options in PageMaker 4.2 is widow and orphan control. As we pointed out elsewhere in this chapter, a widow is the first line of a paragraph left by itself at the bottom of a column or page, and an orphan is the last line of a paragraph at the top of a column or page. The default widow and orphan line control is 1. That means if one line from a paragraph is left at the top or bottom of a page, an extra line will be added or the widow will be moved to the top of the next page. Figures 8.11 and 8.12 show how PageMaker controls orphans, and Figures 8.13 and 8.14 show widow control with one line.

Values other than 1 express the number of lines that constitute an orphan or widow as well. For example, if you indicate three lines for widows, when three initial lines or less of a paragraph fall at the bottom of a page, the lines will be moved to the top of the next page.

You may encounter different definitions of widows and orphans in the literature on typesetting. In fact they are sometimes used in the reverse of our definition. Also, orphans/widows are sometimes used to include unsightly word fragments or short lines at the end of paragraphs as in Figure 8.12. These have to be removed by changing

Orphans and widows in page makeup refer to paragraphs that have only a single line from the paragraph at the top or bottom of the page. A line of less than full measure looks the worst, and widows and orphans can be defined as more lines than a single one.

FIGURE 8.11 Orphan left at top of second column.

Orphans and widows in page makeup refer to paragraphs that have only a single line from the paragraph at the top or bottom of the page. A line of less than full measure looks the worst, and widows and orphans can be defined as more lines than a single one.

FIGURE 8.12 Line automatically added to eliminate orphan

In se perpetuo Tempus as revolubile gyro Iam revocat Zephyros, vere tepente, novos. Induiturque brev Tellus reparata iuventam, Iamque soluta gelu dulce virescit humus.

Orphans and widows in page makeup refer to paragraphs that have only a single line from the paragraph at the top or bottom of the page. A line of less than full measure looks the worst, and widows and orphans can be defined as more lines than a single one.

FIGURE 8.13 Widow at bottom of firstcolumn

In se perpetuo Tempus as revolubile gyro Iam revocat Zephyros, vere tepente, novos. Induiturque brev Tellus reparata iuventam, Iamque soluta gelu dulce virescit humus.

Orphans and widows in page makeup refer to paragraphs that have only a single line from the paragraph at the top or bottom of the page. A line of less than full measure looks the worst, and widows and orphans can be defined as more lines than a single one.

FIGURE 8.14 Widow pushed to top of second column

the sentences or paragraphs by hand. The important thing to remember is that *anything* that detracts from the look of the page
because it is left hanging by itself should be corrected.

Kerning, Spacing, and Hyphenation

Letter spacing is the amount of space between characters. In general,
kerning is the adjustment of letterspacing. Track kerning is a way of
automatically increasing or decreasing the spacing between all words
and letters. Pair kerning is adjusting space between selected characters so that they are aesthetically pleasing. Letter spacing can be
adjusted through the Spacing Attributes dialog box (Figure 8.9) and
can be done from within either a style or paragraph. Finally, spacing
between words can be adjusted in PageMaker.

Hyphenation is related to spacing. If PageMaker determines that any
more space in a line will make the type unacceptably tight, words in the
hyphenation dictionary will be hyphenated automatically. The purpose
of the hyphenation in conjunction with kerning and spacing is to give
the publication an even, readable, and pleasing appearance.

Kerning, spacing, and hyphenation can be done automatically as
well as manually. The great bulk of all spacing is done automatically,
but there will be situations where you will have to make manual
changes because too much or too little space is in a paragraph. In the
next section we will examine how to deal with the problem of tight
and loose lines that crop up in your publication.

Tight and Loose Lines

A new feature introduced in PageMaker 4.0 is the automatic highlighting of lines that are deemed too "tight" or too "loose." A tight
line does not leave enough space between the characters or words,
giving a crowded appearance to the line. Alternatively, a loose line
has too much space between the letters and words. Either type of line
makes the publication look less than it optimally should.

To set up automatic highlighting of tight and loose lines, select
the *Loose/Tight Lines* option under *Show Layout Problems* in the Prefer-

ences dialog box in the **Edit** menu. After setting the option, automatic highlighting of loose or tight lines appears in your text. Using a 200 percent magnification of some text, Figure 8.15 shows a highlighted loose line.

Since this is a loose line (too much space in the line), it will be necessary to determine how to put more text in the line. The easiest solution would be to take out the hyphenation from the word *programs* and push the entire word into the loose line. Since Page-Maker automatically hyphenates words according to a dictionary, we cannot simply backspace over the hyphen. Instead, we have to go to the Hyphenation dialog box and change the hyphenation to manual. The change will affect only the text that has been selected or the line where we have the Text tool cursor. Therefore, before opening the Hyphenation dialog box, we will place the Text tool cursor in the highlighted line. From the **Type** menu we select *Hyphenation . . .* or press ⌘-Ⓗ on the keyboard. Figure 8.16 shows the change we will make by clicking the *Manual Only* option.

In the *Manual Only* mode for hyphenation, we can take out the hyphen that was placed there automatically with the dictionary. Under the *Manual Plus Dictionary* mode, the dictionary forces a hyphen in certain circumstances. Since we want to get rid of the hyphen in the word *pro-grams,* we will need to use the *Manual Only* option for de-hyphenating the word. With the hyphen gone in *programs,* the text realigns itself as shown in the example in Figure 8.17.

If you are using a specialized terminology, such as found in science, where Latin words are often used, you may have to add a word to your dictionary. For example, suppose you have a situation as

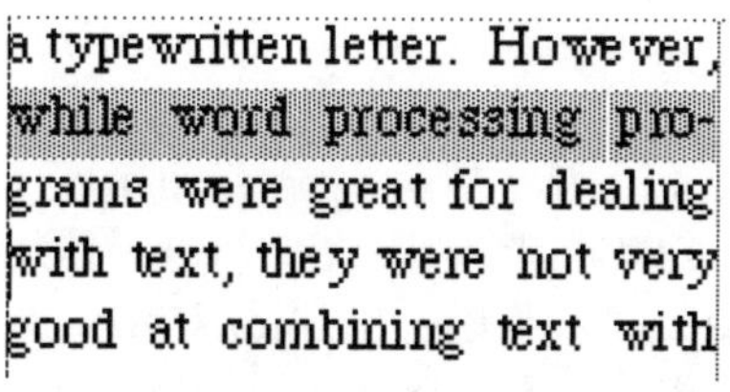

FIGURE 8.15 Automatic highlighting of bad word spacing

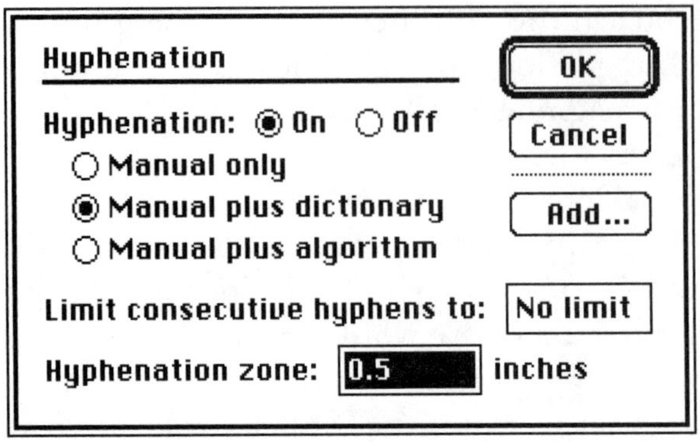

Hyphenation		OK

Hyphenation: ⦿ On ◯ Off
  ◯ Manual only
  ⦿ Manual plus dictionary
  ◯ Manual plus algorithm

Limit consecutive hyphens to: | No limit |

Hyphenation zone: | 0.5 | inches

Cancel

Add...

FIGURE 8.16 Hyphenation dialog box

omitted from a typewritten
letter. However, while word
processing programs were great
for dealing with text, they were
not very good at combining text

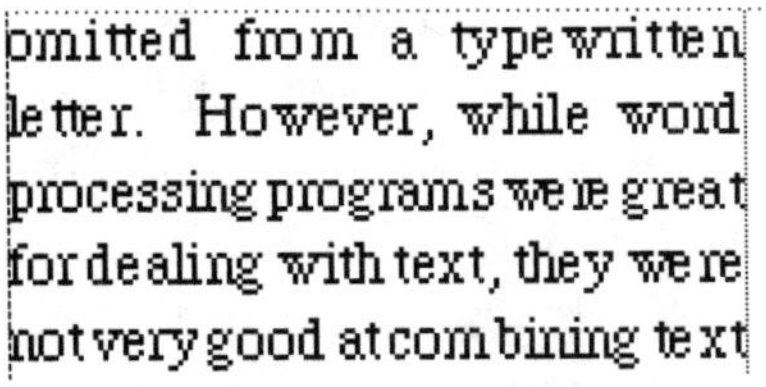

FIGURE 8.17 De-hyphenating sometimes can correct spacing problems.

shown in Figure 8.18. If the word *verbum* is hyphenated, it will probably be enough to tighten the highlighted line.

Usually, the easiest way to handle loose and tight lines is with the manual technique discussed earlier. However, if you have several nonstandard words, it may be easier to add them to your hyphenation dictionary. Then they will be hyphenated automatically and save you the work of manual hyphenation.

To add a word to the hyphenation dictionary, first select the word in your text you want to be hyphenated. Next, click the Add . . . button in the Hyphenation dialog box to bring up the dialog box shown in Figure 8.19.

The selected word appears in the Word box with two tildes (~~) indicating where the hyphens will be placed in the event the word is to be hyphenated. If you don't like where the hyphens are to be placed, change them by erasing the tildes and/or putting in your own.

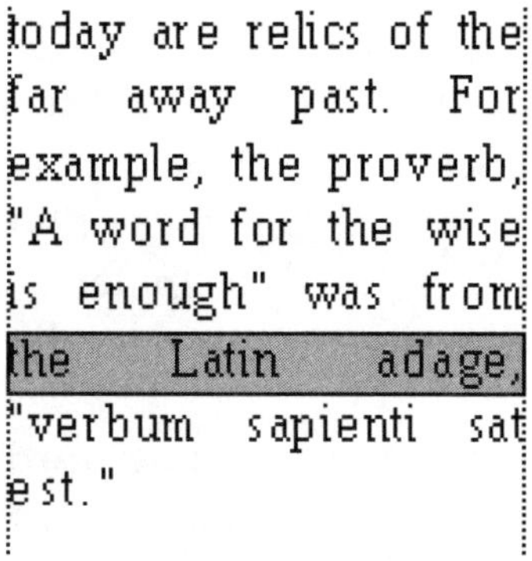

today are relics of the
far away past. For
example, the proverb,
"A word for the wise
is enough" was from
the Latin adage,
"verbum sapienti sat
est."

FIGURE 8.18 Unknown words are not automatically hyphenated.

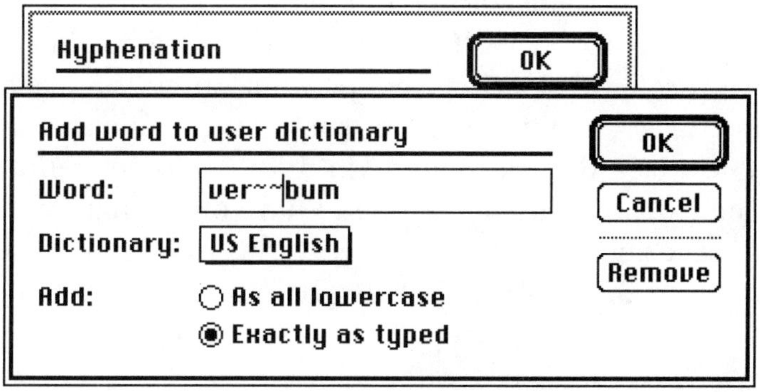

Hyphenation ▭ OK ▭

Add word to user dictionary ▭ OK ▭

Word: ver~~bum

Dictionary: US English

Add: ○ As all lowercase
⦿ Exactly as typed

Cancel

Remove

FIGURE 8.19 Adding a word to hyphenation dictionary

With the word in the hyphenation dictionary, it will hyphenate
the word when it is required, as shown in the following illustration:

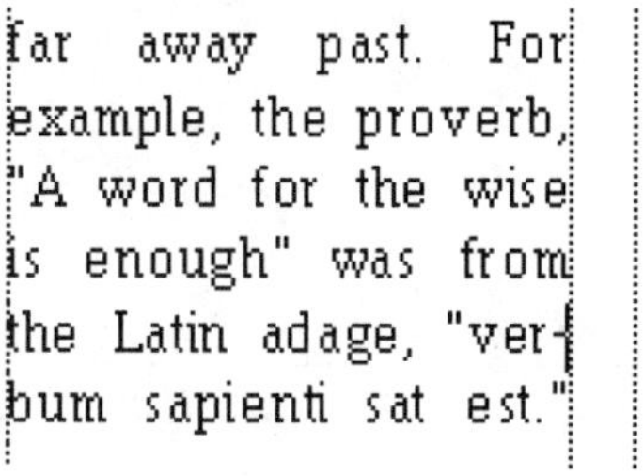

far away past. For
example, the proverb,
"A word for the wise
is enough" was from
the Latin adage, "ver-
bum sapienti sat est."

Dictionary Editor

A new item in PageMaker 4.2 is the Dictionary Editor. It allows you to create new dictionaries for special vocabularies used both in spell checking and hyphenation. To access the Dictionary Editor, find the icon in the Utilities folder within in the Aldus folder in the System folder. Figure 8.20 shows the folders to open to get the Dictionary Editor.

After launching the Dictionary Editor, adding words is simple. Type the word in the Word window. Use tildes (~~) to separate the word into hyphen breaks. Click the Add button, and the word is now in the dictionary. Figure 8.21 shows the dialog box of the Dictionary Editor.

Once you have added all the words you want, save your dictionary. If you use the AldEng.udc file name, it will be added to the default user dictionary. If you save it under a different name that will only be used with specific types of publications, such as a computer, typesetting, scientific, or other special-use language, then you will have to place the AldEng.udc in another folder before your new dictionary can be used. It's fine to have more than one user dictionary for a single language, but each has to be in a separate folder. Figure 8.22 shows the Save dialog box for the Dictionary editor.

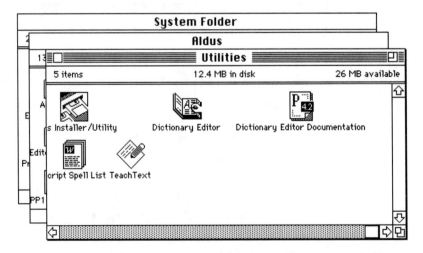

FIGURE 8.20 Dictionary Editor icon in the Utilities folder

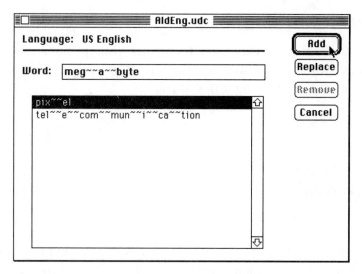

FIGURE 8.21 Adding words in the Dictionary Editor

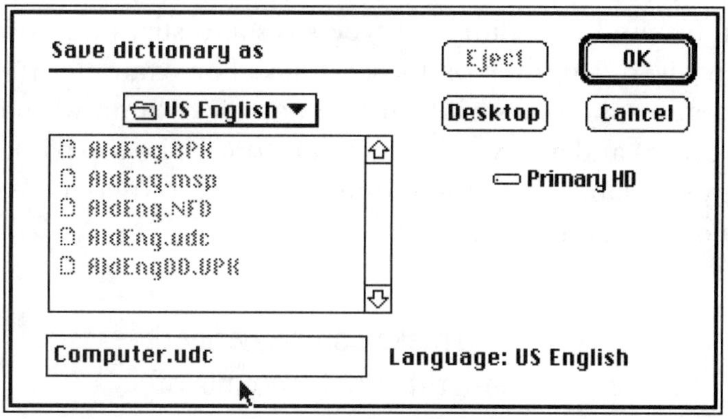

FIGURE 8.22 Save under a unique name or use existing dictionary

Be sure to take advantage of this feature if you are using a lot of nonstandard words. It will save the time of manually hyphenating words, and far fewer instances of loose and tight lines will occur because most of your words will be found in the hyphenation dictionary. It will also speed up the process of spell checking if the words you use are in the user dictionary.

Track Kerning

Track kerning is a method for giving your publication an professional look through spacing use. The *Track* option in the **Type** menu provides the following types of tracks:

- No track
- Very loose
- Normal
- Tight
- Very tight

Tracks can be assigned to selected text, the next text you type, or to styles. The track selection can be through the Type Specifications dialog box for either selected text or styles and also, more directly, through the *Track* option in the **Type** menu pointed out above.

In deciding how to set the track kerning for your publication, keep in mind that different type sizes and styles will look different when given a tighter or looser track. For example, the following illustration shows a serif font in a narrow column with a very loose track (top) and a very tight track (bottom). The top paragraph looks pretty good, but the bottom one is far too crowded to be easily read, let alone be aesthetically attractive.

Tracks can be defined with different amounts of looseness.

Tracks can be defined with different amounts of looseness.

While a tight track on a serif font may be crowded, sans serif fonts, such as Helvetica, look much better. In the next illustration, the top paragraph has a tight track and the bottom paragraph, in a

Times font, has a loose track. However, they both look appropriately spaced.

> Different fonts can be tracked differently.
>
> Different fonts can be tracked differently.

When you use larger fonts or fonts with special styles, track kerning has different results. For example, the following illustration has the word *Holiday* in a 24-point bold sans serif font. The top sample is tracked as tight, the middle one as normal, and the bottom one as loose. Notice how the width increases as you look from the top to the bottom.

> **Holiday**
> **Holiday**
> **Holiday**

In setting up a track the prime consideration is how the publication looks. There may be situations where you have to "fill" or "crowd" type into a publication. Sometimes a change in the track will accommodate filling or stuffing space in a fixed area; however, it is not advisable to do so at the expense of the publication's appearance. If you need more space, it is a better idea to use a smaller font or smaller font size or to cut material than to use too tight a track. For example, if your publication needs a little more room, try changing from a serif font such as Bookman to Times Roman, a relatively small serif font. Likewise, to fill in blank space, a larger font or font size will probably do a better job than loose tracking.

Manual Kerning

Manual kerning allows you to get spacing between letters or words as perfect as possible. It would be difficult to use manual kerning on everything; but with certain applications, it may be worth the effort. For example, in preparing print copy for an advertisement where several different type sizes and styles are used, there is not enough text to make the fine changes too burdensome. However, you wouldn't want to try and manually kern all of the text in a book.

To perform manual kerning, you will use the numeric keypad on your keyboard. The increments are in 1/25 and 1/100, with 1/25 being coarse and 1/100 units being fine. The following table shows the kerning available:

TABLE 8.1 Manual kerning key strokes

Increment	*Keyboard*
+1/25	⌘ → or ⌘ SHIFT DELETE
−1/25	⌘ ← or ⌘ DELETE
+1/100	SHIFT ⌘ → or OPTION SHIFT DELETE
−1/100	SHIFT ⌘ ← or OPTION DELETE
Clear	⌘ OPTION 3 with selected range of text

To see how this works, we will look at a piece of copy with and without manual kerning. The top paragraph in Figure 8.23 has too much space between the letters *T* and *r* in the word *Track*. Placing the cursor of the Text tool between the *T* and the *r*, press the ⌘ ←. You will see the *T* and the *r* come closer together.

Place the cursor between *with* and *Jack* and try reducing the space between the words. You will notice that the *letters* in the two words and the words come closer together. To reduce the word spacing only, use the spacing options in the Paragraph dialog box.

Try adding space between letters using manual kerning to practice the procedure. Usually this type of kerning is used for very fine

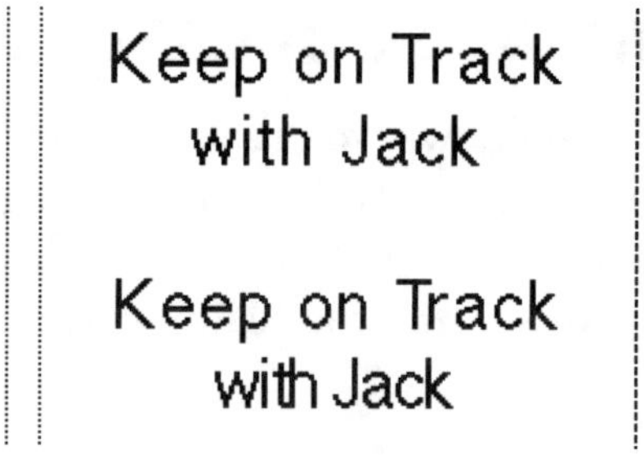

Keep on Track
with Jack

Keep on Track
with Jack

FIGURE 8.23 Fine tune with manual kerning

tuning, and you should rely on track kerning and automatic kerning for most of you documents.

Pair Kerning

In the Spacing Attributes dialog box (accessed through the Paragraph Specifications dialog box) is a *Pair Kerning* option box. If this box is checked, then certain pairs of letters are automatically kerned so that they are more aesthetically spaced. For example, the *Tr* pair that we adjusted in Figure 8.27 showed we had to manually delete space in a *Tr* pair in the word *Track*. With smaller size fonts this is not as much a problem; but with larger fonts and font sizes, certain pair space is more noticeable. If it is desirable to have smaller point text automatically pair kerned, specify a smaller point size in the Auto Above box next to the Pair Kerning label. For example, if you want an 11-point text automatically kerned for pairs, then type in **Auto above 10 points**.

Kern Disadvantages

Track kerning and pair kerning, will slow down text composition in PageMaker. If track or pair kerning is not really needed—the text looks fine with no track or pair kerning—then do not use it. Because PageMaker lets you automatically highlight overly loose and tight lines, you can manually fix your text to look excellent. However, if track and/or pair kerning adds to the appearance of your work, by all means use it. Just don't use it when it is not needed.

TABLE OF CONTENTS AND INDEX CREATION

PageMaker 4.2 has considerable power to create a table of contents and an index for your publication. By flagging paragraphs and words, you determine what should be included in a table of contents and/or an index. Then PageMaker automatically creates the table of contents or index for you.

Table of Contents

Planning ahead helps a good deal in setting up a good table of contents (TOC). If you design your headers to be included in the TOC, then you can have a consistent and good-looking table. For our example, we will have three levels of headers:

- Chapter—all caps flush left
- Level 1—caps and small caps flush left
- Level 2—indent 0.25 inch

Each header is included in the TOC automatically so that when it comes time to create a TOC, there will be no need to go back through the document and include any topics. If for some reason a new subtopic has to be added, it can be done through the Paragraph Specifications dialog box—**Type** menu, Paragraph . . . or press ⌘-Ⓜ on the keyboard.

Figure 8.24 shows a sample document with the three levels of headers.

- Chapter—ALL ABOUT AIRPLANES
- Level 1—Aerodynamics
- Level 2—Lift

Since the style definitions have already been selected to be placed in the table of contents, all that has to be done to create the TOC is to select *Create TOC* . . . from the **Options** menu. The Create Table of Contents dialog box (Figure 8.25) appears with several options. The title of the table defaults to "Contents," and you can change that to whatever you want. If a TOC has already been placed, you can opt to

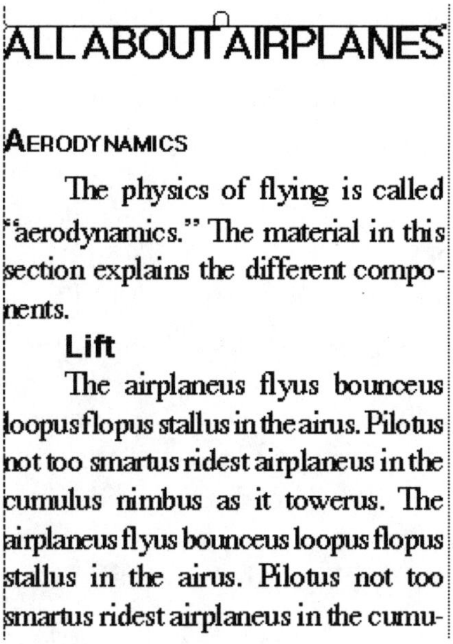

ALL ABOUT AIRPLANES

AERODYNAMICS

The physics of flying is called "aerodynamics." The material in this section explains the different components.

Lift

The airplaneus flyus bounceus loopus flopus stallus in the airus. Pilotus not too smartus ridest airplaneus in the cumulus nimbus as it towerus. The airplaneus flyus bounceus loopus flopus stallus in the airus. Pilotus not too smartus ridest airplaneus in the cumu-

FIGURE 8.24 Headings can be automatically made TOC items.

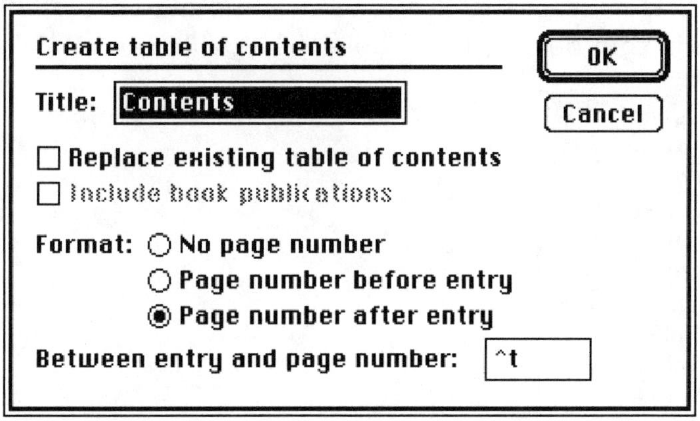

Create table of contents

OK

Cancel

Title: Contents

☐ Replace existing table of contents
☐ Include book publications

Format: ○ No page number
○ Page number before entry
◉ Page number after entry

Between entry and page number: ^t

FIGURE 8.25 Create TOC dialog box

have it replaced with the new one. If there are several other linked documents in a book, they should be included unless it is a document with multiple tables of content. The page-number format may be selected at this time as well. For initial drafts, the *No Page Number* option may be selected, but typically the default with the page number following the entry will be used.

The final item in the Create Table of Contents dialog box determines what, if anything, will be placed between the entry and the page number. The default is a tab indicated by the ^t character. The tab is preceded by a string of dots or other leaders you can change by editing the TOC styles that will appear in your style palette once you have created your TOC (see Figure 8.26). Other characters in the extended character set are in Appendix C of your PageMaker 4.0 manual.

Once you have selected the *Create TOC . . .* option, you will get the loaded icon, just like you do when you place text. When you place the TOC, it flows just like any other word-processed file. Figure 8.27 shows the results created from our sample, with the page numbers spread out to provide a more realistic idea of what you will see in your table of contents.

Sometimes you will get a different heading in the TOC than in your publication. Note in Figure 8-26 the styles with TOC in the name. This means that they are styles employed in the TOC based on styles in your document. Although they will generally keep the same

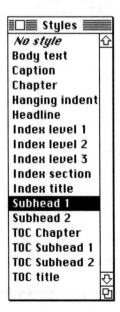

FIGURE 8.26 New styles are added when TOC and index are created.

Contents

ALL ABOUT AIRPLANES **1**

Aerodynamics **3**

Lift 6

Drag 9

Thrust 12

Gravity 14

Axis **16**

Pitch 21

Yaw 26

Bank 30

Controls **37**

FIGURE 8.27 TOC with page numbers

style as in the document from which the TOC is derived, sometimes they will have special TOC styles. Of course you can create your own TOC styles. If you want changes, edit the TOC style; not the entire table of contents itself.

For example, the best way to edit the TOC if you want Subhead 2 entries indented is to edit the TOC Subhead 2 style. In that way, all of the entries will be changed with a single edit. All of the regular editing tools are available to edit the TOC.

Index

Making an index is a little more involved than creating a table of contents. Each item that is to be included in the index must be flagged. We will begin with a simple indexing example and then show how to index on different levels.

To add a simple index entry, all that is required is to select the word you want in the index and select *Index Entry* . . . from the **Options** menu or (more sensibly) press ⌘ ⓖ on the keyboard. For example, suppose you selected the word *lift*. Figure 8.28 shows the Add Index Entry dialog box that appears. Click the Add button, and your word will be included in the index.

In some cases you will want to make cross references, and when you select the Cross-reference button, the Add Index Entry dialog box changes to that shown in Figure 8.29.

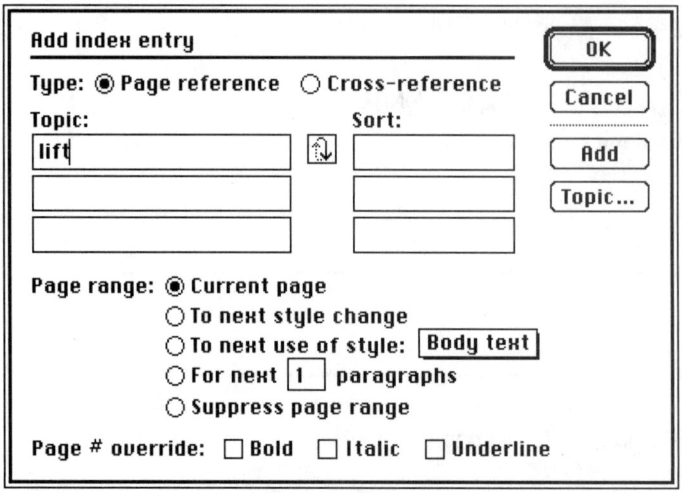

FIGURE 8.28 Initial dialog box for index entry with Page reference selected

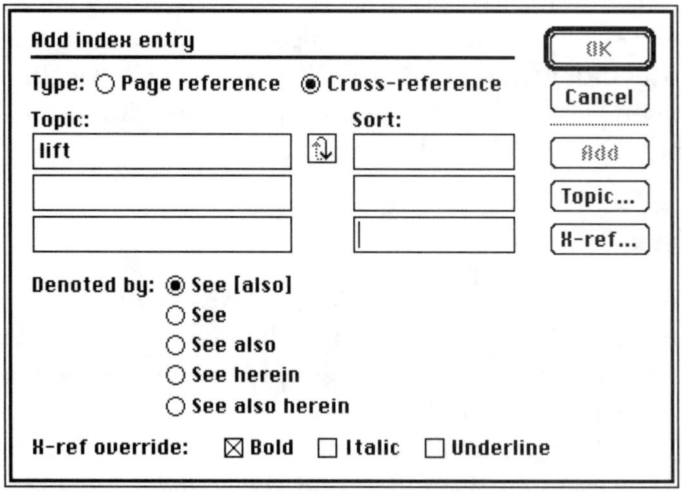

FIGURE 8.29 Initial index entry dialog box with Cross-reference button selected

When you do select a cross-reference, you can choose from five denotation phrases shown in Figure 8.29. When your reference is placed in the index, it will appear with the cross-reference. That is, the word will direct the reader to another part of the index for more information. Depending on the denotation (e.g., *see, see also,* etc.), the reader will be better able to find what he or she seeks.

To select a cross-reference, select the X-ref . . . button. The Select Cross-reference Topic dialog box appears. Depending on what topics are already present, you will choose or create the desired cross-reference. For example, Figure 8.30 shows a cross-reference to Aerodynamics (Level 1) and Gravity (Level 2). The following would appear in the index, given that set of selections:

lift See also Aerodynamics: Gravity:

Multiple-Level Indexing

A very powerful and useful part of the new PageMaker index option is the ability to make up to a trilevel index. That means that under one topic, you can have subtopics. For example, the following shows a multiple-level index that can be created automatically with Page-Maker:

```
Mammals        44
        Domestic        88
                Dogs              93, 103
```

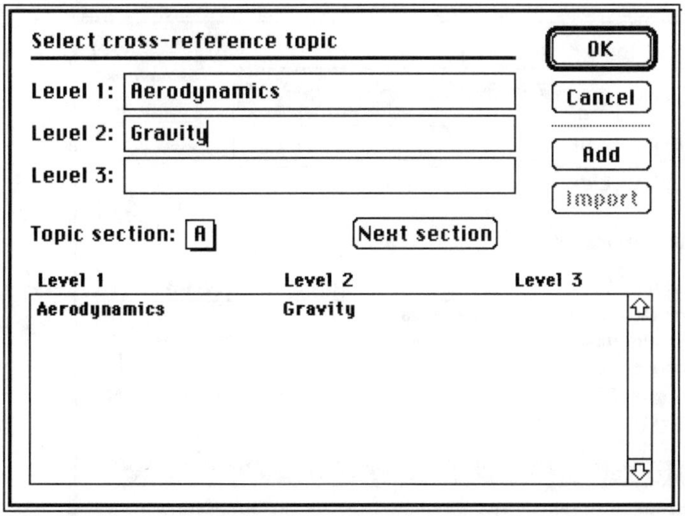

FIGURE 8.30 Establishing cross-reference

Such combinations and multiple-level indexing makes your index far more professional and useful to the reader. Using cross-references, you might also have under the entry Dogs "See also Mammals: Domestic." By combining multiple-level indexing with cross-referencing, your index can be made almost foolproof.

In order to see how to use multiple-level indexing, we will use the text in Figure 8.31. It will show the context and purpose of multiple-level indexing.

To get started, open the Add Index Entry dialog box and click the Topic . . . button. This will open the Select Topic dialog box shown in Figure 8.32. For multiple-level entries, you do not select the word to be entered as with single-level entries.

Private Planes

Private planes come in many different sizes and for different purposes. Cessna aircraft include the Commuter, Skyhawk, Cardinal, Skylane, and Skymaster. Piper has the Cub, Cherokee, Dakota, Tomahawk, and Archer. The Grumman Tiger has been reintroduced by another company.

FIGURE 8.31 Sample text for indexing

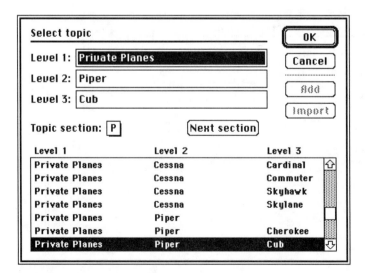

FIGURE 8.32 Topics have one, two, or three levels

Type in the Level 1, Level 2, and Level 3 entries. If you already have entered topics, select the topic letter (the letter with which the topic begins). In Figure 8.33, "Private Planes Piper" is already entered; so all that would have to be done would be to click it in the topic box to fill Level 1 and Level 2 boxes at the top of the dialog box. If you had already selected "Cub" before opening the Index dialog box, it would be erased when you selected the Level 1 and Level 2 entries. In our example, all you would have to type in would be "Cub" in the Level 3 box. Once you have all levels typed in, click the Add button. The Add Index Entry dialog box now has the three levels entered as shown in Figure 8.33. You again click the Add button to install the triple-level index entries.

Once you have made all of your entries, the final step is to create the index. That is done by selecting *Create Index . . .* from the **Options** menu. If you have an existing index, you can replace it; and if you have a book publication—a list of files in the book publication list—they can be indexed as well. Click OK and you will see a loaded Text icon containing all the text for your index. Then flow the text as you would any word-processed text. Figure 8.34 shows part of the index created with the sample text from Figure 8.31.

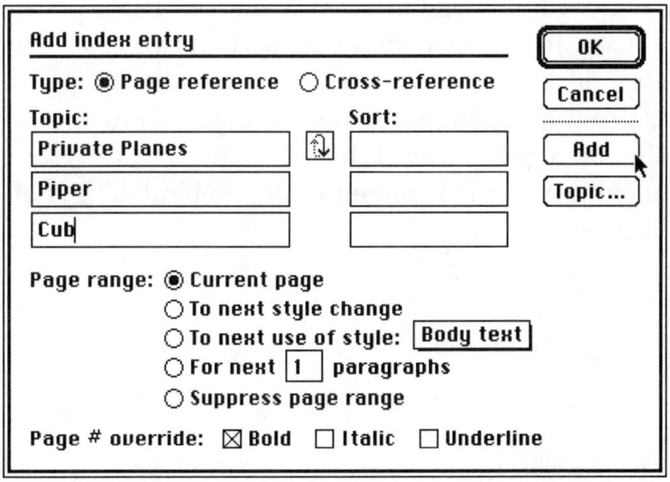

FIGURE 8.33 Click Add to enter three-level page reference

P

Private Planes
  Cessna
      Cardinal 24–25
      Commuter 25–27
      Skyhawk 24, 28–29
      Skylane 30
  Grumman
      Tiger 49–53
  Piper 31
      Cherokee 32–35
      Dakota 35–36
      Tomahawk 37

FIGURE 8.34 Three-level index

We removed the double references in the sample index in Figure 3-34. For example, *Grumman* and *Grumman Tiger* began on page 49, so we removed the page number. However, Piper began on page 31 where it was discussed separately from Piper Cherokee and the other Piper aircraft.

More advanced indexing can be done, but here we want to show indexing on a general level. It is very important to experiment with the indexing, especially the multiple-level indexing, before creating an index yourself.

GRAPHICS

One of the most important features of PageMaker is its ability to place graphics on the same page with text. We will examine the many different ways PageMaker 4.2 can place graphics in combination with text, what types of graphics it can place, and how to prepare graphics for placement. Then we will examine the variety of ways graphics can be used in a publication.

TYPES OF GRAPHIC FILES THAT CAN BE PLACED

One of the nice features of a Macintosh is the limited number of graphic files. Essentially, there are four different formats for graphic files; Encapsulated PostScript (EPS), paint, draw (PICT), and Tag Image File Format (TIFF). PageMaker can accept any of those types. Unlike other computers though, the Macintosh does not require an extension name with the file types, and so you may not know what type of graphic file you are placing until you load the graphic. Of course, you can use extension names to help you ahead of time know what kind of graphic file you will be placing. Figure 9.1 shows the different types of files with extension names to let you know the kind of file you are placing before it is part of a loaded icon.

If you do not know the type of graphic you are placing, your loaded icon will tell you when you select it to load. The next section

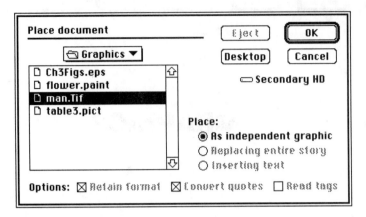

FIGURE 9.1 Different types of graphics can be placed.

shows the icon you will see and explains the different types of graphics being placed.

 Paint/bitmap files Paint files are one of the most common types of graphic files. These files contain pictures that are mapped in bits. When changed in PageMaker, they are easily distorted, but they are easily edited in paint programs such as Aldus SuperPaint. Scanned images are often saved as paint files since they lend themselves to touch-up work.

 Draw/object-oriented files This type of file works very well with PageMaker. Programs like McDraw II and the draw element of SuperPaint create this type of file. They can be changed with PageMaker tools and still remain clear and proportionate when printed.

 Tag image file format (TIFF) This type of format is also common for scanned images. TIFF graphics may not look very good on the screen, but they can be changed in size and still look good when printed.

 Encapsulated PostScript files (EPS) This type of file can be placed in your PageMaker document, but you will need a PostScript printer, such as one of Apple's LaserWriter series printers, to print an EPS file. When it appears on the screen, you might not be able to see the graphic image. Instead you will see a gray box with "Title," "Creator," and "Creation date." You can get excellent printed resolution with PostScript files regardless of how you change the size of the graphic.

 Scrapbook Files When you take a graphic from the Scrapbook, it appears with a number, indicating the number of items loaded from the Scrapbook. Since Scrapbook files maintain the formatting information, you can get anything from a TIFF file to a text file. As each file is placed, the counter in the Scrapbook icon decreases by 1. To access the Scrapbook File, first select the System Folder as shown in Figure 9.2.

When you place a graphic, you either see the graphic itself on the screen or a box showing the approximate size of the graphic. Some EPS files display the box without the graphic. The following illustration shows what you can get when an EPS is placed:

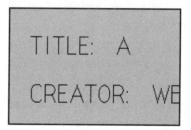

This type of EPS file can be cropped, stretched, and otherwise changed just as any other graphic file. However, because it does not have a screen-linked graphic, all you see is the area where the graphic will be placed. Graphics in this form save room on the hard disk, RAM memory, and your laser printer's memory; and their output is excellent. However, they are more difficult to envision on the screen.

PREPARING GRAPHICS

For the most part, preparing graphics for PageMaker is the same as preparing graphics for any other application. However, the following tips might help.

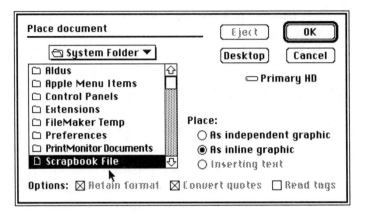

FIGURE 9.2 The Scrapbook File is in the System Folder

- Remove all white space from around the graphic. Even though you can crop white space in PageMaker, it takes up memory in your file.

- Clean up your graphic. Make sure all extraneous marks are erased.

- Electronic "clip art," sometimes called "click art," is available for the non-artistic. Use it instead of giving up on having graphics in your publication.

- Scanners can prepare graphic artwork on disk. Use scanners to reproduce everything from your company logo to public domain artwork.

- If you are preparing a graphic from scratch for a publication, try to scale it as closely as possible for the area in your publication. Even though PageMaker can scale graphics, sometimes distortions occur if graphics are expanded or reduced to fit a space in a document.

- If you are printing with a PostScript printer, use PostScript (TIFF and EPS) files wherever possible to maintain top-quality output.

The preceding tips are general guidelines for preparing graphics. As a rule, remember to do as much as possible before you place a graphic.

SCALING GRAPHICS

One of the important features of PageMaker is the ability to change the size of graphics so that they fit the areas available for them in your publication. However, you must be careful not to distort the graphics when changing their sizes. Using the new Control Palette, you can enter numeric values to scale graphics more precisely to avoid distortion.

There are two basic ways you might distort graphics. First, you can push and pull on them on one dimension or side and create fat or skinny versions of your graphic. Second, you can change the size of the wrong type of graphic. We will see how to correctly change a graphic, and then examine some of the problems.

We will start with a big fat Ali Baba and reduce him proportionately. Figure 9.3 shows the original Ali scanned from a drawing.

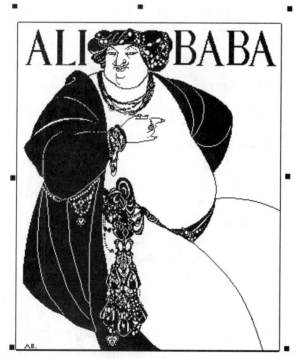

FIGURE 9.3 Originally placed graphic

Select the Pointer tool, and place it in any corner where you see a square handle. Holding down (SHIFT), place the pointer in the corner and move it inward to the center of the graphic. If you do not hold down the (SHIFT) key, there is no guarantee that your graphic will be proportional and you can easily get distortions.

Figure 9.4 shows the smaller Ali ready to fit into a smaller niche in your publication. If you place the pointer somewhere off the graphic and click it, the tabs will disappear.

If you want to rescale a graphic with a precise value in mind, use the new Control palette available with PageMaker 4.2. It is placed on the screen by selecting *Control Palette* from the **Window** menu, or by pressing ⌘-①.

It is less intuitive for scaling graphics, but great for setting a graphic to an exact size or proportion. For example, suppose you want to reduce Ali Baba to 20 percent of its original size. First select the graphic by clicking it with the mouse. Click the Proportional box on the right side of the palette to keep the correct proportions. Click the Reference Point icon (second icon from the left) in the center or one of the corners. Type in **20** where the percentage value is. The following illustration shows the correct settings in the Control palette for such a change:

		◀▶X: 1.258 in	◀▶W: 0.931 in	20%	⊠ Proportional
		↕Y: 0.446 in	↕H: 1.108 in	20%	

The main advantage of using the Control palette is that you can scale a graphic to a precise value. However, in working with the Control palette, you may find it to be more difficult for precise scaling on the screen and fitting or filling available space. Now if you know that you have exactly 1.45 inches of vertical space for a graphic, the Control palette is the tool to use. However, if you are just trying to rescale a graphic to fit a gap, it is probably easier to use the Pointer tool.

Proportional scaling of graphics is generally important no matter what tool you use. To see some problems created when you do not proportionally reduce a graphic, we will examine a graphic pie chart. Figure 9.5 shows the original chart.

FIGURE 9.4 Graphic in reduced scale

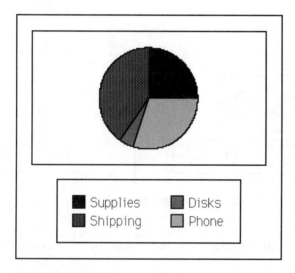

FIGURE 9.5 Undistorted pie chart

In Figure 9.6, the same chart is shown when it was pushed inward from the side (top) and bottom (bottom) graphic tabs without holding down (SHIFT).

Of course, you may want to intentionally show fat or skinny graphics for special effects.

Cropping Graphics

In addition to changing the size of graphics, you may also change them by cropping. Cropping cuts your graphics down to size for inclusion into your publication. You may crop graphics before or

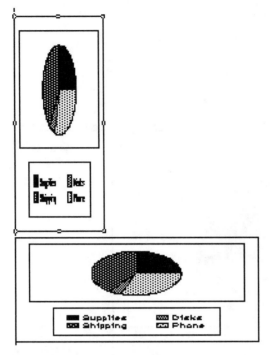

FIGURE 9.6 Distorted vertical and horizontal graphic

after altering their size, or you may even find it necessary to crop
before and after scaling.

 To crop a graphic, choose the Cropping tool from the
lower right-hand corner of the toolbox. Place the Cropping tool icon on any of the tabs in the graphic, and hold
down the mouse button and drag the tab inward toward
the graphic. You will see parts of the graphic disappear.

To see how this works, we will employ Ali Baba again. Figure 9.7
shows that the graphic extends beyond the bounds of the publication
to the right. There is also a good deal of white space above Ali's head.

To crop the right, place the Cropping tool icon pointer on one of
the tabs and drag the tab to the left until it removes the white space.
Do the same on the top. Figure 9.8 shows the double-pointed arrow
that appears when the top is cropped downward.

FIGURE 9.7 Uncropped graphic

FIGURE 9.8 Note double arrow when cropping.

Finally, now that the cropping is completed, you may scale the graphic down with the Pointer tool or Control palette so that it fits in the page. Figure 9.9 shows this final step in a typical cropping and scaling application.

Using the Control palette for cropping is just like scaling except that part of the graphic is cut away. When the Cropping tool is selected from the Toolbox or the Crop icon in the Control palette is selected, the Control palette appears as shown in the following illustration:

| | | ◀▶X: 1.681 in | ◀▶W: 4.028 in | |
| | | ◆Y: −6.66 in | ◆H: 2.236 in | |

Instead of cropping with the Cropping tool, it is done by setting the value in the Control palette to what you want. Note the position of the double arrow in the Reference point outcome, and then set the value to the amount you want cropped or uncropped. The little arrows to the left of the values are nudge icons. Using these arrows,

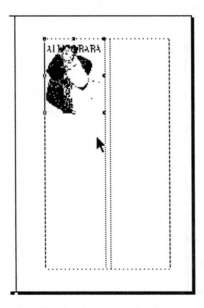

FIGURE 9.9 Scaling to fit after cropping

you crop a value by 1 pixel. If you press the nudge icon while holding down the ⌘ key, you crop it 5 pixels.

Recovery from overcropping is simple. Select the Cropping tool, place the crop tool on one of the graphic tags, and drag the tab outward away from the overcropped portion of the graphic. You will see the cropped graphic reappear. You may uncrop a graphic even if the publication has been saved to the disk and you are working on it in a new session. For example, in Figure 9.10 an overcropping has cut off the wing of a flying fish.

To get the missing wing back, the crop tool is used to pull back on the right side tab of the graphic. Figure 9.11 shows the graphic with the cropped portion recovered.

FIGURE 9.10 Overcropped graphic

FIGURE 9.11 Correct cropping

TEXT WRAP AND GRAPHICS

The real key to working with PageMaker and graphics is the integration of text and graphics. We will be dealing with both independent and inline types of graphics integrated with text. First, we will deal with text wrap, a general feature of text and graphics. Actually, text wrap refers more to the "halo" around a graphic than it does text.

To initiate text wrap, select *Text Wrap* . . . from the **Element** menu. Figure 9.12 shows the Text Wrap dialog box with three wrap and three text flow options. We will examine each of these options in turn, with an example showing adjustments to the graphic with text wrap and flow selections.

 The first wrap option is one where the text and graphic interflow with one another. Figure 9.13 shows text intermingled with graphics. This option is typically used where the graphic is very light and in the background behind the text. A company logo underlying text is an example of where this type of interflow would be effectively used.

 A second wrap option occurs where the text flows around the graphic. When this selection is chosen, there is a default standoff of 0.167 inch suggested in the Text Wrap dialog box. Looking at the graphic in Figure 9.14, you can

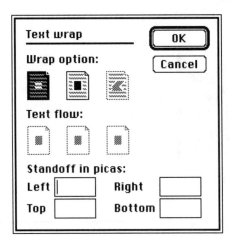

FIGURE 9.12 Text Wrap dialog box

see a broken line around the graphic. This is the "stand-off" that separates the text from the graphic.

There are a lot of gaps and spaces around the graphic and between the text in Figure 9.14, and it would not be suitable for publication in this form. By using the Pointer tool and dragging the standoff handles, the standoff can be customized. This allows some of the text to be inter-mingled with the graphics yet still be readable. Figure 9.15 shows how the graphic looks with a customized standoff "halo" that has been adjusted to the text. Also, the graphic has been scaled down a bit so that the text is not spread out so much.

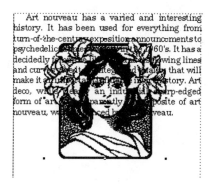

FIGURE 9.13 Text intermixed with graphics

FIGURE 9.14 Graphic with standoff from text

Art nouveau has a varied and interesting history. It has been used for everything from turn-of-the-century exposition announcements to psyche- delichip- pies post- ersin the 1960's. It has a de- cidedly feminine lilt to it nd its flowing lines and curves give it an in- tegrated quality that will make it an impor- tant in- fluence in art his- tory. Art deco, while clearly an industrial sharp- edged form of art and apparently the opposite of

FIGURE 9.15 Customized standoff

The text flow we have been using in Figures 9.13 through 9.15 is the *Surround* option. The other two options have the text above and below the graphic, as in Figure 9.16, or have the text stop at the top of the graphic and the rest of the text flow onto the next column or page.

Art nouveau has a varied and interesting history. It has been used for everything from turn-of-the-century exposition announcements to

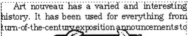

psychedelic hippies posters in the 1960's. It has a decidedly feminine lilt to it, and its flowing lines and curves give it an integrated quality that will

FIGURE 9.15 Customized standoff

Entering Text in a Graphic Field

If you attempt to type text in PageMaker 4.2 directly onto a graphic, chances are it will bounce right off. However, there are many occasions where your publication may need to have text entered directly onto a graphic to label it or to use it as a border.

Fortunately PageMaker provides a simple way of placing text on top of graphics even if there is a standoff "halo" around the graphic. The technique involves "drawing" a text window with the Text tool completely inside the graphic. If even a part of the text window is off the graphic, the entire window will bounce off. The following illustration shows a flower border that might be used in a wedding announcement. Holding down the mouse button, drag a text block in the area where you want the text to go. (The rectangle disappears as soon as you release the mouse button.)

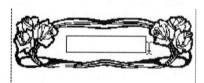

Once the text block area has been defined, you can now type in any text required. There will be a separate text window and a graphics block as shown in the following illustration:

The final result, shown in the next illustration, appears as though it were a single entity with no separate blocks for graphics and text. You will find the technique especially valuable when making drop caps and labelling graphics.

Image Control

While most of your graphic preparation should take place before placement with PageMaker, there are several things you can do once the graphic is placed. In fact, you may be able to do things with PageMaker 4.2 that you could not do with your graphic package. The major image adjustment tool in PageMaker is image control. It allows you to change the lightness and contrast of an image as well as screen patterns. Image control works only with black-and-white graphics.

To get started working on a graphic's image, select the graphic with the Pointer tool and click *Image Control . . .* from the **Element** menu. Figure 9.17 shows a typical Image Control dialog box after some manipulation of the lightness and contrast. The default is 0 percent for lightness and 50 percent for contrast. To see if you have the correct settings, click the Apply button before clicking OK.

To see how image control could be used in a practical application, we will employ the poetry of Emily Dickinson. Beginning with a graphic image of a flower, we will lighten the flower until we can superimpose readable text onto it. Figure 9.18 shows the original graphic.

Next, the graphic will be selected with the pointer, and we will increase the percentage of lightness to about 80 percent. Figure 9.19 shows this new lighter image.

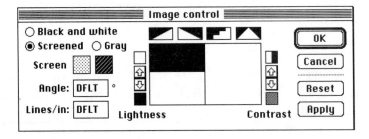

FIGURE 9.17 Image control dialog box

FIGURE 9.18 Original graph

Next, we superimpose the text over the graphic as shown in Figure 9.20. As you can see, it was necessary to lighten the flower even more and to use a dark bold text font so that it was not lost in the graphic.

The best way to work with the image control element is to first experiment with it a lot. After setting different controls, see how it looks on your screen by clicking Apply. Keeping the image on the

FIGURE 9.19 Graphic with increased lightness

This quiet Dust was Gentlemen and Ladies And Lads and Girls — Was laughter and ability and Sighing And Frocks and Curls

FIGURE 9.20 Text superimposed over graphic

screen with the Image Control dialog box off to the side so that you can see the changes in the image, you will be able to make adjustments without wrecking your graphic. If you get stuck, you can always click the Cancel or Default buttons to get everything back to the way it was originally.

INDEPENDENT AND INLINE GRAPHICS IN TEXT

An important feature of PageMaker is inline graphics, as noted in Chapter 5, "Preparing and Placing Text." The basic difference between inline and independent graphics is the ability of inline graphics to stay in one position relative to text. This prevents graphics from sliding away from captions or otherwise ending up where they are not wanted.

Placing Inline Graphics

Up to this point we have showed only how independent graphics are placed in PageMaker. In Chapter 5, "Preparing and Placing Text," we saw that inline graphics can be placed if they are placed as part of a word-processed document. However, independent graphics can be transformed into inline graphics. We will use the example of a chart you want to label with text. Tying the graphic to the text will allow changes elsewhere in the publication since any position change in the text will cause a position change in the graphic as well. We will begin with the chart at the top of page 205. It is an independent graphic placed conventionally.

Next we will add a legend below the chart to explain what is represented, as shown in the second illustration on page 205.

Now that the label is in place, to insure that the label and the graphic stick together, you have to change the independent graphic into an inline graphic. To accomplish that, select the graphic only and then cut it. Next, select the Text tool and paste the graphic in above the caption. Simply click at the insertion point and then paste it as you would to insert text in the same position. (Use *Paste* from the **Edit** menu or press ⌘-Ⓥ on the keyboard.) Since the graphic has

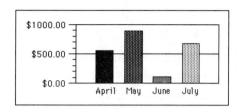

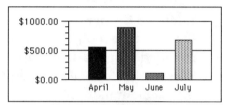

Monthly Sales in $100 Increments

been pasted in with the Text tool, it is now an inline graphic. The trick is to use the Text tool when pasting it in instead of the Pointer tool. It is a simple procedure and an important one when you want your graphics and text to stay together in large documents where you will be shifting text.

Changing from Inline to Independent Graphics

To change an inline graphic into an independent graphic, select the graphic with the Text tool and cut it. Then, with the Pointer tool selected, paste it wherever you want it. You essentially reverse the procedure of changing from independent to inline graphics, and the key is in pasting the graphic back into the document with the Pointer tool selected.

PAGEMAKER GRAPHIC TOOLS

The graphic tools supplied with PageMaker 4.2 are relatively simple ones; and while they are limited in what they can do, you may be surprised by their versatility.

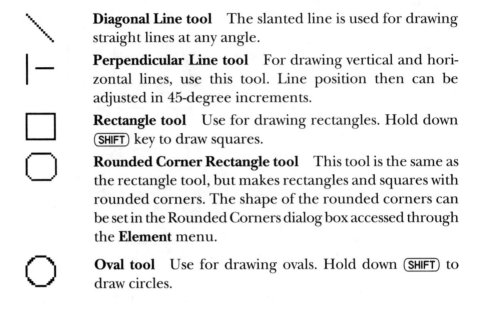

Diagonal Line tool   The slanted line is used for drawing straight lines at any angle.

Perpendicular Line tool   For drawing vertical and horizontal lines, use this tool. Line position then can be adjusted in 45-degree increments.

Rectangle tool   Use for drawing rectangles. Hold down (SHIFT) key to draw squares.

Rounded Corner Rectangle tool   This tool is the same as the rectangle tool, but makes rectangles and squares with rounded corners. The shape of the rounded corners can be set in the Rounded Corners dialog box accessed through the **Element** menu.

Oval tool   Use for drawing ovals. Hold down (SHIFT) to draw circles.

Lines

The **Line** submenu is accessed through the **Element** menu. This menu (Figure 9.21) shows all of the types of lines for all of the tools. For example, if you select a 12-point line and then draw an oval, your oval will be created with a 12-point border.

Besides the more obvious applications for lines, such as drawing borders around text, they have a number of other uses as well. For example, using 12-point lines, the following illustration shows a simple logo created with the Perpendicular Line tool. (The lines have been selected so that the tabs show and you can see how it was made.)

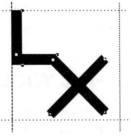

You can make interesting charts and graphs with the various drawing tools. For example, a candy-striped graphic can be created. The shapes in Figure 9.22 show the progression from a filled rectangle to a barber pole.

Use the following steps to create the "barber pole" effect.

- **Draw a rectangle with a solid fill.**

- Using a hairline-size line, draw an oval with a paper fill on top of the rectangle.

- With a 12-point reverse line, use the perpendicular line tool to draw 45-degree angles across the length of the cylinder. If the reverse lines obscure any of the oval on top, select the oval and press X-Ⓕ or select *Bring to Front* from the **Element** menu.

FIGURE 9.21 Lines available in PageMaker 4.2

FIGURE 9.22 From rectangle to barber pole

Once the first striped cylinder is completed, it can be duplicated with the *Copy* command and then scaled to different sizes. Using the Pointer tool click the bottom of a cylinder on a tab. Push the tab upward until the cylinder is the desired size. Figure 9.23 shows a screen-view of how the graphic can be used to make a chart.

Candy Cane Sales for Four Quarters

FIGURE 9.23 A graphic chart

You can also make "talk balloons" with the PageMaker graphic tools. Figures 9.24 to 9.26 show the three steps in creating a balloon. First use the oval and diagonal line tools as shown in Figure 9.24.

Next, using the paper fill and reverse line, draw a small oval over the intersection between the talk balloon and the pointer. Figure 9.25 shows how it should look when completed.

Finally, make a text block inside the balloon and type in your copy.

FIGURE 9.24 Make an oval and a pointer.

FIGURE 9.25 Blank out part of the oval.

See Moe for
your hairpiece!

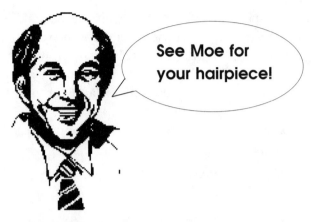

FIGURE 9.26 Add text inside of balloon.

It is important to remember that when a line is selected, it is selected for all shapes. For example, using a broken line makes a handy tool for creating "cut-outs," as shown in Figure 9.27.

While the graphic tools are relatively simple, remember that there is a good deal you can do with them. Don't let their simplicity fool you.

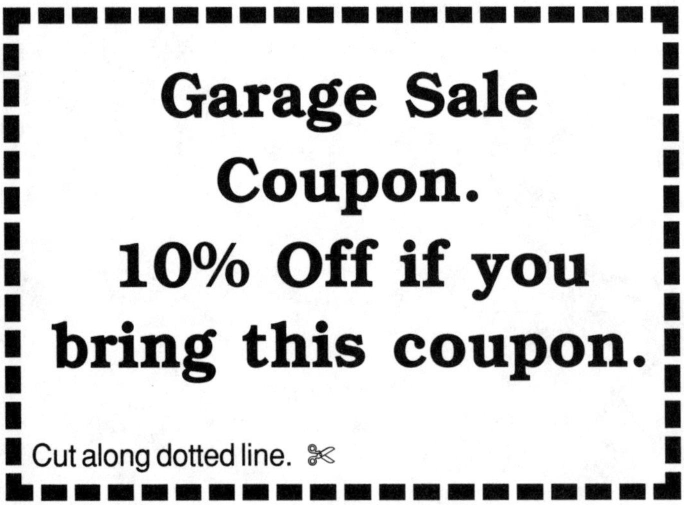

Garage Sale
Coupon.
10% Off if you
bring this coupon.
Cut along dotted line.

FIGURE 9.27 Use broken lines for "cut-out" items.

Fill

The other submenu in the **Element** menu is **Fill**. *Fill* refers to the pattern that will occupy the interior area of ovals and rectangles. Figure 9.28 shows the patterns available to fill in enclosing lines.

In Figure 9.25, we used a "paper" fill to cover up the intersection between the talk balloon and the pointer. Since it was invisible, it made the intersection appear as though a single unit made up the talk balloon. Other figures are quite visible. For example, the following illustration shows some different things that were done with a filled circle and several filled rectangles:

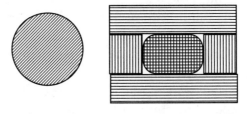

FIGURE 9.28 Fill menu

Depending on your application, the fills can be used in various ways. One of the most common applications of fills is to create screens for highlighting text. Text is placed on top of a screen and, depending on the dots per inch (dpi) of the output, the screens appear as various shades in the background.

Layering Text and Graphics

One of the problems in using text and graphics is in getting the layers right. For example, if you want a screen to underlie a text block, you have to have the text in front and the screen in the back. Otherwise you will end up with the condition shown in Figure 9.29.

To move text or graphics to a different layer, use the *Bring to Front* or *Send to Back* options in the **Element** menu. If you are doing a lot of switching, it's easier to use ⌘-F and ⌘-B, respectively, on the keyboard. For example, with the text selected as in Figure 9.29, a ⌘-F would bring the text to the front, as illustrated in Figure 9.30.

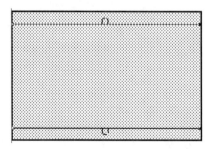

FIGURE 9.29 Text block behind graphic screen

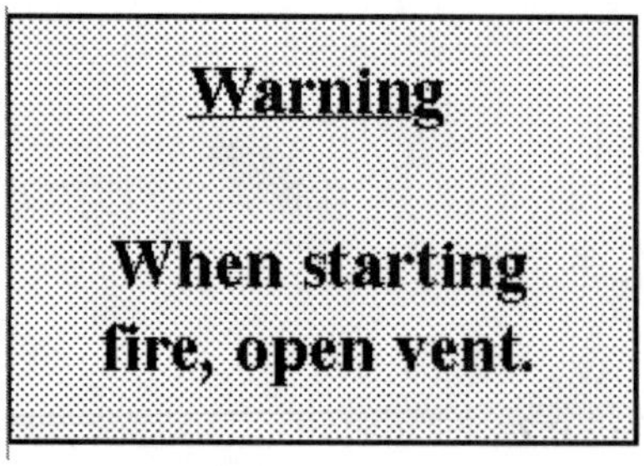

FIGURE 9.30 Text brought to front

If you have several layers of text blocks and graphics, it may be difficult to get to the level you want. The best way is to send the top element to the back until the one you want is on top.

COLORS

The last aspect of graphics we will examine is color—how to get different colors on your screen and how to color different parts of your publication. In Chapter 11, we will discuss color separation.

Color palette

The main tool you will use when working with color is your Color palette. You can set the default color of your text, either as a style or directly through the Type specifications dialog box. For adding a color other than the default one for text or for any graphic, select the text and click the desired color in the Color palette. For example, the following illustration shows a Color palette with "Blue" darkened. Selected text or graphic would be colored blue. Only the Text tool can be used for selecting text for coloring. Text blocks selected with the Pointer tool will not be colored. Graphic blocks, on the other hand, are selected for coloring with the Pointer tool.

The color you see on your screen will be determined by the type of monitor you have. Black-and-white and grayscale monitors will show no colors at all, but the grayscale monitors will show differences in colors as shades of gray. The standard Apple color monitor gives fewer colors than a high resolution monitor. So, you cannot expect a high WYSIWYG (What You See Is What You Get) correlation between colors on the screen and colors that are shown on a color monitor or called out for a printed page.

You will also notice that the Color palette has no effect on certain colored graphics. For example, if you have placed a colored object-oriented graphic in your publication and select it, it will not turn to the palette color. However, a black-and-white version of the very same graphic will be changed to the selected color, and a TIFF graphic changes in multiple colors.

Before continuing, be advised that the color that you see on the screen and the actual color printed may be very different. The color printing process will be explained in Chapter 11, "Files, Printing, and Scripting," but it is important to understand that even a very good color monitor may have difficulty reproducing the exact color you will see on the printed page. However, you can get an approximate idea of what your publication will look like in color from your screen colors.

Defining Colors

Defining colors is both simple and complex. It is simple because PageMaker provides four different ways to define and edit colors. It is complex because there are so many different combinations and possibilities that it is difficult to know exactly what to select. Mixing colors to get the shade you want can also be a bit perplexing. However, the tools for doing so are available, and all it takes is a bit of practice.

To get started defining or editing a color, select *Define Colors . . .* from the **Element** menu. The Define Colors dialog box shown in Figure 9.31 appears with the palette color shown in the color window.

From the dialog box, select to add a new color to the palette, edit an existing one, copy a color from an existing palette, or remove a color from your palette. Since defining a new color and editing an old one involve essentially the same procedures we will look at them together.

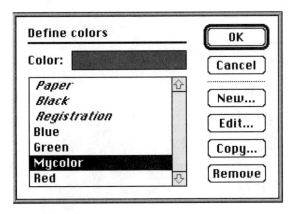

FIGURE 9.31 Define colors dialog box

New and Edit

From the Define Colors dialog box, if you select either *New* or *Edit* you will be placed in the Edit Color dialog box. There are three models of the dialog box and a Pantone . . . button choice to provide the four ways to create or edit a color. (A shortcut for editing is to point to the color in the color palette you want to edit, press ⌘ and double-click the mouse.)

One method used for creating or editing a color is RGB, standing for "red, green and blue." It makes a color by mixing it as a percentage of those three colors. Figure 9.32 shows the RGB dialog box.

When working on a color, you will see a colored double-boxed column in the lower right-hand corner of the dialog box. The bottom color is the current color, if any, and the top color is the color that changes in the mix will bring. To return to the original color after mixing, click the bottom color box.

Another mixing combination, called HLS, is based on hue, lightness, and saturation. The hue is first selected to get the general color area, and then lightness (the higher the lighter) is added or subtracted. Finally, saturation is increased or decreased to bring the color to the desired level. Figure 9.33 shows the HLS dialog box.

The best method to use for defining process colors is the one used by commercial printers, namely CMYK. Cyan, magenta, yellow, and black are used instead of red, green, and blue mixtures. (K is

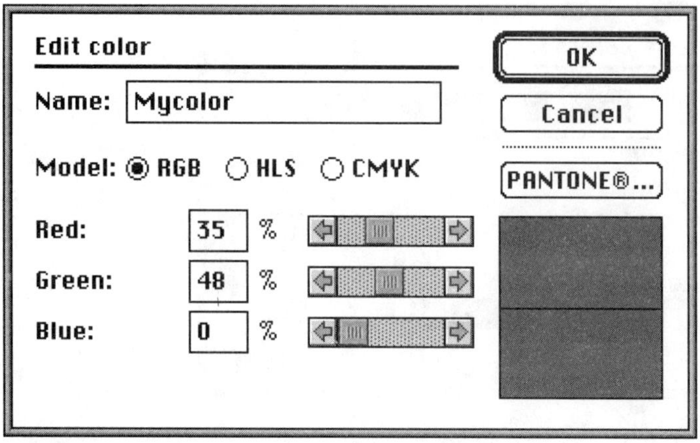

FIGURE 9.32 The red, green, and blue (RGB) options

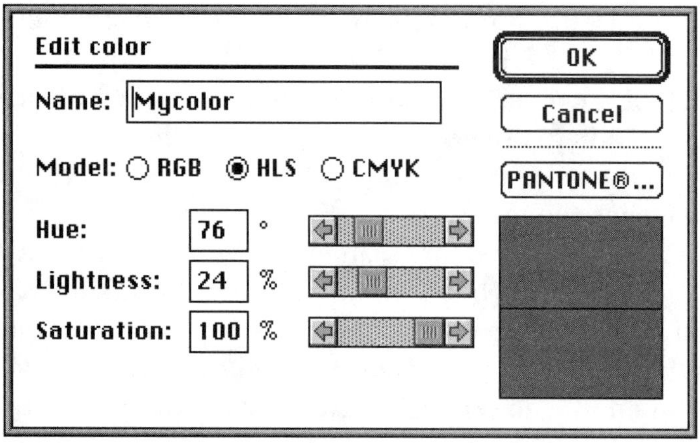

FIGURE 9.33 Hue, lightness, and saturation options

used for black rather than B to avoid confusion with blue.) The use of CMYK requires four plates—one for each color plus black. If four or more colors are required, process colors are less expensive than using spot colors (colors that are mechanically separated), which require a separate plate for each color. Spot colors are less expensive for three or fewer colors. Figure 9.34 shows the CMYK dialog box.

The remaining method of creating and editing colors is to select the PANTONE® . . . button. Pantone® colors are widely used by printers when designating premixed colors. The big advantage of using Pantone® colors is the ability to see exactly what the color will look like when printed. This is done by using the Pantone® Color Formula Guide, available at any art supply store, containing samples of all of the Pantone® colors. For example, Pantone 347 appears on a VGA monitor, with extended memory card, as lime green with a hatch pattern on it. However, in the Pantone® Color Formula Guide, it is a medium green. By holding the patch from the Color Formula Guide up against the screen, it is possible to see exactly the amount of difference the colors will have.

When adding a Pantone® color to your Color palette, be sure to use the New button. Otherwise, you may end up editing one Pantone® color with another. For example, if you have Pantone 471 CV selected in your Color palette and you edit it to Pantone 547 CV, Pantone 471 CV in your palette will now appear as the color for Pantone 547 CV. If you specify Pantone 471 to your printer and are expecting the color of Pantone 547, you will be in for a big surprise when you see the results. Figure 9.35 shows a section of the PANTONE Color dialog box.

Working with the colors in PageMaker 4.2 can significantly help in visualizing what your final publication will look like. When you print material, only a color printer will handle color. What you are really doing

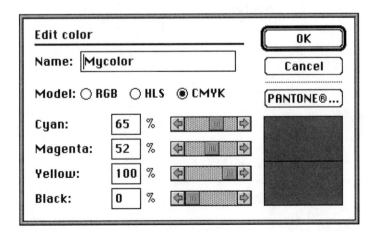

FIGURE 9.34 Cyan, magenta, yellow, and black (CMYK) options

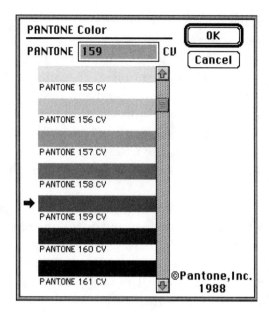

FIGURE 9.35 PANTONE Color dialog box

with color in PageMaker is getting an idea of what your publication will look like when it is finally printed in color by a commercial printing firm. Also, with spot colors, you are separating the different colors in the pages you provide to the commercial printer. Chapter 11 will explain color separation in detail. In the meantime, experiment with different colors to create exciting publications.

STYLE

T his chapter is for those who are new to page makeup even
though they may have a lot of experience with computers. It
can also be a review for those experienced with page design
even though they have no computer experience.

A page's style is just as important as a person's style. Fortunately,
page styles do not change with the same frequency clothing styles do,
but good style, whether old or new, has a pleasing sense to it when it
is encountered. Look at a magazine or newspaper printed in the
early part of the twentieth century, and you will see a style different
from that of contemporary publications. If you look at several different publications, you can see that they have different "looks"—
different styles.

Good style is what is pleasing to the reader's eye. If you are
creating advertisement copy in the form of flyers, magazine ads, or
brochures, you want to use every possible tool to get and keep the
reader's attention. Good style is part of the magnetism that keeps a
person looking at your page. The same thing is true for textbooks,
newsletters, and scientific journals as well. While you may not be
selling anything other than the contents of your publication, you still
want the style, along with the text and graphics, to help carry the
message.

It is not enough to learn how to use PageMaker 4.2 and start
cramming text and graphics together in an effort to get everything to

fit, regardless of how it looks. It is not just a matter of being neat—PageMaker 4.2 makes that simple. Style is being able to have everything flow together in what appears to the reader as a natural and interesting arrangement. In fact, most readers will not even realize if a page looks good or bad. If it looks good, it will have a good, and usually unnoticed, "feel" to it—a natural feel. A publication with poor style will not feel right. Readers may feel slightly uneasy, and may think the publication amateurish or unprofessional. They will not know why, but will have a feeling that something is not quite right. So, while learning to use PageMaker, we will brush up on how to make what you produce with PageMaker look good.

WHAT LOOKS GOOD?

Making a list of what looks good is a starting point only. The following list of the more important components of style in page makeup is not all-inclusive, but it is a useful jump-off point.

- **Type choice**   The most subtle but most important style choice is that of typeface or font. Display fonts should not be used for body text, and body text should not be used for display. Good body faces include serif fonts such as Times Roman, Palatino, New Century Schoolbook, Galliard, Baskerville, Garamond, and Goudy Old Style. Use styles like Cooper Black, Park Avenue, ITC Tiffany, Hobo and similar dramatic fonts for display. Good sans serif fonts like Helvetica, Optima, or Avant Garde make the best header fonts.

- **White space**   Do not be afraid to have part of your publication blank. Space on a page does not automatically have to be filled with text or graphics. Used correctly, white space can add "breathing room," interest, and style to a stuffy, overpacked document.

- **Slugs**   Miles and miles and miles of uninterrupted text is boring. Subheads between paragraphs help break up endless body text, and they help readers find their way through the text.

- **Large type** If you want to grab the reader's attention, use large type every now and then. Don't overdo it, but when there's a point to make—make it BIG.

- **Captions** Boring captions make for boring graphs, charts, and pictures. It's as easy to make an interesting caption as a boring one, so make it worth reading.

- **Quotations** Quotes can be extracted from the text body to highlight key points and to heighten a text scanner's interest in reading an article. The fact that the quotations are out of context makes the reader want to find out what's up. Figure 10.1 shows a PageMaker example.

- **Graphics** Use graphics when appropriate and possible. If you are setting a novel with page after page of thrilling adventure and romance, you don't need graphics. However, graphics break up text, communicate certain concepts more clearly, and make the publication more interesting. Photographs, charts, drawings, maps, and artwork make a better-looking publication.

"... I saw pigs fly...."

Elias Quackenbush

Farmer Elias Quackenbush explained that while the tornado spared his house and barn, it made a direct hit on his pig pen. He said, "Why I never seen nothing like it. Them pigs got picked up and threw all over. When I saw pigs fly by, I jumped in the cellar."

FIGURE 10.1 Use eye-catching quotations

These seven guidelines are designed to help you create the best-looking document possible; however, if any one of them makes your publication look "wrong," by all means do not use it. Rules, especially when it comes to art and style, are meant to be broken if they do not produce the desired results.

TEMPLATES

The old saw about not reinventing the wheel every time you sit down to do a task applies doubly to page design. If the document you design will be used in many applications, putting it in a template means you will not have to redo the design every time you sit down to work on your publication. However, you want to make sure your template looks good, for if your initial creation is poorly done, then all publications using that template will look bad.

In order to see some elements of style, we will look at some sample templates that come with PageMaker 4.2. Guidelines have been omitted so that we can concentrate on what the page will look like when printed. By looking at them, we can get a sense of proportion, placement, and overall style. We'll start by examining a brochure template. Figure 10.2 shows one of the brochure templates supplied with PageMaker 4.2.

Even without the guidelines, you can tell where the three sections flow. One purpose of guidelines is to provide alignment so that when they are hidden during printing, the material placed in accordance with the guidelines will fall into columns, rows, or other ordered arrangements.

The middle section of the brochure best shows the use of white space. You may be surprised to think of the addressing front of a brochure as having white space. Instead we tend to think of envelope fronts and addressing sections of brochures as having areas for the address, return address, and stamp. That is true, but the rest—most of the space in fact—is white space. Imagine how strange it would look if we crowded that area with a lot of text and graphics without white space.

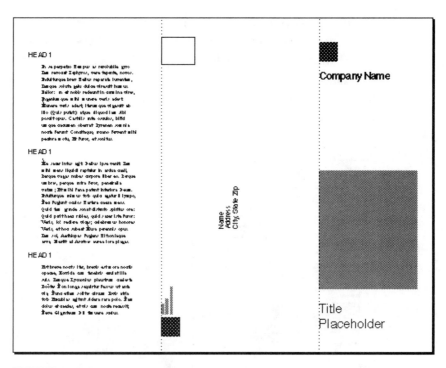

FIGURE 10.2 Brochure template

The other two panels on the left and right also have much white space. The right panel contains white space between the company name and the graphic area below the name. Likewise, the left panel has ample margin space and space between paragraphs. We could crowd more text and graphics in those spaces, but the brochure would not look good if we did.

Also note the balance. Each panel in a brochure is a separate page, and the back side (the middle panel with the address space) does not have to balance with the front and back panels of the brochure. However, each panel should balance within itself. For example, on the right panel, notice how the graphic and title on the bottom half of the panel are balanced by the bold type and logo on the top. The graphic on the bottom is clearly larger than the logo graphic on the top, but the bold font of the company name balances the larger graphic on the bottom.

The next template we will examine is that of a newsletter. The interesting aspect of the newsletter is its two types of pages—one with two columns and one with three. Some pages, including the front page shown in Figure 10.3, have a narrow and a wide column. Other pages, such as the one shown in Figure 10.4, have three equal-sized columns.

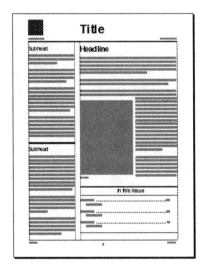

FIGURE 10.3 Newsletter two-column page

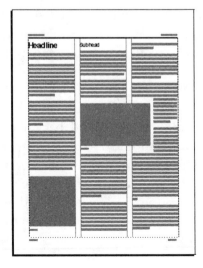

FIGURE 10.4 Newsletter three-column page

Balance

With two different sizes of columns (Figure 10.3), you might think the design would automatically be off balance. However, if you look carefully, you can see that the graphic in the center draws attention to the middle rather than just the right side. It is center-balanced by the title, headline, and graphic. It is also balanced at opposite corners. The heavy logo in the upper left-hand corner is balanced by the larger but lighter table of contents in the lower right-hand corner. The slugs and line separators help balance the narrow column on the left with the wide column on the right.

Examining the three-column page of the newsletter template (Figure 10.4), we see a different type of balance and an interesting use of graphics on a page. The left column is definitely a heavy one with the headline at top and a graphic at the bottom of the page. In order to balance that weighty side, the graphic in the center column extends into the right column. The graphic is larger and so has more weight, and having a part of the graphic in the right column better balances it.

However, the page in Figure 10.4 is a bit more dramatic because it is just enough off balance to create tension. There is not a lot of tension, but there is enough to create interest. Although symmetrical balance is a generally good style guide, the more interesting the balancing act, the more the reader is drawn to it. Asymmetrical balance can be achieved by using balance of interest rather than a balance of weights. A large area of white space with a figure in a corner will draw the eye to the corner. The small graphic figure has an asymmetrical balance with the large white space because the figure is more interesting than the white space.

Proportion

Another key design concept is that of proportion. Good artists and designers have a natural sense of proportion. A good sense of proportion can be achieved by using certain standardized ratios. As a general guide, a 3 to 5 ratio provides the best proportion. A two-column page with 3- and 5-inch-wide columns would be well proportioned. A column with five-eighths taken up by text would be well proportioned if a graphic at the bottom takes up three-eighths of the column.

To do a quick check of proportion use the following formula:

$$L = 5 \times [(L + S) \div 8]$$
$$S = 3 \times [(L + S) \div 8]$$

L is the larger segment and S is the smaller segment. If each equals the formula's results, then they are proportional. (Actually, you only have to test one; and if it is proportional, the other will be also.) Let's take a look at an example. We will start with a 6-inch vertical column. The top 4 inches are taken up by text and the bottom 2 inches are graphics. We will look at the larger segment (L) to see if we come up with the correct proportion. In this case the larger segment is 4 inches.

$$L = 5 \times [(4 + 2) \div 8]$$
$$L = 5 \times (6 \div 8)$$
$$L = 5 \times .75$$
$$L = 3.75$$

The proportion was close, but not quite right. We should have had 3.75 inches of text and 2.25 inches of graphics. It was only a quarter of an inch off, but with PageMaker 4.2, it is simple to increase the size of the graphic and shorten the text so that they are proportional. It is a small difference, but if you are designing a template that will reproduce proportion again and again, it might as well be done right. (Of course, if it looks right with that proportion, then it is right.)

Sequence

Another aspect of style to consider is sequence. Sequence refers to the way the eye naturally moves across a page. It starts in the upper left-hand corner and zigzags from left to right, top to bottom across the page. A way to catch and arrest the eye is with a narrow column on the left side of a page such as that shown in Figure 10.5, which is a template for an instructional manual that comes with PageMaker 4.2.

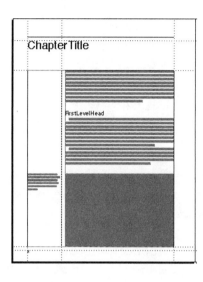

FIGURE 10.5 A narrow left-hand column will arrest the sequence and draw the eye.

The weight of the page is balanced by the chapter heading on the left side and achieves an asymmetrical balance with the interest in the mostly empty left-hand column. Proportionately, the small and large columns are way off—1.75 to 5. However, within a column, you can see good proportion. Figure 10.6 shows the same design on a different page. The wide column has perfect proportion between

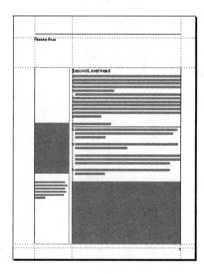

FIGURE 10.6 Balance with positioning of graphic elements

text and graphic. Also note the balance achieved by having a graphic in the narrow column above the graphic in the wide column.

If you examine the pages in the layout of the sample manual (Figures 10.5 and 10.6), you will notice that all of the narrow margins are on the left side. This design helps draw attention by taking advantage of the sequence and asymmetrical balance. However, many books and manuals have narrow left columns on left pages and narrow right columns on the right pages. Although asymmetrical when viewed individually, symmetry is achieved in facing pages when printed and bound in traditional book form. The following illustration shows a fit-in-world view of a design with narrow columns on the outside of each page. Viewing two pages at once, you can see that there is a better balance; the sequence pulls the reader to the left column, then the two middle columns, and finally the last column before the page is turned. However, the asymmetrical balance of the narrow columns, with lots of white space on the wings and the text/graphic-filled wide columns in the center, pull the reader to the center; the marginal comments are noticed but don't interfere with the focal point.

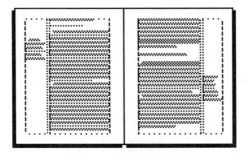

Unity

One of the most subtle yet important features of style is *unity*. In general, unity refers to bringing the various components into an order or harmony so that they appear unified. On the simplest level, graphic components are brought into harmony with text through captions and references to graphics within the text. This is called *compositional unity*.

Another type of unity, *component unity*, refers to avoiding clashes between the spirit, temper, and tone of the design and the page makeup components. Wearing a tuxedo to an informal beach party shows lack of component unity, but shorts and tee shirts at the same affair have component unity. In the same way, typefaces (fonts), choice of graphics, and writing style must all work together to produce component unity.

Consider Figures 10.7 and 10.8. Figure 10.7 clashes in about every way components can clash. The font, Avant Garde, clashes with the art nouveau style of the flowers; and the flowers overwhelm the relatively small font. To top it all off, the topic—a magazine for real men—is hardly unified with the fuchsias. Likewise, the Avant Garde font is not unified with the "he-man" image to be portrayed. The only unifying element is the box that encompasses the components. Otherwise there is no unity at all.

Figure 10.8 has component unity because everything fits the mood of the ad. The text is in a strong, bold Lubalin Graph font. It flows right into the graphic of the football players, and of course the running and tackling football players fit the theme as well. There is no frame around it because it does not need one for unity.

As far as the reader is concerned, the unity in Figure 10.8 will probably go unnoticed. However, a viewer would look at Figure 10.7 and "feel" there was something wrong even though he or she could not point out the lack of unity.

FIGURE 10.7 Text and graphic lack unity.

FIGURE 10.8 Unity of text, font, and graphic

LAYOUTS

Now that we have seen some samples of pages with various design elements illustrated, we will look at the basic elements of a page. Using a facing-page publication, we will examine the various parts and the considerations to be made when planning a layout. We will start with a blank piece of paper and consider each part in turn.

Margins

Using the master pages, you set up the design for the entire publication. Just as when you are writing a story, you must have somewhere to begin. Start with the trim margins. These margins are about 0.25 inches from each edge and are needed for trimming the paper when a book is bound. Figure 10.9 shows these trim margins.

The right-hand trim margin in Figure 10.9 would have to be considered in light of whether a publication has facing or single pages as well as the type of publication. Books require a binding margin so that the reader can see all of the text. Newsletters, on the

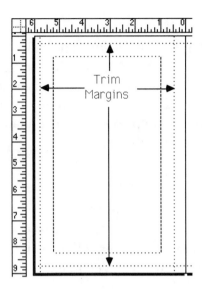

FIGURE 10.9 Trim margins along sides

other hand, require very little binding margin since there are so few pages.

Within the trim margins is the text margin. In PageMaker, the text margin sets the parameters for where the text can be flowed. When setting the text margins in the text page setup process, you must not only give the inside margins a little more room, but you must also keep the trim margins in mind.

Besides the text and trim margins, other types of margins have functions in designing a page.

Header Margin

If your publication is going to have headers, it is necessary to add a margin along the top to specify where the header belongs. Depending on the type of publication, the header margins can be wide or narrow. In some cases you might need more than a single type of header margin. Special margins for chapter and section headings are important for a consistent look in your publication. If you have the standard page headers aligned on a guideline, but nothing similar for chapter headings, your publication will look uneven.

Alley

The space between columns is called the *alley*. The width of the alley defaults to 0.167 inches. If you are using that, or any other alley width, consider how the width will affect the amount of text in the columns in relation to your other margins. Thinking of an alley as margins between columns might help you to conceptualize alleys in your design and to establish alley widths.

Fold

The fold is simply the point where your publication separates facing pages. In the center signature of a newsletter, the fold appears as a single sheet with a crease down the center. For facing pages, it is treated as the page limit on the inside of each page.

Gutter

The inside margins adjacent to the fold on facing pages comprise the gutter. For thick books, the gutter should be wider than for thin books or other slimmer publications because the binding process itself takes up some of the inside margin. Figure 10.10 shows all of the other marginal components.

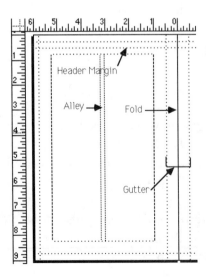

FIGURE 10.10 Page margins

You want to have the extra room in the inside margins so that when the publication is open, the facing pages appear to be roughly equal in terms of the inside and outside margins. This is accomplished by having a little extra space for the margins making up the gutter.

Folio Margin

The final margin to put in your master pages is the folio or page-number margin. Figure 10.11 shows the folio master and the folio margin line on top of the master.

First, decide where you want your left-hand page number to go. Pressing ⌘-OPTION-P, with the Text tool selected, establishes the master-page folios. Place a guideline on top of the folio. This establishes a baseline for the folio on the facing page. Since it is very easy to have page numbers out of alignment on facing pages, use the folio margin to establish aligned page numbers.

If you are used to working with the older version of PageMaker, you should note that the initial page numbers in the master pages are now "LM" and "RM" for left and right master, respectively, instead of "0."

FONTS

The single most common style mistake made by desktop publishing novices is the misuse of fonts. Perhaps the biggest error is using too

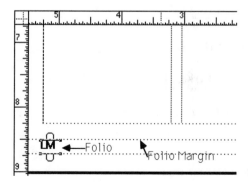

FIGURE 10.11 Folio margin

many fonts in a single publication. Most publications use only two or three fonts. Typically, a publication should have only two fonts; one for the heads and subheads and one for the body text. A publication with fifteen different fonts is confusing and messy and looks like a kidnap note with its profusion of type styles.

In this section we will examine using fonts to make your publication look just right. Different fonts look best with different types of publications. Likewise, different fonts have different jobs in a publication. We will look at what to do and what to avoid in your publication.

Using the Right Font for the Publication

First, we want to examine what fonts to use within a publication. The way things look on your screen can help you get a good idea of what they will look like in type. Therefore, consider investing in screen fonts for the fonts that you have on your printer. We will be examining screen shots of what your font will look like when you are creating your publication for purposes of illustration.

If you use a TrueType fonts in the System 7 environment, what you see on the screen is much closer to what you will see on the printed page than if you do not. For example, Figure 10.12, shows four 18-point fonts—three with TrueType and one without. TrueType will scale text to just about any size, and when you magnify your view of the page, the text will not become distorted. The Bookman font in Figure 10.12 clearly is not what you will expect to get on the page.

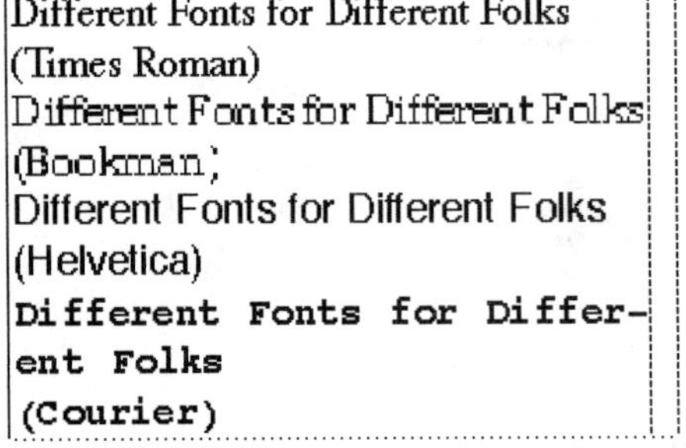

Different Fonts for Different Folks
(Times Roman)
Different Fonts for Different Folks
(Bookman)
Different Fonts for Different Folks
(Helvetica)
**Different Fonts for Differ-
ent Folks
(Courier)**

FIGURE 10.12 Find the font without TrueType

If you do not have a TrueType font, then make sure the correct screen font is installed in your system. Even without TrueType fonts, your screen view of a font will be much clearer if you install the correct size of your screen font. With an 18-point Bookman screen font installed in the System file, you will have a much clearer screen representation as is shown in the following illustration:

Different Fonts for Different Folks
(Bookman)

Not only do the screen fonts give the proportion of the font vis-à-vis the size of the page or column, but they also show whether the font fits the mood of the topic. For example, Figure 10.13 shows different display screen fonts enhancing the message they announce. Of course, these fonts will look a lot better when printed, but since you will be working with the screen images of the fonts in PageMaker, you need to get the most accurate screen representation of the font you can.

Even more so than with the body and header fonts, it is important to have display screen fonts. Otherwise, it is almost impossible to get a good idea of what your publication will look like while setting it up on the screen. Several screen fonts are available from different sources. For those with PostScript printers, Adobe, Inc., has screen fonts for all of its PostScript fonts.

Art Nouveau Antiques On Sale

Board Meeting Today

Medieval Faire

New Movie on Hitler's Humor a Flop

Garden Club Has Prize-Winning Rose

FIGURE 10.13 Screen display fonts show whether the font looks right for the publication.

Fonts for Heads and Bodies

At the beginning of this chapter, we pointed out that a simple and effective rule of thumb in style is to use a bold sans serif font such as Helvetica or Optima for a header font and a serif font such as Times Roman or Palatino for the body. If you look at a number of publications, you will quickly see that some use that combination and some do not. What's more, the publications that do not follow the rule look just fine. The right combination of fonts rests, in the final analysis, on how it looks. However, for beginners in the world of page makeup, certain simple guidelines help keep you from making mistakes that stem from lack of experience.

As you become more sophisticated, you can begin to explore other possibilities. The best guide for understanding style is finding publications that look good to you. For example, in many of the *Aldus Magazine* articles, the same font for heads and body is employed. The header fonts are larger versions of the body fonts and a little darker, but not bold-faced. You will find combinations of sans serif fonts used as body and headers—some using the same font, others using a combination of different sans serif fonts. Again, if it looks "right," "dramatic," and just plain "good" in the context of its application, then it is good. Any designer with an artistic soul will tell you that rules are to be broken. However, before breaking the rules, you need to know what they are.

Using Large Caps

Large caps, including standing caps and drop caps, can add interest to a publication, but are best used sparingly. At the beginning of chapters or articles, a large cap heralds the beginning of something new. However, at the beginning of every sentence or paragraph, they get in the way of the flow of the text.

The type of large cap depends on the publication. You can make large caps with PageMaker, but one of the advantages of PageMaker is the ability to import graphics created with software designed specifically for artwork. The following are some paint-type, bit-mapped standing caps. The first, in Figure 10.14, shows a screen example of how they can be incorporated into publications. You use the auto-

ETH KNELT BY THE pool and looked at her reflection. She was changing in ways she did not understand but felt were part of growing up. There was a restlessness she felt but could not define. Her brothers and parents treated her with the same combination of love and attention that had made her feel secure, but she wanted something more. The problem was that she didn't know what this new feeling of emptiness meant or how to fill its void.

FIGURE 10.14 Large graphic caps can add luster to a publication.

matic Drop Cap in the Aldus Additions if you incorporate an invisible (i.e., reverse) font to be under the graphic font, but it is just as easy to indent the text that is next to the large cap.

It is not uncommon to see the first several words after a large cap all in small caps. The small caps after the giant capital letter at the beginning of the sentence provide a transition from the large to the small. It is a style convention that many page designers use. Figure 10.15 shows several other large graphic caps.

FIGURE 10.15 Large graphic caps

Large caps can be found in many sources. Those created with object-oriented paint programs, PostScript, or scanned into TIFF files provide the best results. However, as shown in the illustrations, the humble bit-mapped graphics can do a credible job as well with certain publications.

Leading

Leading , the amount of space between lines, can be a genuine style problem. Normally, you can be safe with the 120 percent leading given in the autoleading default in PageMaker 4.2. (The 120 percent means the space from the same point line-to-line is 120 percent of the size of the font used.) Before deciding on leading space, however, print out sample pages to see how it looks. Different types of fonts have slightly different sizes and different height-to-width ratios. Times Roman is smaller than Bookman, and the autoleading looks different depending on which font you are using. Different size columns look different with different leading.

The most common style mistake is to tighten or shorten a publication by using less leading. The idea may be to give the reader the most text for his or her buck, but doing so may give the reader a headache as well. As a rule of thumb, a little more leading will do less harm to a style than a little less leading. So when in doubt, add a point or two of leading. The reader will appreciate it, and your publication will look better.

The best tactic to use in deciding how leading affects your style is to start with the autoleading and then adjust it up and down a few points. Print out the pages and see which one looks the best. Rely on your intuitive sense of style to see how the leading looks in the context of your overall publication.

LINE LENGTH

The optimum number of characters for a line depends on the size of the font, the width of the column, and type face. This is as much a matter of readability as it is style. The table below shows desirable line lengths in picas for lines for different point sizes of fonts. (This table, incidently, was made with the Table Editor). These figures are only rough recommendations, and the type face you select will further influence the optimum line length. However, the range between minimum and maximum line length is a good guide for any type face. (The numbers in the first row are point sizes and the numbers in the rest of the rows are picas.)

Point Size	6	8	10	12	14
Minimum	8	9	13	14	18
Optimum	10	13	16	21	24
Maximum	12	16	18	22	28

To convert the table figures from points to inches, use the following conversions:

12 points = 1 pica
6 picas = 1 inch
72 points = 1 inch

Divide the numbers in the last three rows of the table by 6 to get a quick idea of how many inches your column should be for different size fonts.

A useful rule of thumb is to use about nine or ten words or 55–60 characters per line. If you find your lines are longer, you can break up pages into columns. To check the accuracy of this method, look at some magazines and other publications. Exceptions to this rule of thumb are found in some books where the lines are slightly longer.

CHAPTER 11

LINKING FILES, PRINTING, AND SCRIPTING

T his chapter covers three diverse, but important subjects. First, we will examine linking files to their original source so that changes will be reflected in the PageMaker publication. This is similar to Edition files discussed in Chapter 2, "System 7 and PageMaker 4.2." In fact, if you are using System 7, then you may want to use Edition files instead of the PageMaker links. Links also refer to linking PageMaker files together into "books." A book can be automatically renumbered in PageMaker 4.2.

Next, we cover printing with PageMaker. Some features are new, but, most of the printing is pretty much like printing anything else with the Macintosh.

Finally, we introduce scripts. Scripts are like super-macros or simple programming languages. They add a whole new dimension to what you can do with PageMaker, and they can make your work a whole lot easier.

LINKING FILES

One of the most important features in PageMaker 4.2 is the ability to link files. One file placed in PageMaker can be linked with another containing a graphic, word-processed text, or a table produced with Table Editor. If you make a change in the graphic, text, or table file,

PageMaker can automatically update the placed files in a PageMaker document.

For example, suppose you have placed a graphic file in a Page-Maker publication. Once it is placed, you realize there are some important changes that have to be made to the file. You make changes with the graphic program that was used to create the original graphic. Instead of having to remove the graphic from PageMaker and replace it with the revised one, PageMaker 4.2 will do that automatically.

Working Links

To see how the linkage process works, we will start with a publication that has some text and graphics. The names of the graphic files are: flower.paint (a bit-mapped graphic), man.Tif (a TIFF file), and Table.Pict (a PICT file). The text file is Origdoc. To examine the linkages, select *Links . . .* from the **File** menu, or press (SHIFT)-(⌘)-(=). The Links dialog box appears as shown in Figure 11.1.

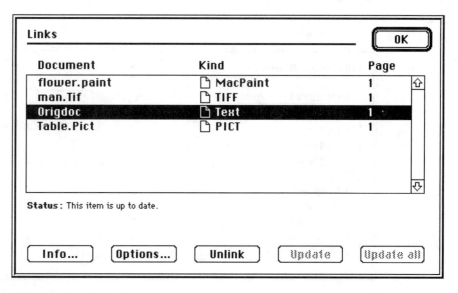

FIGURE 11.1 Links dialog box

The Links dialog box shows all of the files in your current publication that are linked to a graphic or text source. The status line under the file box tells you whether or not the selected item is up-to-date. If it is not up-to-date, the Update buttons will become active. By clicking an Update button, you can update some or all of the non-current files.

The Link Info . . . button brings up the Link Info dialog box and shows the files in the current directory. The path to the selected file is listed under the name box along with all the information about the file. Figure 11.2 shows the Link Info dialog box.

In the Link Info dialog box you can change the linked file. For example, if you do not want to make changes to your original file but you want to make all of the changes in a revised file, you can select the revised file as the linking file. Just select the new file you want and click the Link button. This will replace all of the contents of the PageMaker placed text or graphics with the new file's contents. For example, in Figure 11.2 we changed the linked file from Origdoc (Figure 11.1) to Revisedoc. Whenever changes are made to Revisedoc, they will be incorporated into the PageMaker placed file. Figure 11.3 shows that the Links dialog box now shows a new file has replaced Origdoc as the linked file.

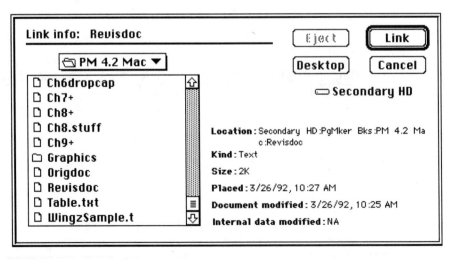

FIGURE 11.2 Links Info dialog box

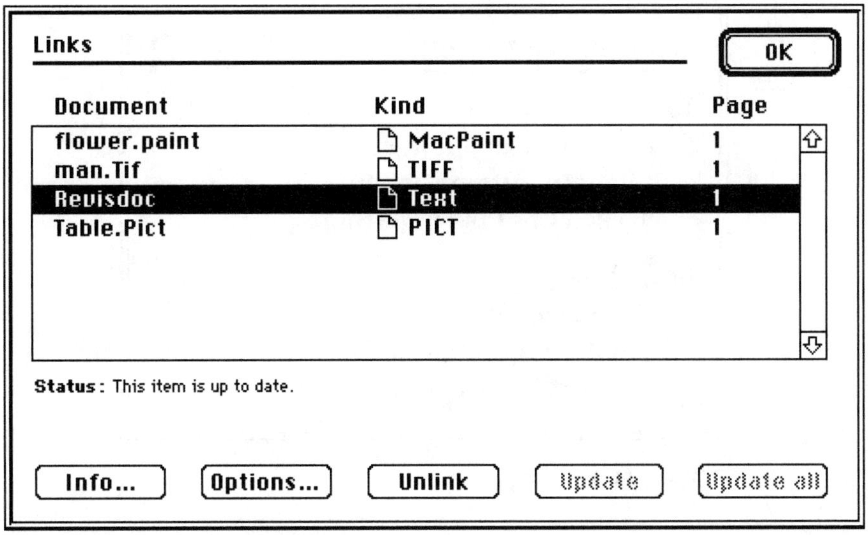

FIGURE 11.3 New linkage replaces the original.

You could also use the link feature to replace the contents of a newsletter, form, inventory list, or any other PageMaker publication where the same format is used over and over again. If the graphic sizes and amount of text were fairly standard, this would save a lot of time placing materials.

Returning to the Links dialog box, the last button to examine is Link options . . . The Links Options dialog box shown in Figure 11.4 provides options for automatic update and alert before updating.

You can change the default for the link options with the Link Options: Defaults dialog box, shown in Figure 11.5. With nothing

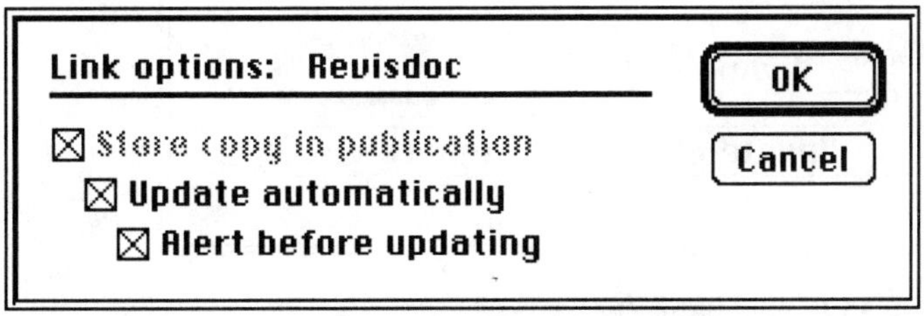

FIGURE 11.4 Links Options dialog box for selected item

Link options: Defaults

Text:
☒ Store copy in publication
  ☒ Update automatically
    ☐ Alert before updating

Graphics:
☒ Store copy in publication
  ☒ Update automatically
    ☐ Alert before updating

[OK]
[Cancel]

FIGURE 11.5 Setting Link options defaults

selected, choose *Link options . . .* from the **Element** menu. This allows
you to set up a different default linkage.

When the automatic update with alert before updating is selected, the Document Modified dialog box, Figure 11.6, appears
subsequent to a file change after the PageMaker document has been
reopened. It allows options for updating or ignoring some or all
changes.

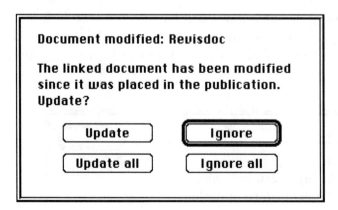

Document modified: Revisdoc

**The linked document has been modified
since it was placed in the publication.
Update?**

[Update]   [Ignore]

[Update all]   [Ignore all]

FIGURE 11.6 Alert before updating

Book Linkages

Another type of linking can be done with *Book Link* found in the **File** menu. In publications with several parts, such as a book with several chapters or a long report with numerous sections, the book link ties them together for purposes of:

- Creating a table of contents
- Creating an index
- Printing

When your publication is linked with book, you not only save time, but you also have a consistent index and table of contents. Figure 11.7 shows the Book Publication List dialog box.

The arrangement of the book list tells PageMaker 4.2 which part of the book to print first, second, and so on. The Move Up and Move Down buttons let you position the selected segment. Once completed, use the table of contents and index creating functions of PageMaker to create a TOC and index. Then remember to include both the TOC and index in the book links!

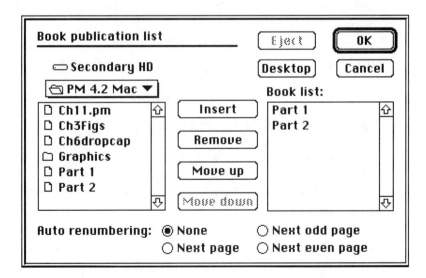

FIGURE 11.7 Book Publication List dialog box

The Auto renumbering buttons are new to PageMaker 4.2. They allow you to automatically renumber an entire book. That is, if you have several different files all with their own numbering, you can automatically renumber all of them. If you select *None,* then there will be no renumbering. If you select *Next Page,* if a file in a book ended with page 54, the next one would begin with 55. To force an odd or even page to begin in the next file, select *Next Odd Page* or *Next Even Page.* For example, many publications require that new chapters or sections begin on the right-hand page and be an odd number. By choosing *Next Odd Page* for renumbering, the first page of the next file will begin with an odd number, even if PageMaker has to generate a blank page preceding it to do so.

PRINTING

Printing with PageMaker 4.2 is very simple, but there are so many options that setting things up may be a little complex at first. However, once you get your printer set up, most of the printing will be a matter of making a few clicks with the mouse. This section will explain how to use all of the various options with PageMaker 4.2. For purposes of illustration we will use a PostScript printer, and for most applications there will not be any differences between a PostScript and non-PostScript printer as far as the commands are concerned.

Setting Printer Parameters

The first thing to do is to select your printer, using the *Chooser* option in the menu. Find your printer icon, and click it. Figure 11.8 shows the selection of a LaserWriter icon. The printer itself is a LaserWriter Plus, shown in the printer window.

The Print To dialog box shows several options. Be sure that your printer is selected in the printer window. If not, point to the printer window and press on the mouse button to open the window and select your printer as shown in Figure 11.9.

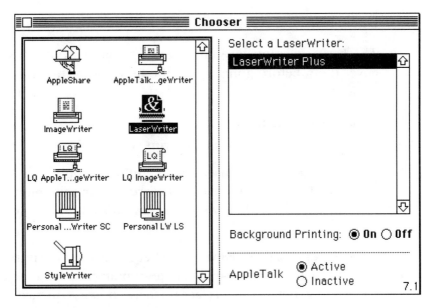

FIGURE 11.8 Selecting a printer from Chooser

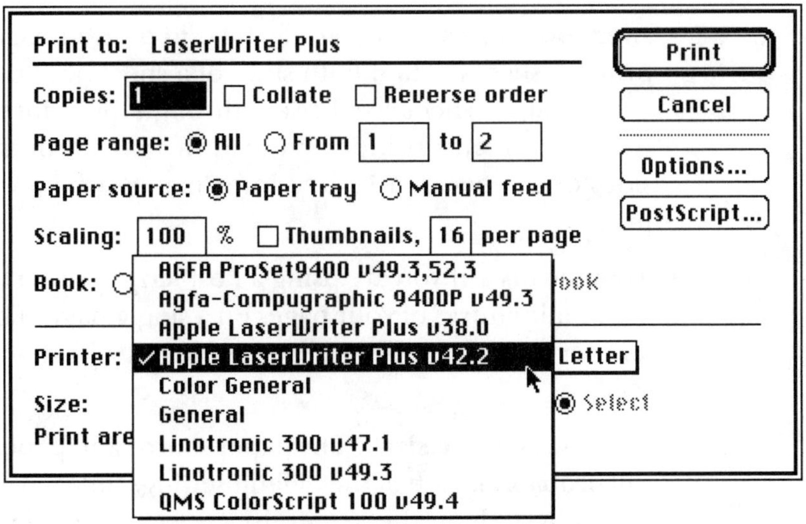

FIGURE 11.9 Printer dialog box

Basic Printer Selections

The basic selections are fairly self-explanatory, but we will quickly cover them before going on to the more powerful and interesting options.

- **Print entire book**   The Book check box allows you to print the whole book with a single print command.

- **Collate**   This is used when multiple copies are printed. It prints one complete copy before printing the next copy. This procedure takes a long time, and it's a lot faster to collate by hand.

- **Reverse order**   Paper path alternatives on some printers deliver printed sheets face-up but in descending sequence. Selecting this option delivers sheets face-up in ascending sequence.

- **Range**   When you want to print only part of a publication, use this option and specify the page range.

- **Scaling**   When a publication is to be printed at other than 100 percent, set the scale to the desired size.

- **Even/odd pages**   When only the odd or even pages are to be printed, such as when both sides of a sheet of paper are to be printed and a sheet is to be sent through the printer twice, use the even or odd printing instead of both. Printing on both sides of a sheet in a laser printer may not be good for your printer.

- **Thumbnails**   If you are using a PostScript printer, this option prints miniatures of your pages on a single page. This provides an overview of your layout, and it lets you check sequence for style.

- **Paper source and size**   The paper source and paper size boxes will probably be left at the default settings unless paper is being manually fed or the paper is a special size. Likewise, the orientation will be left at portrait.

Aldus Options

The Options . . . button opens the Aldus Print Options dialog box.
The options include several printing choices available depending on
the nature of your Macintosh and publications. The *Color/Grayscale*
option only works if you have a color/grayscale monitor. Even
though most laser printers are not color ones, the *Color/Grayscale*
option will work with black-and-white laser printers and provide
grayscales not available on Macs with black-and-white monitors.
Figure 11.10 shows the options available.

Options

The options require a good deal more discussion than the basic
settings. This is especially true with the color separation options. We
will briefly cover the less-used, simpler options and then examine in
more detail color separation using spot color overlays and knockouts.

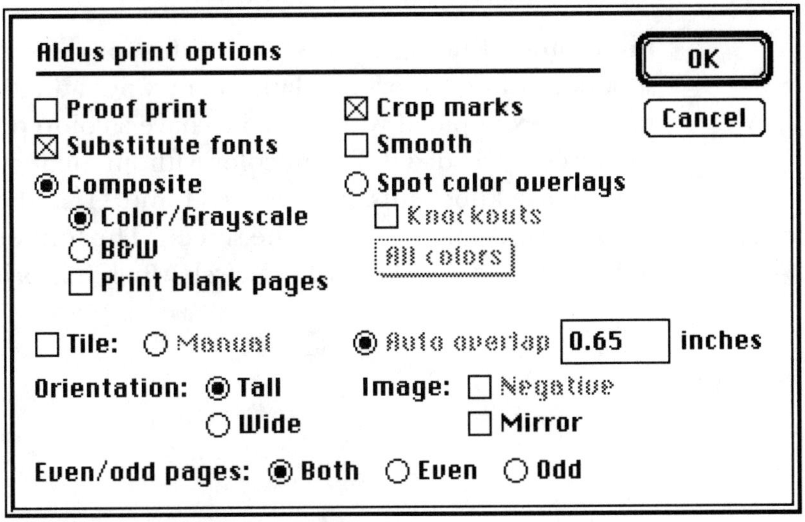

FIGURE 11.10 Aldus Print Options dialog box

- **Printing Blank** Pages   Blank pages are common in books. This option lets you save paper when you print drafts. However, blank pages should be brought to the printer so that your publication will have the right number of pages. It is usually a good idea to have PageMaker print blank pages so you do not accidentally forget to place them in your publication. Also, even though blank pages do not have page numbers, they should be counted in the numbering sequence.

- **Mirror image and negative**   Mirror image prints everything so that it appears as though you are viewing it through a mirror. Certain types of commercial printing require camera ready copy in a mirror image, and it can be used for special effects with graphics. The negative printing reverses black-and-white dots.

- **Crop Marks**   Crop marks are markings on the page to show the printer where your page limits are. For example, if you are printing on an 8.5- by 11-inch piece of paper and your publication is 7.5- by 9-inch, you can use crop marks on the 8.5- by 11-inch sheet to show where to trim. The crop marks consist of horizontal and vertical lines in the corners of the page.

- **Knockouts**   Knockouts are used with spot color overlays. In situations where colors overlap, you may not want the colors to mix. For example, if you wanted to have a colored bar overlay a colored circle of a different color without mixing, you would want to use knockouts. Figures 11.11 and 11.12 show how the graphics and colors look on the screen. The following illustration shows the knockout of the circle when it is printed:

- **Spot color overlay**   When you have different colors in your publication, you can have PageMaker print out separate pages

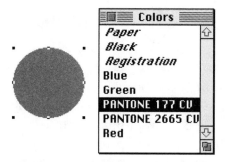

FIGURE 11.11 Pantone 177 colored circle as seen on the screen

FIGURE 11.12 Pantone 2665 color bar overlay circle as seen on the screen

for each color. This is a mechanical separation technique as opposed to process separation. Every page is labeled with the page number and the color overlay. For example,

Page 2 - PANTONE 471 CV overlay

is printed on the page that only has objects with the color PANTONE 471. In this way, the printer can print each color from your camera-ready pages. Each page also has four registration marks—one each at the top, bottom, and both sides. This helps the printer assure alignment when printing the different colors to the final pages. The following illustration shows the registration mark you can expect to find in the nonprinting portions of the page (8.5- by 11-inch pages do not show the registration marks):

- **Tile** The tile option is for big documents that have to be pieced together like tiles in a mosaic. This involves piecing together two or more 8.5- by 11-inch pages into a single big page. You can specify the overlap manually or have it done automatically. The manual setting requires you to establish a "zero point" for each tile.

As was stated at the outset, most of the printing you will be doing will not involve changing a lot of options. The color separation is usually done only on the last and perhaps second-to-last draft. Once your have your printer set up and running with PageMaker, the various parameters you can change will only occasionally be used.

PostScript Printing

If you plan on taking your publication disks to a service bureau or compositor to output on a high-density printer (e.g., 1200, 2400 dpi), you may be required to provide your publication as a PostScript file. Depending on the type of output device available, you will be given a number of different options. Figure 11.13 shows the available PostScript printing options on PageMaker.

Once you have selected the options, click the File name . . . button. This is important since you will want a different file name for your disk output than the name currently being used for your document. For example, suppose the name of your file is Newsletter4. When you print a PostScript file to the disk, you will want a different name; otherwise, the file would be overprinted with a PostScript file that could not be read by PageMaker except as a graphic to be placed in PageMaker. Be sure to ask your service bureau or compositor what parameters to use and not to use. Parameters will vary depending on their output device. You may also be asked to change the output device from the Printer dialog box.

For the most part, printing is a matter of choosing the number of copies desired, selecting the range of pages and possibly the scale,

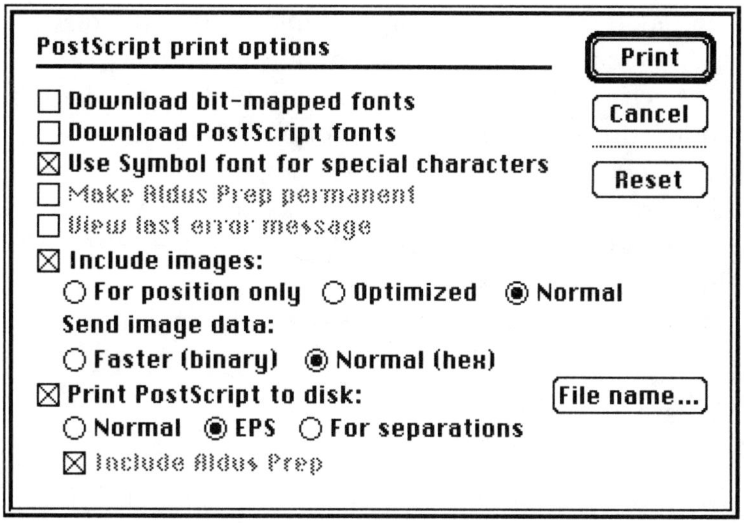

FIGURE 11.13   PostScript Print options

and clicking OK in the Print dialog box. However, there are some very interesting options that we need to consider, especially when preparing a publication for color separation.

SCRIPTS

PageMaker 4.2 has a new script language you may wish to employ. The script language is like having a very powerful macro capacity or even a programming language made to use just with PageMaker. As a new PageMaker user, you may want to wait a while before trying to tackle it. When you're ready to give it a try, the following discussion will give you the rudiments of the language and how to use it.

First, let's discuss what you might have for your own script. The best way to approach the problem is to think of anything with Page-Maker that is done repetitively and involves several steps. For example, if you have a publication that has a nondefault format, you might want to have a script that will create such a format. If you have a more complicated task, such as making fractions or drop caps, then a script would save you a lot of time. Those scripts are supplied with Aldus Additions. Setting up special tabs, indentations, font combinations, or just about anything else that you do with the mouse and keyboard can be done automatically with a script.

A script works like a robot who goes through all of the steps you would with the menus and palettes. For example, the script command *save* goes to the **File** menu and saves the current document. Likewise the *saveas* command, works just like *Save as . . .* does in the **File** menu. It's easier to press ⌘-Ⓢ or select *Save* from the **File** menu than it would be to run a script that does the same thing, but suppose you want your document to be saved on your hard disk and backed up to a floppy disk. The script,

```
save
saveas "Floppy: Backup"
```

would do that for you. It wouldn't save a great deal of time, but it would save a little. More sophisticated scripts will do more.

Scripting Rules

This section gives a brief explanation of the rules for writing scripts. If you are familiar with computer programming, you will find the rules very simple. Those of you new to programming probably will find it to be simpler than you thought.

- **Separate Commands**   Each command is separated by a carriage return or a semicolon. For example:

  ```
  close
  new
  ```

  or

  ```
  close; new
  ```

- **Parameter separators**   Parameters are separated by commas, parentheses, spaces, or tabs. For example:

  ```
  pagesize 6i, 9i
  ```

  or

  ```
  PageSize (6i) (9i)
  ```

  or

        PAGESIZE 6i 9i

or

        PaGeSiZe   6i   9i

The parameters are the parameters you would enter in the dialog boxes from the menus. Some are specific to the language such as

    new 5

where 5 is the number of pages in a new file. However, the parameters are pretty intuitive if you know PageMaker well.

- **Caps, lowercase, and formatting**   You can use uppercase or lowercase or a combination of each as shown in the above examples of parameter separators. Also, the formatting is ignored by PageMaker, and so things like font size or style and indentations have no effect. However, the commands must not be split. All command words must be single words. For example, the command *pagesize* cannot be broken into two words such as *page size*.

- **Comment lines**: Two hyphens (--) are used in front of comments. They can be on the same line as commands, but after each carriage return, comment lines must have the two hyphens. In the following example the commands are *save, close,* and *new 3,* and everything else is a comment. For example:

            save --Before you close be sure to save
            close
                    --After closing
                    --you can open a
                    --new file
            new 3

Running Scripts

Scripts can be run from selected text or from a file. To run a script as selected text, first select the text in PageMaker as illustrated.

```
save
close
new
pagesize 6i, 9i
pagemargins .75i, .5i, .5i, .5i
```

Next, select *Aldus Additions* from the **Options** menu and choose *Run Script . . ..* You will get a dialog box that has two buttons for launching scripts. Figure 11.14 shows how the dialog box looks when there is selected text.

The Run selected text button is selectable, and so you can click it to run the script you have written in PageMaker. Since the script saves the file before closing it and opening another, your script will be saved on the page. Had you not saved the file, the script would be lost—which in some cases is just what you want.

If you are going to be using a script a good deal, save it as a text file. This can be done by exporting a text file from PageMaker, writing it with a word processor and saving it as a text file, or even using TeachText that comes with PageMaker 4.2. Writing scripts and running them as selected text is a way to debug your script prior to saving it as a file.

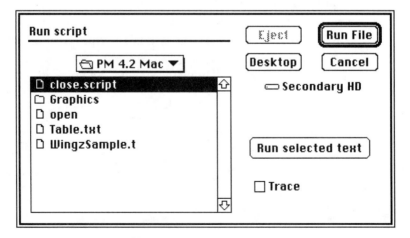

FIGURE 11.14 Run script dialog box

If you have written something wrong in your script, you will get an error message as shown in Figure 11.15.

The "Addition error" refers to an error in Aldus Additions; not an arithmetic error. If you do get such an error, click the Trace box in the Run script dialog box (see Figure 11.14). When you run the script again, you will get a dialog box that lets you execute the script one step at a time. Figure 11.16 shows a Trace script dialog box with

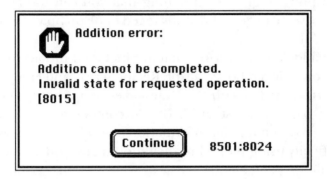

FIGURE 11.15   Aldus Addition Error message—not a math error

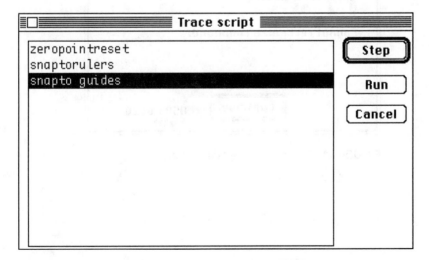

FIGURE 11.16   Trace Script window with error highlighted

the step selecting an error. (The command has been broken with a space between "snapto" and "guides.")

When the error occurs, you will get the Error in script dialog box and can see which command led to the error by noting the selected command in the step in the Trace Script dialog box. Figure 11.17 shows a typical dialog box announcing the error.

There is much more to scripting than the simple introduction here. With the commands that follow, you can get your feet wet and see if scripting might be something that you can use and want to learn. If so, you can get a more advanced book on how to write scripts for PageMaker.

Take a look at the scripts that are included in PageMaker. The files Crayon Colored Boxes.script, Recipe.script, and Fractions.script are all scripts written with the PageMaker Script Language. On the following pages is a list of all of the commands available in the language. Without further information on their parameters, you will have difficulty using them, but they should give you an idea of what you can do.

FIGURE 11.17 Error in Script dialog box

addition	copy	getbasedon
after	copystyles	getbook
alignment	createindex	getcase
all	createtoc	getcolor
allcaps	crop	getcolorinfo
allsides	custom	getcolornames
apartcoarse	cut	getcolorpalette
apartfine	decimal	getcolumnguides
arabic	default	getcontrolpalette
aslowercase	delete	getcroprect
astyped	deletehoriz	getdefaultdir
auto	deleterulerguides	getdictionary
autoflow	deletevert	getexportfilters
autooverlap	deselect	getfillstyle
back	diagfew	getfont
basedon	diaglots	getfontdrawing
baseline	dictionary	getfontlist
before	dontcare	getguides
between	dots	gethorizguides
bold	downnext	gethyphenation
book	downone	getimageframe
both	editcolor	getimportfilters
bothpages	editoriginal	getindents
bottom	editstory	getlasterror
bottomleft	eightpoint	getlasterrorstr
bottomright	eightypct	getleading
box	eol	getletterspace
bringtofront	eps	getlinebreak
case	even	getlinebreakloc
center	export	getlinestyle
char	faster	getlinkinfo
ciceros	fillstyle	getlinkoptions
clear	fit	getlinks
close	font	getlockguides
closercoarse	fontdrawing	getmasteritems
closerfine	force	getmeasureunits
cmyk	fortypct	getnextstyle
color	fourpoint	getobjectlist
colorpalette	fpo	getoverrides
column	front	getpageimage
columnbreak	getadditions	getpagemargins
columnguides	getalignment	getpagenumber
controlpalette	getautoflow	getpagenumbers

getpageoptions
getpagerect
getpages
getpagesize
getparaoptions
getparaspace
getpminfo
getpmstate
getpreferences
getpubname
getpubwindowrect
getpubwindows
getrotation
getroundedcorners
getruleabove
getrulebelow
getruleoptions
getrulers
getscreenfont
getscrollbars
getselectlist
getsize
getsnaptoguides
getsnaptorulers
getspaceoptions
getstoryeditpref
getstorylist
getstorytext
getstyle
getstylenames
getstylepalette
gettabs
gettargetprinter
gettextbounds
gettextwrap
gettextwrappoly
gettoolbox
gettrack
gettypeoptions
gettypeposition
gettypestyle
getvertguides
getview

getwidth
getwordspace
getzerolock
getzeropoint
grayout
guide
guidehoriz
guides
guidevert
hairline
halfpoint
hashfew
hashlots
highres
horizfew
horizlots
hyphenation
import
inches
inchesdecimal
indents
independent
indexauto
indexautoname
indexformat
inline
inserting
insertpages
irregular
italic
jumpover
justify
last
leading
left
leftbottom
leftpage
lefttop
letterspace
line
linestyle
linked
linkoptions

lm
lockguides
loose
loweralpha
lowerroman
manualfeed
manualkerning
manualonly
manualtiling
masterguides
masteritems
measureunits
mediumdash
millimeters
minisave
minisaved
move
movecolumn
multiplepaste
nested
new
newstory
next
nexteven
nextodd
nextpage
nextstyle
none
nonumber
normal
normalimage
normalpostscript
normalres
normaltrack
notrack
nudge
numberafter
numberbefore
odd
off
on
onepoint
open

optimized	removepages	snaptorulers
original	removestyle	solid
outline	replacing	spaceoptions
oval	resize	squares
page	resizepct	story
pagemargins	reverse	storyeditpref
pagenumbers	revert	strikethru
pageoptions	rgb	style
pagesize	right	stylebegin
pantone	rightbottom	styleend
paper	rightpage	stylepalette
papertray	righttop	subscript
para	rm	superscript
paraoptions	rotation	tabs
paraspace	roundedcorners	template
paste	ruleabove	tenpct
pasteboard	rulebelow	text
picas	ruleoptions	textblock
place	rulers	textcursor
placenext	run	textedit
plusalgorithm	runin	textenter
plusdictionary	save	textselect
position	saveas	textwrap
preferences	saved	textwrappoly
preservechar	scroll	thickdash
preserveline	scrollbars	thickthin
prev	select	thindash
previous	selectall	thinthick
print	selectextend	thinthickthin
printcomposite	sendtoback	thinthin
printoptions1	sendtopage	thirtypct
printoptions2	sent	tight
printpostscript	seps	toolbox
printsetup	setwidth	top
printspotcolors	shadow	topleft
proportional	showpages	topofcaps
pub	sixpoint	topright
publication	sixtypct	track
quit	size	twelvepoint
rect	sizebump	twentypct
redraw	smallcaps	twopoint
relink	smaller	typeoptions
remote	snaptoguides	typestyle

underline	vertfew	wordspace
unlink	vertlots	zerolock
upnext	veryloose	zeropoint
upone	verytight	zeropointreset
upperalpha	view	
upperroman	word	

INDEX

A

About This Macintosh option memory
audit, 6
Actual-size page view, 40, 42-44
Adding text
by drag-placing, 105-106
making room for added text, 110-
111
with Text tool, 104-105
Addition error message, 257
Adjusting text, 109-123
cut or cleared text, 111-112
ripple effect, control of, 1213-114
in Story View mode, 125
Adobe, Inc., screen fonts for, 235
Alias, 9-10
Alignment
of paragraphs, 156
templates and, 222
Alley margins, 232
Alphabetic characters as page-
numbers, 64
Apostrophes and quotes, 81
Apple menu memory audit, 6
Application menu memory audit, 6
Apply button for tabs, 162
Arrow tool, 65
ASCII files, 70
exporting files, 122-123
import/export filters for, 122-123
Attributes option of Find routines, 133
Autoflow option for text flow, 81
Autoleading, 160
default, 238
Avant Garde 12 point font, 10-11

B

Balance, 225
Beginning windowshade handle, 86
Bit-mapped fonts, 10-12
Bit-mapped standing caps, 236-237
Black-and-white displays, 8-9
graphics and, 213
Blocks of text. *See* Text blocks
Boldfacing in Story View mode, 125
Book linkages, 245-246
Bookman font, 234-235
Borders
lines for, 206
for tables, 146-148
Bringing up page, 22-23
Bring to Front option, 101-102
Broken lines, 210
Buffer
Clear command, 109
Copy command and, 107
Cut command and, 107
and Paste/Replace operation, 108-
109
Business cards
margins on, 37
sizing page for, 32

C

Calendars, sizing page for, 32
Capital letters. *See also* Large caps;
Standing caps
in script language, 255
Captions
inline graphics and, 75-777
for style, 221

Cells in tables, 138

Chaining style sheets, 163-164

Changing text. *See* Adjusting text

Chapter heading margins, 231

Ciceros, measurement in, 50

Clear command, 109
    adjusting cleared text, 111-112

Clip-art graphics, 21, 190

CMYK method for defining colors, 215-216

Coffee table books, 32

Collate option for printing, 248

Color displays, 8-9
    graphics and, 213-214

Color/Grayscale printing option, 249

Color palette, 213-214

Colors, 213-218
    CMYK method for defining, 215-216
    defining colors, 214-218
    Pantone button for, 215, 216-218

Column break before paragraph option, 156

Columns, 56-59. *See also* Table Editor
    alley margins, 232
    autoflow option for text flow, 81
    balance, 225
    custom columns, 58-59
    guides and, 59
    line length and, 238-239
    margins and, 37, 232
    multiple columns, 56-57
    proportion and, 225-226
    resizing text blocks within, 87, 89
    sequence and, 226-228
    two-column page as default, 22

Compatible word processors, list of, 69-70

Completing text placement, 25

Component unity, 229

Composite page numbers, 62-64

Compositional unity, 228

Convert quotes option, 81

Copy command, 107
    for line drawing, 208-209

Create Publisher options, 15

Crop marks option for printing, 250

Cropping graphics, 26-28, 192-197

Cropping tool, 65, 194
    use of, 66-67

Cross-references in index, 181-183

Custom columns, 58-59

Cut command, 107
    adjusting cut text, 111-112
    making room for added text, 110-111
    and unthreading text, 112-113

Cut-out items, broken lines for, 210

Cylinders, line drawing in, 207-208

D

DCA format, 69

Decimal measurement system, 50-51

Defaults
    for columns, 56
    fit-in-window page view as, 41
    leading defaults, 238
    for page numbers, 38
    for standoff for graphics, 30
    for style sheets, 151-153
    two-column page as, 22

Defining colors, 214-218

De-hyphenating words, 169

Deleting with Story Editor, 129-130

Descriptive-section composite page number, 64

Diagonal line tool, 66, 206

Dictionary. *See also* Spell checking
    hyphenation dictionary, 169-171

Dictionary Editor, 172-173

Double-sided pages, 35-36
    master pages, 40

Downloading fonts, 12
Drag-placing, 83-85
    adding text by, 105-106
    for headlines, 115
Draw files, 187, 188
Drawing tools, 65
Drop caps, 115-119
    style and use of, 236-238

E

Editing, 106-109. *See also* Adding text;
    Story Editor
    Clear command, 109
    Copy command, 107
    Cut command, 107
    Paste command, 108-109
    selecting text for, 103-104
    in Story View mode, 125
    styles, 154-157
    table of contents, 181
    tabs, 161-162
    with Text tool, 102-109
    undoing edit, 107
Edition files, 15-16
Editions option, 15
Element menu, Text Wrap option from,
    29
Encapsulated PostScript (EPS), 187, 188-
    189
End-of-story windowshade handle, 87
Enlarging text blocks, 87
Entire story, replacement of, 78-79
Erasing text with Clear command, 109
Even/odd pages printing option, 248
Excel, 137
Export filters. *See* Import/export filters
Exporting files, 122-123
Export tags, 122-123

F

Facing pages, 35-36
50 percent of actual page size
    magnification, 42
File extensions for graphics files, 187
Files
    exporting, 122-123
    linking files, 240-246
File sharing, 18
Fill in graphics, 211-213
Filters. *See* Import/export filters
Finding text with Story Editor, 131-133
Find option in Story Editor, 131-133
Fit-in-window page view, 40-41, 42
Fit-in-world page view, 41
    grabber hand inoperative in, 47
Fixed-size fonts, 10-12
Flow of text. *See* Text flow
Fold margins, 232
Folio margin, 23
Fonts, 10-14
    into blocks of text, 114-121
    for bodies, 236
    component unity and, 229
    downloading fonts, 12
    greeked text, 45-46
    for headlines, 115
    for heads, 236
    LaserWriter Font Utility, 12-14
    line length and, 238-239
    new editing features, 4
    screen fonts, 234-235
    scripts for, 253-254
    in Story View mode, 125
    style and, 233-238
    track kerning and, 174-175
    width control of, 119-120
Footers. *See* Headers and footers
Formatting options, 80-81

400 percent of actual page size
    magnification, 44
Further-story windowshade handle, 86

G

Global changes in Story Editor, 133-135,
    152-153
Grabber hand, 47
Graphics
    balance and, 225
    CMYK method for defining colors,
        215-216
    colors in, 213-218
    columns affecting, 59
    component unity and, 229
    cropping graphics, 26-28, 192-197
    dragging graphics line, 85
    entering text in graphics field, 201
    fill, 211-213
    formats for graphics files, 187-189
    guides and, 59
    handles on graphic image, 28
    image control in, 202-204
    independent graphics
        changing from inline to, 205
    initial graphic placement, 25-26
    inline graphics, 75-77
        changing from independent to, 205
        placing of, 204-205
        in Story View mode, 125
        text wrap and, 198-204
    layering text and graphics, 212-213
    lines in, 206-210
    linking files with, 241-244
    margins for, 37
    moving graphic blocks, 29
    overcropping, recovery from, 197
    Pantone button for, 215, 216-218
    placing graphics, 21-22
    preparation of, 189-190

proportionally scaling graphics, 191-
    193
proportion and, 225-226
scaling graphics, 191-197
    after cropping, 196
stand-off for, 29-30
in Story View mode, 125
style and, 221
superimposing text on, 202-204
talk balloons, 209-210
text blocks and insertion of, 89-92
text wrap and, 198-204
tips for preparing, 190
tools for, 205-213
uneven columns due to, 58
graphics
    independent graphics, 75-77
Grayscale displays, graphics and, 213
Greeked text, 45-46
Grids
    alignment in paragraphs, 158-159
    in tables, 148
Guides, 51-56
    columns and, 59
    peeling guides, 51
Gutters
    margins, 232-233
    in tables, 138

H

Hand-drawn graphics, 21
Handles. *See also* Windowshade handles
    on graphic image, 28
Hanging indents, 152
Hard carriage returns, 71-73
Harmony and style, 228-230
Headers and footers
    cut or cleared text adjustments with,
        111-112
    fonts for, 236

margins, 231
ripple effect, avoidance of, 112-113
Headline fonts, 115
Hierarchy for placing stories, 77-78
HLS dialog box for colors, 215
Horizontal page dimension, 34
Horizontal scroll bar, 47
Hyphenation, 168
dictionary, 169-171
Dictionary Editor, 172-173
and loose lines, 169
for specialized terminology, 169-170
for style, 163

I

IDs for networks, 18
Image control with graphics, 202-204
Import/export filters
for ASCII files, 122-123
in Story menu, 128-129
updated word processing programs
and, 70
Inches
line length in, 239
measurement in, 50-51
Indentation
hanging indents, 152
for paragraphs, 156
scripts for, 253
tabs, setting indent with, 73, 161-162
Independent graphics. *See* Graphics
Index graphics in Story View mode, 125
Indexing, 181-186
and book linkages, 245-246
cross-references in index, 181-183
multiple-level indexing, 183-186
new features, 4
Initial graphic placement, 25-26
Initial text placement, 23-24

Inline graphics. *See* Graphics
Inserting text in stories, 79-80
Invitations, sizing page for, 32
Invoice forms, margins on, 37
Italics
for alias, 10
in Story View mode, 125

J

Justification of text, 54-55

K

Keep lines together paragraph option,
156
Keep with next . . . lines paragraph
option, 156
Kerning, 168. *See also* Track kerning
disadvantages of, 177
manual kerning, 176-177
pair kerning, 160, 168, 177
Knockouts option for printing, 250

L

Labels
for inline graphics, 204-205
sizing page for, 32
Large caps, 115-119. *See also* Drop caps
style and use of, 236-238
Large type for style, 221
LaserWriters
Font Utility, 12-14
setting printer parameters, 247-247
Layers
selecting text in, 99-102
of text and graphics, 212-213
Layouts, 230-233
Leaders, 161
custom leaders, 161

Leading, 160
    style and, 238
Lettered-section composite page
        number, 63
Letterheads, stationary pads for, 16
Letter spacing, 160, 168
Lines
    in graphics, 206-210
    style and length of, 238-239
    tight or loose, 168-171
Linking files, 240-246
    book linkages, 245-246
    with graphics, 241-244
Loose lines, 168-171
Lowercase letters in script language, 255

M

Macintosh System 7, 5
Macros. *See* Script language
MacWrite Versions 5.0 and II, 69
Magnification of page, 40-45
    greeked text, 45-46
    shortcuts for, 41, 44-45
    text insertion point, clicking on, 48
Manual kerning, 176-177
Manual text flow option, 81
    working flow with, 82-83
Margins, 33
    alley margins, 232
    for custom columns, 58-59
    drag-placing text with, 106
    fold margins, 232
    folio margin, 23
    gutter margins, 232-233
    for headers, 231
    layout style for, 230-233
    right justification of text, 54-55
    setting of, 36-38
    text margins, 231
    trim margins, 230

Master page, 39-48
    composite page number on, 63
    magnification of pages, 40-45
    moving around, 47-48
    page numbers, placing of, 59-64
    text insertion point, clicking on, 48
    viewing master pages, 40-45
Match Case option of Find dialog box,
        132
McDraw II files, 188
Measurement systems, 50-51
Memo forms, stationary pads for, 16
Memory. see also Random access
        memory (RAM)
    color display and, 8-9
    System 7 using, 5-6
MicroSoft Works Version 2.00a, 69
MicroSoft Word Versions 3.02 and 4.0, 69
Millimeters, measurement in, 50
Mirror image and negative option, 250
More-to-place windowshade handle, 87
Moving graphic blocks, 29
Multiple blocks of text, 94-95
Multiple columns, 56-57
Multiple-level indexing, 183-186

N

Network Identity, 18
Networking with System 7, 17-20
New features
    for PageMaker Version 4.0, 3-4
    for PageMaker Version 4.2, 4
New item, placing story as, 78-79
Non-Arabic numbers as page numbers,
        64
Nonstandard sized pages, 32-33
Numbering pages. *See* Page numbers
Numeric keypad for manual kerning, 176

O

Object-oriented graphics files, 188
Options menu in Story Editor, 127-128
Orientation of page, 33
Original story placement, 78-79
Orphans
    control of, 166-168
    paragraph option, orphan control as,
        157
Oval tool, 66, 206
    talk balloons with, 209-210
Overcropping, recovery from, 197
Overlapping text blocks, 99-102

P

Page break before paragraph option, 156
Page Dimension option, 33-34
Page numbers
    composite page numbers, 62-64
    folio margin, 23
    non-Arabic numbers, 64
    placing of, 59-64
    setting up, 38-39
    styles of, 62
    in table of contents, 179-180
Pages. *See also* Master page
    autoflow option for text flow, 81
    facing pages, 35-36
    greeked text, 45-46
    magnification of pages, 40-45
    moving around page, 47-48
    nonstandard sized pages, 32-33
    review of page setup, 39
    sequence of, 226-228
    setup of page, 32-33
    shortcuts for viewing, 41, 44-45
    size of page, 23, 33-35

text insertion point, clicking on, 48
two-column page as default, 22
Paint files, 187, 188
Paint-type standing caps, 236-237
Pair kerning, 160, 168, 177
Pantone button, 215, 216-218
Paper fill, 211-212
Paper source/size printing options, 248
Paragraphs. *See also* Orphans; Widows
    controls, 165-173
    grid alignment in, 158-159
    options for placing, 156-157
    rules for, 157-163
    spacing attributes for, 160
    styles, 156-157
    tabs in, 161-162
Parameter separators in script language,
        254-255
Passwords for Network Identity, 18
Pasteboard, drag-placing text on, 106
Paste command, 108-109
    making room for added text, 110-111
    and unthreading text, 112-113
Paste/Replace operation, 108-109
Perpendicular line tool, 66, 206
Picas
    line length in, 238-239
    measurement in, 50
PICT files, 187
    tables exported as, 149
Place command, 3
    initial text placement, 23-24
    for stories, 77
Placing stories, 77-80
    options for, 78-80
    text and graphics, 21-22
Pointer tool
    for moving graphic blocks, 29
    use of, 66

PostScript
    bit-mapped fonts with, 11-12
    graphics from, 190
    printing options, 252-253
    screen fonts for, 235
    thumbnails printing option, 248
    width control and, 119
Print entire book option, 248
Printing, 246-253
    Aldus options for, 249
    basic selections for, 248
    crop marks option, 250
    knockouts option, 250
    mirror image and negative option, 250
    PostScript options, 252-253
    printing blank pages option, 250
    setting printer parameters, 246-253
    spot color overlay option, 250-251
    Start Page option turning off printing, 12, 14
    tile option, 252
Printing blank pages option, 250
Prior-story windowshade handle, 86
Program linking, 18
Proportional leading, 160
Proportionally scaling graphics, 191-193
Proportion and style, 225-226
Publish/Subscribe feature, 15-16

Q

Quotes
    convert quotes option, 81
    for style, 221

R

Random access memory (RAM)
    adding RAM through virtual memory, 6-9
    System 6 and, 5

System 7 using, 5=6
Range printing option, 248
Ratios for proportion, 225-226
Read tags option, 81
Rectangle tool, 206
Reference line for ruler, 50
Regular-page composite number, 63
Repeat Tab option, 162
Replacing entire story, 78-79
Replacing text
    and Paste/Replace operation, 108-109
    Story Editor, find and replace option in, 133-135
Retain format option, 80-81
Rethreading text, 114
Reverse order printing option, 248
RGB dialog box for colors, 215
Right justification of text, 54-55
Ripple effect of text changes, 113-114
Roman numerals as page numbers, 64
Rotation of text, 120-121
    Story Editor, changing rotated text with, 130-131
Round corner tool, 66, 206
Rows. *See* Table Editor
RTF format, 69
Rulers, 48-51. *See also* Guides; Zero point measurement systems, 50-51
    reference line, 50
Rules for paragraphs, 157-163
Running heads, guides for, 56
Running scripts, 255-258

S

Sample page
    completing text placement, 25
    initial text placement, 23-24
    step-by-step process, 22-30
Sans serif fonts, 236
Scaling. *See also* Graphics
    for printing, 248

Scanners, graphic art from, 21, 190

Scrapbook files, 189

Screen fonts, 234-235

Script language, 253-258

    caps, lowercase and formatting of, 255

    comment lines for, 255

    errors in scripting, 257-258

    parameter separators for, 254-255

    rules for scripting, 254-255

    running scripts, 255-258

    separate commands in, 254

Scroll bars, 47

Searching for text with Story Editor, 131-133

Section heading margins, 231

Select All option, 103-104

Selecting text for editing, 103-104

Semiautomatic flow option for text, 82

Send to Back option, 102

Separators in script language, 254-255

Sequence, 226-228

Set Width window, 119

75 percent of actual page size magnification, 43

Shades in tables, 146-148

Sharing Setup control panel, 18

Shortcuts

    with style sheets, 152

    for tools, 67

Shortening text blocks, 89

Single-sided pages, 35

    master pages, 40

Size of pages, 32-35

Slugs and style, 220

Small caps, use of, 237

Soft carriage returns, 72-73

    for drop and standing caps, 117-118

Space band, 160

Spaces replacing tabs in word processor file, 73

Spacing attributes for paragraphs, 160

Speed improvements, 4

Spell checking

    adding new words to dictionary, 135-137

    Dictionary Editor, 172-173

    for paragraphs, 156

    for specialized terminology, 169-170

    in Story Editor, 135-137

Spot color overlay option for printing, 250-251

Square corner tool, 66

Standing caps, 115-119

    selecting text block of, 102

    style and use of, 236-238

Standoffs

    in graphics, 29-30, 198-199

    halos, 199

Start Page option turning off printing, 12, 14

Stationary pads, 16-17

Stories

    inserting text in, 79-80

    placing stories, 77-80

Story Editor

    adding text with, 104

    carriage returns and, 72

    change operation, 133-135

    entering text, 129-130

    find and replace option, 133-135

    finding text with, 131-133

    global style changes with, 133-135, 152-153

    menus, 125-129

    Options menu, 127-128

    rotated text changes with, 130-131

    selection of, 124-125

    spell checking in, 135-137

    Story menu, 128-129

    styles sheets for, 152

Story menu, 128-129

Story preparation problems, 74
Story View mode, 125
Style, 219-220
    balance and, 225
    captions for, 221
    fonts and, 233-238
    graphics and, 221
    large caps and, 236-238
    large type for, 221
    layouts, 230-238
    leading and, 238
    line length and, 238-239
    margins, 230-233
    proportion and, 225-226
    quotes for, 221
    sequence and, 226-228
    slugs and, 220
    templates for, 222-224
    type choice and, 220
    unity and, 228-230
    white space and, 220
Style sheets, 150-177. S*ee also* Paragraphs
    chaining of, 163-164
    creating, 153-157
    defaults for, 151-153
    editing styles, 154-157
    hyphenation, 163
    new styles, creation of, 163-165
    paragraph styles, 156-157
    rules for, 157-163
    transferring, 165
    type style specifications, 154-156
    using style sheets, 164-165
Subscribe to option, 16
Subscript type, 155-156
Sum option of Table Editor, 144-145
Superimposing text on graphics, 202-204
SuperPaint files, 188
Superscript type, 155-156
Surround option, 200
System 6, 5

System 7, 5
    Edition files, 15-16
    fonts and, 10-14
    LaserWriter Font utility, 12-14
    networking and, 17-20
    stationary pads, 16-17
    TrueType fonts in, 234-235

T

Table Editor, 137-149
    borders for tables, 146-148
    cell references in, 138
    contents of table, editing of, 143-148
    data editing with, 142-143
    exporting data with, 149
    grids in tables, 148
    importing data with, 140-141
    making tables with, 137-142
    manual data entry, 142
    narrowing columns and rows with,
        138-140
    preparing tables for PageMaker, 149
    shades in tables, 146-148
    Sum option of, 144-145
Table of contents
    book linkages, 245-246
    creation of, 178-181
    editing of, 181
    paragraph option, include table of
        contents as, 156
Tabs
    apply button for, 162
    automatic alignment of tab bar, 4
    with drop caps, 116
    indents, setting of, 161-162
    in paragraphs, 161-162
    Repeat Tab option, 162
    scripts for, 253
    spaces replacing, 73
    in table of contents, 180

Tag Image File Format (TIFF), 187, 188
Tags
    Export tags, 122-123
    problems with, 74-75
    read tags option, 81
Talk balloons, 209-210
Templates
    balance and, 223-224
    stationary pads, 16-17
    for style, 222-224
Text. *See also* Adding text; Adjusting text;
    Editing; Rotation of text; Text
    blocks
    completing text placement, 25
    drag-placing of, 83-85
    in graphics field, 201
    greeked text, 45-46
    initial text placement, 23-24
    inline graphics, 75-77
    inserting text in story, 79-80
    layers, selecting text in, 99-102
    placing text, 21-22
    right justification of text, 54-55
    superimposing text on graphics, 202-
    204
    Text Wrap option, 29-30
    threaded text, 95-99
    working flow of text, 82-83
Text blocks. *See also* Editing
    Cut command with, 107
    enlarging text blocks, 87
    expanding, 98
    fonts and, 114-121
    graphics, insertion of, 89-92
    layers, selecting text in, 99-102
    moving, 92-95
    multiple blocks, selection of, 94-95
    overlapping text blocks, 99-102
    resizing shapes of, 87-92
    rotation of text in, 120-121
    selecting, 103-104

shortening of, 89
shrinking of, 96-97
standing cap, selecting text block of,
    102
n talk balloons, 209-210
threaded text, 95-99
Text files
    tables exported as, 149
Text files from word processors, 70-71
Text flow, 81-83
    around graphics, 198-200
Text margins, 231
Text tool, 65, 102-109
    adding text, 104-105
    exporting files with, 122-123
    selecting text with, 103-104
    use of, 66
Text Wrap option, 29-30
    graphics and, 198-204
Threaded text, 95-99
    rethreading text, 114
    and ripple effect of text changes,
    113-114
    unthreading text, 112-113
Thumbnails printing option, 248
Tiffany 18 point font, 10-11
Tight lines, 168-171
Tile option for printing, 252
Toolbox, 65-67
    functions of tools, 66-67
    for graphics, 205-213
    new features, 4
    in Story View mode, 125
Top of caps leading, 160
Track kerning, 168, 174-175
    options for, 174
Transferring style sheets, 165
Trim margins, 230
TrueType fonts, 110-12, 234-235
25 percent of actual page size
    magnification, 41

Two-column page as default, 22
200 percent of actual page size
        magnification, 44
Typesetting, computerized, 3
Type specs option, 115
Type style specifications, 154-156

U

Undoing edit, 107
Uneven columns due to graphics, 58
Unity and style, 228-230
Unthreading text, 112-113
Updated import filters for word
        processors, 70

V

Vertical page dimension, 34
Vertical scroll bar, 47
Viewing
        master pages, 40-45
        for sequence, 228
Virtual memory, adding RAM through,
        6-9

W

Weight of page and style, 227
White space, templates showing, 222-223
Whole Word option of Find dialog box,
        132
Widows
        control of, 166-168
        paragraph option, widow control as,
        157
Width of fonts, 119-120
Windowshade handles. *See also* Text blocks

on completing text placement, 25
cut or cleared text adjustments with,
        111-112
for flow of text, 83
for initial text placement, 24
reading, 86-87
for threaded text, 95-99
Wingz, 137, 140
Word fragments, 166
WordPerfect Version 1.02, 69
Word processing
        compatible word processors, list of,
        69-70
        exporting files, 122-123
        formatting with, 69
        hard carriage returns, 71-73
        page makeup and, 2
        problems with importing text from,
        71-75
        soft carriage returns, 72-73
        spaces replacing tabs, 73
        story preparation problems, 74
        tags, problems with, 74-75
        text files from, 70-71
        updated import filters, 70
Word spacing, 160, 168
Writing style, 229
WYSIWYG correlation for colors, 214

Z

Zero point, 49-50
        for custom columns, 58
        for page numbers, 61
Zero standoff for graphics, 29
Zooming for overlapping text blocks,
        99-102